Theories and History of Architecture

Manfredo Tafuri

Theories and History of Architecture

ICON EDITIONS

HARPER & ROW, PUBLISHERS

NEW YORK

Cambridge
Hagerstown
Philadelphia
San Francisco

1817

London
Mexico City
São Paulo
Sydney

This work was first published in Italy under the title *Teorie e storia dell'architettura*, 4th edition. Copyright © 1976 by Guis. Published by Laterza & Figli Spa, Rome and Bari.

Translated from the Italian by Giorgio Verrecchia.

FIRST U.S. EDITION

LIBRARY OF CONGRESS CATALOG CARD NUMBER: 79-2638

ISBN: 0-06-438580-9   80 81 82 83 10 9 8 7 6 5 4 3 2 1

ISBN: 0-06-430108-7 pbk   80 81 82 83 10 9 8 7 6 5 4 3 2 1

To Giusi

SADE

To sort out the true from the false
we must know ourselves
I
don't know myself
When I think I have discovered something
I begin to doubt
and I reject it
Everything we do is but a larva of our
intentions . . .

MARAT

We must pull ourselves out of the ditch
by our boot-straps
turn inside-out
and see everything with new eyes . . .

Peter Weiss, *Marat–Sade*

Contents

Foreword

This book by Manfredo Tafuri has probably done more to influence current ideas and theories on architecture on the continent of Europe than any other publication since Christian Norberg-Schulz's difficult and controversial book *Intentions in Architecture* was published in the early 1960s. Indeed a whole mystique has grown up about it and, although published over a decade ago in Italian, no English language publisher has seen fit to issue it earlier or to see it as an essential document *de partir* before the republication in English of Tafuri's later and more ideological books. *Theories and Histories of Architecture* has, of course, appeared in other languages than English over the past few years – a useful French translation was produced in 1978 – but my own enthusiasm for an English version stems not simply from the thoroughness of its scholarship and relevance of its statements, but also because, almost by accident, I came across a fastidiously cyclostyled copy prepared by Dutch students for circulation in one of the Dutch schools of Architecture. They claimed, justifiably, that the arguments and methodologies proposed by Tafuri should be understood by all students pursuing a desire to understand the past and to see Modern Architecture in an extended context. I am still of the opinion that this book is one of the most comprehensive accounts of the state of architectural theory and criticism and that the methodology it suggests, and adopts, for a discussion of the history of ideas is of great significance to a deeper understanding of present architecture.

However in transferring the book from Italian to English a number of problems have arisen that both the translator and myself feel should be shared with the reader. The occasional rhetorical ring of Italian we both felt needed to be preserved but there seem to be few phrases in English which capture this effect without sounding weak, as anyone will know who has suffered a performance of Grand Opera with an English libretto. Furthermore, Professor Tafuri's analysis digs deeply into the vocabulary of Linguistics and Structuralism, and we have found it, appropriate to use the internationally acceptable terms used in these specialist areas.

A few further translation problems occurred in transferring quotations from various language sources into English; sometimes Professor Tafuri uses the original English sources but on other occasions he has used translations into other languages (mainly of course Italian), for his references. We have on the whole attempted to go back to original texts whenever possible, although it must be admitted that it proved entirely impossible with a minor number of shorter quotes. This version of the book adheres fairly strictly to the make-up of the Italian paperbound version (fourth edition, 1976) and follows the style of the original in retaining the illustrations as an appendix to the text. To improve readability we have however grouped reference notes at the end of each chapter.

It is to be hoped that the usefulness of *Theories and Histories of Architecture* will be enhanced by the opportunity the publisher has taken of publishing it in English simultaneously with the essays written by Professor Tafuri and others on *The American City from the Civil War to the New Deal*, which, as readers will find, cogently applies the method of historical enquiry (but with a wider Marxist interpretation) outlined and used in this book.

Dennis Sharp
Hertford 1979

Note to the second (Italian) edition

I realise now, roughly two years after the publication of the first edition of the present volume, that too many things in it were left unsaid and that many among those said were incomplete. The following point has to be made clear: these pages are only a first step towards the acknowledgment of what architecture, as an *institution*, has meant up to now. First in the anticipation of ideologies and in begging the questions, then as a process directly involved in modern production processes and the development of the capitalist society.

I re-emphasise this conceptual element in order to avoid misunderstanding: I am speaking of Architecture, of *all* architecture, as an institution. With the following consequence (carefully ignored by the sugary official 'Marxism' – from Fisher to Goldmann and Della Volpe, by the Marcusian school – from Mitscherlich to his followers, by the 'vulgar' sociologism of Hauser, and by the recent groping in the dark of America's 'progressive' architects): *just as it is not possible to found a Political Economy based on class, so one cannot 'anticipate' a class architecture (an architecture 'for a liberated society'); what is possible is the introduction of class criticism into architecture.* Nothing beyond this, from a strict – but sectarian and partial – Marxist point of view. Any attempt to overthrow the institution, the discipline, with the most exasperated rejections or the most paradoxical ironies – let us learn from Dada and Surrealism – is bound to see itself turned into a positive contribution, into a 'constructive' avant-garde, into an ideology all the more positive as it is dramatically critical and self-critical.

When I started the present work I thought the best way to deal with such a theme would be to define all the obstacles *contained* in the discipline, all its inevitable contradictions, all its institutional ambiguities, seen against the background of the concrete, objective, historical decline of the positive guiding role of architecture, after the crisis of the programmatic utopianism of the avant-gardes. (This crisis, I would make clear, was not due to 'betrayals' or 'squandering', but to the simple fact that, in its progressive realisation, the dream-ideology has to turn into an intervention technique in order not to be erased by the processes of development.)

I see now that the main limitation of this volume has been in trying to maintain the specific quality of the analysis. I was made particularly aware of this by the strong criticisms of establishment culture at the time of the first edition; but certainly not through the content of its criticism, which, in its matter-of-course defence of all the worn-out, and not yet worn-out, myths of the Modern Movement and of the reforming mediation of the intellectuals, puts itself too clearly on the other side of the barricade to be taken seriously (not to mention its backwardness on specific grounds). Nevertheless these criticisms have clearly shown that the construction of the volume allows too many arbitrary interpretations: the ways in which architecture, *as a discipline*, is involved in the question of development, the ways in which the city shapes itself as a 'social' manifestation and as machinery of production, even the analysis of the relationship between the avant-garde and architecture, can obviously still be read as abstract scientific contributions.

Clearly all this must be corrected, and not by simply adding to the existing material; the reader will find the text of the second edition almost unchanged, apart from a few revisions and necessary corrections. I prefer to define briefly, once and for all, the correct interpretative key, and mention that I consider this book only a very first step towards a rigorous reading that should embrace the whole history of architecture in all its ideological aspects. (I would like to repeat that I use the term *ideology* specifically as the structure of the false intellectual conscience.)

Architecture as ideology, as an institution that 'fulfils' the ideology, as a discipline in crisis because of the new integrative techniques of the world of production and of anti-cyclical planning: the parable, read with different eyes, usually acquires dramatic overtones in current literature. From this springs, mainly, the effort to contain with artificial devices – which are bound to fail – the fall of architecture towards silence, towards the negation (also artificial) of itself: read in this key it becomes clear that the analysis of the anti-historicity of the avant-gardes in the first chapter does not amount to a superfluous homage to a worn out idealistic historicism.

But it is also obvious that, today, irony and silence have lost their cathartic power. The perfection of the *sphere* and the infinite polyvalence of the *maze* are equivalent; such pathetic survival expedients show only that architecture can look forward, at most, to the prospect of being entirely absorbed by the private sphere. Clearly, 'the unpronounceable avant-garde is the other face of mass gossip' (Fortini). And not because 'the *pugno penetrante* has been locked in the stables' (Fortini again), but because it has never left them. It is time to seriously confront the dialectic between architecture and the avant-garde (during the only period in which it had any meaning: between 1910 and 1930), which is outlined from a limited perspective in this book. It is in this relationship in fact, that one sees most clearly all the positive and active meanings, all the anticipated values shouted by the historical avant-gardes, in the very moment in which they recognise the need to suppress themselves, and to advance into subversive and revolutionary praxis.

Is it really necessary to point out how antithetical were the proposals of the *Neue Welt* and the anticipated Revolution? The '*pugno penetrante*' can't be used to blow up the stables: rather, it turns them, in the shortest possible time and with the greatest possible publicity, into a model farm. The 'negation' of the avant-garde is (we won't bother with those who mix up objective roles and *soul saving* mystical flights) the wobbly pivot in the *upheaval* of immediate reality. Schwitters's *Merz* pictures or the *bricolages* of Rauschenberg may start from the apocalyptical denunciation of the marketing of values, but only in order to take on, introject and sublimate such marketing, to give it a 'social' face, to open it to the sacral function, to solve, in the end, the problem of reintegrating the 'negative' at mass level. The avant-garde chains itself to the magic role of Midas.

The use of negation: this new value, or, better, this new operating technique, has a constant function in the transformation of the capitalist-bourgeois crisis into models of development. From 1920 to about 1935, architecture was in the forefront in the battle of the dialectical conversion from Negative to Positive. Its crisis only comes at the precise moment in which, facing the reality of the *Plan*, the role of foreseeing or ideologically mediating the Plan ceases to exist. (This should make clear how useless it is to confront the honest apologists of worn out myths with mockery and irony.)

Perhaps no other discipline has assimilated more than architecture the *ideology of labour*, helping the penetration of superstructured mystifications in support of the advance of the social Capital into the

Country of *realised Socialism*. It is for this very reason that, in the first chapter, I do not make distinctions between the European Constructivists and the Russian avant-gardists. The poetics of the object, the ideology of the *Vesc*, not only put these movements objectively on a par – in spite of their professed very different goals – but prepare the ground, as objectively as possible, for the most recent disciplinary techniques involved in changing the generic, social, group and generation struggles into productive development.

At this point I feel obliged to mention that my criticism of architectural ideology is not in the least apocalyptic. Desperate nihilism belongs to those who, realising the wearing out of the myths at the base of their personal faith, can see in front of them only irrevocable *destiny*. But the first condition for such a misunderstanding is the identification of particular disciplines – art and architecture among the foremost – and of the present institutions with perennial and metahistorical 'values'. One of the specific tasks of the criticism of ideologies is the destruction of the myth of the perpetual and metahistorical validity of institutions and 'values'. This activity too is of course transient, tied to the historical conditions of the class struggle, but only indirectly involved in this struggle; it can reach its objectives only through patient and constant activity, all the more valid, the more conscious it is of its own objective, insuppressible ambiguity.

The absolute separation of criticism from activity, postulated in *Theories and History* and starting from the internal articulations of architecture, has, therefore, this second meaning: it demonstrates the impossibility of any *negation* grafted onto the reality of the discipline, and it gives the warning that only by acting with a false conscience is it possible to speak of anticipation, of disciplines as prefigurations of revolutionary realities, that the only architectural 'revolution' possible today is the concrete adhesion to a rationalisation and development clearly not neutral and without *a priori* guarantees. Demonstrating also that even 'to be as crafty as doves among bursts of laughter' has only one short-lived consequence: the confirmation of the *availability* of institutions.

Accordingly, this book is not concerned with architects as such (or historians): anything in it that may appear contrary to this assumption has to be taken as the residue of cultural and political positions that the author left behind, at least in intention, quite a while ago.

This may clarify further the reason why I consider artificial and unreal the question of the *method* of critical analysis (*see* chapter 5). One must *use* all the tools perfected by bourgeois culture, and use them in depth: this is what I wanted to demonstrate to those still living under the delusion of the possible application of Marxist guarantees to traditional disciplines. (Today, though, I would add a series of notes on the specific meaning of structuralism and its possible use in historical analysis, limiting even further the range of its applicability.)

Beyond the false problems, even beyond the too easy polemics, remains only the possibility of a lucid and detached reading of a change (of architectural culture in its global sense) that, the more one researches its most intimate articulations, the more unified it appears in its internal dialectic.

The following pages will just touch upon this theme, as the premise of an urgent second 'political' reading of the entire history of modern architecture.

Note

Fundamental to the analysis of the 'active' role of negation is the essay by Alberto Asor Rosa 'L'uomo, il poeta', in *Angelus Novus*, 1965, no. 5-6, pp. 1-30, and the essay by Massimo Cacciari 'Sulla genesi del pensiero negativo' in *Contropiano*, 1969, II, no. 1, pp. 131-200. In the same number of *Contropiano* cf. M. Tafuri 'Per una critica dell 'ideologia architettonica' (pp. 31-80) where the theme of the present volume is carried on and moved to a more specific area. See also Francesco Dal Co 'Hannes Meyer e la "venerabile scuola" di Dessau', a preface to the collected works by H. Meyer, with the title: *Architettura o rivoluzione* (Marsilio, Padua 1969), the first chapter of a common study in process at the Istituto di storia dell 'architettura dell' Istituto Universitario di Architettura di Venezia (followed by the more recent collective volume *La città americana dalla guerra civile al New Deal*, Laterza, Roma, Bari 1973).

Note to the fourth (Italian) edition

There is always a difficult relationship between an author and his work. Once written and launched on the round trip that inevitably 'completes' it and returns it changed, the text has run away from the hand that made it. It does not belong to that hand any more. At least, this is the annoying sensation felt by the writer. It would *not* be worth mentioning if, from this annoyance, there did not come the strong need once again to take possession of the text, to crack it and take it apart, to get out of it what, in the first version, was left unsaid. (The note to the second edition expresses this very clearly.)

In the period from the publication of the first edition of *Theories and History* in 1968 up to 1976, several new problems have arisen in the architectural debate. It takes a certain amount of courage to re-offer a text written about nine years ago without substantial alteration: one is tempted to pass it off as evidence of a cultural journey whose more recent results can be seen by anyone. Yet, in reading it again (allowing for my inability, at this stage, to give an account of the mass of new contributions on the theme) I realise now that the problems that were pressing then have not substantially changed.

The position of the reader is, of course, different. But the link between *Theories and History* and the more recent *Progetto e utopia* is still a direct one: the first is only the *prologo in cielo* of the second. So I offer to the more severe of my critics the chance to strike all along my intellectual itinerary: but I feel it is my duty – to myself above all – to offer this interpretative key, also because any naïvety in this volume will have the value of unmistakable historical truth.

Beyond this, the book that is being re-offered to the readers has preserved, in my opinion, its topicality. The theme of 'crisis' that transpires from each of its pages needs to be explained today as the crisis that, more and more, invests the capitalist division of labour and, on reflection, architecture. The latter, which in 1967-8 seemed to be tossing and turning in an uneasy slumber, seems today, still caught in a general uncertainty, accentuated by the slow process of change in an economic sector such as the building trade (*structurally* behind the times). What seems to be most valid, in my opinion, in *Theories and History*, is the effort to show how ineffectual are the brilliant gymnastics carried out in the yard of the model prison, in which architects are left free to move about on temporary reprieve.

The problem is, then, to find the machinery capable of assuming as an essential datum the crisis of its own disciplinary tools. But remembering also that its only meaning is in the premise of a new relationship between intellectual work and urban administration, able to cross, without delays and nostalgias, the mined ground between the building of the future and the myths of the 'roaring twenties'.

Introduction

That architectural criticism finds itself, today, in a rather difficult situation, is not a point that requires much underlining. To criticise, in fact, means to catch the historical scent of phenomena, put them through the sieve of strict evaluation, show their mystifications, values, contradictions and internal dialectics and explode their entire charge of meanings. But in the period we live in, mystifications and brilliant eversions, historical and anti-historical attitudes, bitter intellectualisations and mild mythologies mix themselves so inextricably in the production of art that the critic is bound to start an extremely problematic relationship with his accepted operative practice, particularly in considering the cultural tradition in which he moves. In fighting a cultural revolution there exists an intimate complicity between criticism and activity.

The critic who has embraced the revolutionary cause points all his weapons against the old order, digs out its contradictions and its hypocrisies, and builds a new ideological stack that may lead to the creation of myths: in every revolution myths are the force-ideas necessary to force the situation. But when the revolution – and there is no doubt that the artistic avant-gardes of the twentieth century have fought for a revolution – has reached its goals, criticism loses the support it had found in its total commitment to the revolutionary cause. Then, in order not to lose its purpose, criticism will have to turn to the history of the reforming movement, showing its shortcomings, contradictions, betrayed goals,

1

failures and, particularly, its complexity and fragmentation. Now the generous myths of the initial Heroic period, having lost their role as powerful ideas, are reduced to subjects of debate.

In our case, facing so many explosions of intricate movements, agitations, new questions, and the resulting multiform and chaotic panorama of architectural international culture in the seventies, the main disturbing problem for those critics who do not wish to bury their heads in the sand, or live in an escapist peace with worn out myths, is still the historical assessment of the present contradictions. This implies a courageous and honest scrutiny of the very foundations of the Modern Movement: in fact, a thorough investigation of whether it is still legitimate to speak of a Modern Movement as a monolithic corpus of ideas, poetics and linguistic traditions. One must not, then, turn away from the vista of laborious, uncertain and frustrated efforts that architects have accumulated. It may be one's duty to speak of escapism, renunciations, withdrawals and the waste of usable assets. But this is not enough. The critic that stops at these considerations, which are so obvious as to be almost useless, has already betrayed his foremost task, which is to explain, to diagnose exactly and to avoid moralising in order to see, in the context of negative facts, what are the mistakes we are now paying for, and which are the new values nesting in the difficult and disconnected set of circumstances we live in, day by day. The main danger, in this case, is being caught in the very ambiguity from which one tries to extract a logical structure and a meaning, as pre-conditions to any future operation directed towards a new working hypothesis.

Today it is even more necessary for the critic to be open-minded, to accept, without the falsifying veil of prejudices, totally confused proposals. Today, as never before, there is a need for stricter attitudes, for a deep sense and knowledge of history, as well as for a watchful eye, in order to sort out, in the vast context of historical movements, broad research or single projects, the influences dictated by fashion – and even cultural snobbism – from the forces of renewal.

The architect can always find some sort of coherence in the contradictions of the 'job' of planning, but the critic content with such a situation would either be simply sceptical, or unforgivably superficial. By researching on a firm basis the possibilities contained in the poetics and codes of contemporary architecture, it is possible to salvage a cultural positivism and constructivism, even is often limited to marginal questions. But the critic conscious of the transient and *dangerous* situation of modern architecture, cannot allow himself illusions or artificial enthusiasms in the same way as he cannot allow himself – and this is perhaps more important – apocalyptic or intimist attitudes. (The critic is like the person who has decided to walk on a tight-rope while constantly changing winds do their best to blow him down.) The image is not at all rhetorical: since the Modern Movement discovered its own multiformity, with relative shock, the initial partnership between committed criticism and new architecture and, indeed, the identification of criticism with an activity that shares its premises and problems, has necessarily weakened. The merging of the character of architect and critic in the same person – almost the norm in architecture, unlike other techniques of visual communication – has not entirely covered up this rupture: the split personality of the architect who writes and theorises and also practises is commonplace.

It is for this reason that the *pure critic* begins to be seen as a dangerous figure: and to be labelled with the stamp of a movement, a trend, or a poetic. As the kind of criticism that needs to keep its distance from the operative practice must constantly de-mystify that practice in order to go beyond its contradictions or, at least, render them with a certain precision, one sees the architects trying to *capture* that criticism; trying, in fact, to exorcise it. Trying to avoid capture may be interpreted as fear by the ignorant or dishonest. But the critic, in order to return to his proper task – objective and unprejudiced historical diagnosis and not the job of prompter or 'proof-reader' – needs, on the contrary, a great deal of courage, because in attempting to historicise the dramatic meanings of the present moment, he is walking on mined ground.

It is useless hiding from the fact that the threat hanging over the head of those wanting to 'understand' by radically demolishing every contemporary myth, is the same as that felt by Vasari in the second half of the sixteenth century: more and more one is invited to answer the tragic question of the historical permissibility of the Modern Movement's continuity with tradition.

Merely to pose the question of whether contemporary architecture finds itself, or not, at a radical turning point has value as a symptom. It means that one feels, at the same time, inside and outside the historical tradition, steeped in it yet beyond it, ambiguously involved in a figurative revolution that, entirely founded on the permanent opposition to every acquired truth, turns its weapons upon itself. As Rosenberg wrote, contesting the false radicalism of Sir Herbert Read:

Neither revolutionary art nor revolutionary criticism can get out of it: revolutionary art is a contradiction. It declares that art is art in being against art; and then tries to establish itself as the soundest kind of art. It demands of the critic that he take 'explosiveness' as an aesthetic principle, and that he protects this principle against being blown to bits by the 'conscious negation' of principles.

At war with themselves, revolutionary art and criticism cannot avoid the ridiculous. Yet upon the contradiction of revolution depends the life of art in this revolutionary epoch, and art and criticism must continue to embrace its absurdities.[1]

But, perhaps, it is not quite enough just to accept the ridiculousness of the situation. The task of criticism, has, in fact, changed. If the problem is to operate a sort of changing selection without *a priori* leanings, in order to identify the structure of the problems that are confusedly faced and then left untackled by the new generations and by the few culturally alive masters of the 'third generation' of the Modern Movement, one cannot give, once and for all, the terms of comparison for the foundation of an historical analysis. Criticism is bound, like architecture, continually to revolutionise itself in the search for adequate parameters.

It is no longer possible to trust what has been the traditional safety valve of criticism: the absolution or condemnation of the work in itself. The futility of such a dogmatic attitude on the part of the critic is even clearer. Having said this, let us avoid a possible misunderstanding: we do not at all mean to say that we should get rid of judgment and be content with a sort of relativistic limbo where *tout se tient*. What we would rather emphasise is the difficulty of anyone who is bound to be in daily touch not with badly- or well-finished work, but rather with endless unfulfilled intentions, with new impulses bogged down in the most disheartening and traditional contexts, with reticent intuitions and with intentionally unrealisable projects. Is it possible to evaluate in a traditional way such a disconcerting vista, or is it not, rather, the specific task of the critic to understand its intrinsic meaning, and establish some order through a temporary suspension of judgment?

In an unprejudiced examination of the current situation of architectural culture, the inconsistency and elusiveness of so much current production makes it obvious that one is facing a tacit and perhaps unconscious effort to state, on the one hand, the ineffective nature of architecture, and on the other, to find however confused, a new and unforeseen dimension for architectural activity. It is because of that we have spoken of the possible new availability of the critic: a rigorous and controlled availability, of course, but adequate to the tasks set by the historical moment.[2]

At this point there emerges the essential question of a rigorous formulation of the critic's basic tools. After all, the criticism of modern architecture has been obliged to proceed, almost until today, along rails laid on unprejudiced empiricism: perhaps this was the only viable route as, too often, the art of our century has jumped the fence of ideological conventions, of speculative foundations, of the very same aesthetics available to the critic. So much so that the only authentic criticism of modern art came, especially between 1920 and 1940, from those with enough courage not to derive their analytical methods from existing philosophical systems but from direct and empirical contact with the thoroughly new questions of the avant-gardes.

One must not judge this empirical criticism in a hurry. Through it Pevsner, Behne, Benjamin, Giedion, Persico, Giolli, Argan, Dorner and Shand went, before World War II, beyond the limitations of the thinking of their time, deriving, from the poetics of modern art, the ability to read the new phenomena in the light of an open process, of perpetual mutability, of vindication of the casual, the non-rational, the gestural and the absurd. Post-war criticism has been able to graft onto this empirical tradition, the contributions of Lukacsian realism, existentialism, relativism, Husserlian phenomenology, some Bergsonian recouping of the past, a re-vitalised Fiedlerian pure-visibilism, Croce, and, more recently, *Gestalt psychology*, structural linguistics, semantics, semiology, information theory and anthropological structuralism.

Critical eclecticism then? Perhaps; but, at least, not completely negative. This eclecticism has shown that, in part, the questions posed by modern architecture are more advanced than those successively faced by the traditional methods; and in part it has shown the operative independance of criticism, so much so, that the philosophers themselves have admitted to receiving stimuli and new concepts from it.[3]

But once glimpsed, the crisis of critical operability (because it is no longer possible to take a single position in favour of one current in modern architecture), once discovered, the imminent dialectic of contemporary art, empiricism and eclecticism begin to look like dangers, like instruments unable to provide a rigorous criticism. Lately, architectural critics have shown a symptomatic interest in the researches that have introduced, in the social sciences and the analysis of linguistic and visual communications, methods analogous to those of the empirical and experimental sciences. Today semiology and structuralism are also on the agenda in architectural studies. And one can show immediately the positive contributions made by them to the analysis of planning: first of all they satisfy the need for a scientific basis, and the need for objectivity is particularly felt in times of deep uncertainty and restlessness. Secondly, they offer a systematic commitment to understanding the phenomena that justify the poetics of anguish and crisis, by now become evasive and inoperative through wear and tear. Any criticism, to do more than whining, must, basically, make a diagnosis. And as diagnostic methods – once recognised as such and not as fashionable doctrines or as a single dogmatic *corpus*– structuralism and semiology have already shown their efficiency. But they have also shown the danger and the ideology hiding behind their apparent lack of ideology. Once more, then, criticism is called upon to give its contribution: to choose, and to place within a well-founded historicism the materials on offer.

If it is true though, as François Furet[4] has written, that the fascination felt by the French leftist intelligentsia for the structuralism of Lévi-Strauss is due to the fact that 'simply and progressively the structural description of a man-object has taken the place, in history, of the advent of the man-god', it is true also that a large part of modern art had foreseen this substitution: from Dada and some aspects of De Stijl, and from Russian constructivism, to Le Corbusier, if one reads it correctly. And one cannot say that the acceptance of the end of the myth of humanist anthropocentrism, has not led, so far as those artistic experiences are concerned, to a new and more authentic attitude in man towards the world structured by him.

Somehow we could consider Lévi-Strauss the Parmenides of this neo-Eleatic flavoured (*malgré soi*) philosophy: structure and order against disorder in history, the permanence of Being against the phenomenology of Becoming, the stability of the common mechanisms to which man is reduced against Sartrian dialectical reason (but one is already beginning to see the first skirmishes of the neo-Zenoni demolishing paradoxes). For the moment we are interested in understanding the meaning of some considerable nodes between the structuralist *vogue* and certain phenomena at the centre of artistic and architectural culture. To justify these nodes it is not necessary to rely on the hypothesis of direct influences, which are almost certainly non-existent. The very fact that it is not possible to demonstrate such a direct exchange, becomes, at this point, an independent point of interest, showing the existence of a common horizon created by a common attitude to the present historical condition.

It is of particular relevance to note, here, that ethnological structuralism in its original meaning, Foucault's 'archaeology of human sciences', the anti-humanist orgy of Pop Art, the search for a *new* objectivity by Kahn and his followers, insist – all of them – on the same ideal area (and we would have said ideological, if this term would not take on here the tone of polemical paradox). To discover that this ideal area is all based on anti-historical knowledge and activity might frighten or disconcert. But we shall be far less disconcerting if we try to go further, to dig deeper into the phenomena and not to be led by inadequate ideological pulls.

Has modern art not presented itself, from the very beginning, in the European avant-garde movements, as a true challenge to history? Has it not tried to destroy not only history, but even itself as an historical object? Dada and De Stijl are not all that antithetical if seen from this very particular point of view. But this is not all. The gap between Louis Kahn's myth of Order, with his hermetic delving into the material offered by history so as to de-historify, to the extreme, architectural planning; and the neo-plastic mysticism tending to resolve oppositions and contrasts in a messianic appeasement, is not as crucial as it may first appear, when we compare works like the Salk laboratories and the Schröder house.

The traditional anti-historicism of the avant-gardes finds, then, a kind of confirmation in the very experiences that are trying to overcome it. And there is a reason. 'Myth is against history' Barthes tells us, and myths carry on their mystification by hiding the artificial (and the ideological artificiality) behind the mask of a fake 'naturalism'.[5] If we accept these premises, then the present moment, so totally bent on avoiding, through *new myths*, the commitment of understanding the present, cannot help turning even the researches that, with renewed vigour and rigour, try to plan a systematic and objective reading of the world, of things, of history and of human conventions into *fashion and myth*.

In architectural culture, in particular (but the point applies to all techniques of visual communication), looking for a more advanced criticism seems to compromise the very basis of the critical spirit. In 1957 Argan wrote:

> If we have a crisis on hand, it is not the crisis of criticism, and not just from yesterday, that has upset the great ideologies, conceptions and systems. And this should not be, by itself, a cause for despair: criticism is built on crises, and one should only think of it as criticism that goes beyond its own results. The outcome of the crises is unforeseeable: criticism does not allow predestined salvations or condemnations. However salvation – salvation of the critical spirit inherited from the Enlightenment by modern art and culture – is likely, if criticism is to be criticism of experiences and not of hypotheses: if it will show itself to be, even in art, historical criticism.[6]

Well, twenty years after Argan stated his lucid diagnosis, we can say that, today more than ever, art and architecture have been dominated by the ineffability of hypothesis, and have been so little creators of experiences.

Nor, we must add, has criticism perhaps ever assumed such a minimal historicist character as the one that goes hand in hand with the proliferation of architecture.

From this brief survey, it follows that the critic who wants to make historical the experiences of contemporary architecture and who tries to rescue historicity from the web of the past, finds himself against the current. To what degree then does this opposition involve the historicity of the Modern Movement? And to what degree is the separation from the flow of praxis symptomatic of a deep crisis of *operative criticism*, or is there an opening, in criticism, for a new operative *modus*? And again, what is the relationship that history and criticism can legitimately start with the new sciences and the theories of communication, and still preserve their specific prerogatives, their specific roles, and their specific methods?

These are, basically, the questions at the core of this book: in it, perhaps, one should look for guidelines and temporary solutions more than for definitive answers. We are convinced that methodologies of history should closely relate with the tasks that history itself, in the problem of its development, offers to those who refuse to be swallowed up by the daily mythologies, and by the mythologies – similar and opposed – of catharsis that many would like to conjure up from the gradual and silent annihilation of 'historical reason'.

Notes

[1] Harold Rosenberg, *The Tradition of the New*, Horizon Press 1959. In the same essay ('Revolution and the Concept of Beauty'), Rosenberg denounces the ambiguous links between political revolutions and artistic revolutions, referring to the confusion – today considerably reduced – present in the American culture of the forties and fifties. But his diagnosis still contains a relevant truth when he states that 'The result' (of those ambiguities) 'is an atmosphere of bad conscience, of dupery and self-dupery. It is not too much to say that bad conscience about revolution is the specific malady of art today.'

[2] This availability is made even more necessary by the artistic experience's continuous permutation of semantic areas, often one superimposed on the other. For this reason the crisis of every defined aesthetic, sanctioned by the semantic criticism historicised by Plebe and taken by Garroni to a 'plural notion of art', needs an extremely complex critical attitude and an aesthetic 'that suggests an open artistic field, open and unpredictable' (as later recognised by Anceschi). (Cf. Armando Plebe, *Processo all'estetica*, La Nuova Italia, Florence 1952; Emilio Garroni, *La crisi semantica delle arti*, Officina Ed., Rome 1964, pp. 109 ff.; Luciano Anceschi, *Progetto di una sistematica dell'arte*, Mursia, Milan 1962 and 'Critica, Filosofia, Fenomenologia' in *Il Verri*, 1967, no. 18, pp. 13–24.) Within

this sphere, criticism, having lost the hope of finding pre-existing support in a rigorously philosophical aesthetic, finds new autonomy and new responsibilities.

³ On this subject, the results of the round table at the INARCH, Rome, March 1961 are of considerable interest. (Discussions by G. Calogero, R. Assunto, R. Bonelli, A. Plebe.) They partially appeared in *L'Architettura cronache e storia*, 1961, VII, no. 71, pp. 336–7.

⁴ François Furet, 'Gli intellettuali francesi e lo strutturalismo', in *Tempo Presente*, 1967, no. 7, p. 14.

⁵ We are obviously referring to Roland Barthes's *Mythologies*.

⁶ Giulio Carlo Argan, *La crisi dei valori* (1957), now in *Salvezza e caduta dell'arte moderna*, Il Saggiatore, Milan 1964, p. 38.

1

Modern Architecture and the Eclipse of History

From the few points already mentioned one can begin to see a singular phenomenon: the difficulties of criticism come from the very context of modern art, and the most vulnerable type of criticism is, without doubt, historical criticism. The historians who refuse the role of fashionable commentator, and who try to historicise their criticism, know what we mean. Despite the fact that, for some time now, through the efforts of the masters of modern art criticism – Pevsner, Giedion, Argan, Zevi – the air-tight division between the history of architecture and criticism of contemporary phenomena has disappeared, and, despite an adequate articulation within historiography, one cannot ignore the obstacles continually thrown in the path of criticism by the operative practice.

We are not referring only to the speed of the *consumption* of images, research and movements. The problem with assessing contemporary architecture historically comes from its initial choice: presenting itself as a radically *anti-historical* phenomenon. For some time now, many historians have felt the need to attack polemically this assumption of the avant-gardes of this century. In April 1961 the *Journal of the Royal Institute of British Architects* printed a fundamental essay by Pevsner with the symptomatic title: 'Modern Architecture and the Historian, or the Return of Historicism'.[1] The English historian notes with concern how history, in reappearing on the scene of modern architecture, becomes oddly responsible for the most absurd revivalist phenomena. Paradoxically, after the anti-historical and technological ideology of the

11

initial phase of the Modern Movement, the reintroduction of history seemed to cause, according to Pevsner, a backward leap towards a revival of the Victorian mentality.

The following year Sibyl Moholy-Nagy compared the function of the historian in architectural didactics to the stiffly formal gentleman who, during a royal banquet, proposes a toast to the king before the start of the ceremony:

> . . . for about the span of a generation, from 1920 to 1955, the function of the historian in architectural teaching has been that of the pathetic proposer of toasts. His task was to bow, more or less self-consciously, to a cultural continuity by then without any real links with what architecture thought to be its real mission. This mission consisted, according to the masters of the modern architecture of the twenties, in starting from scratch. The muse of Gropius, Mies van der Rohe, Le Corbusier, Aalto, Oud and dozens of others did not allow illicit flirtations with history.[2]

The price to be paid, according to Moholy-Nagy, is the new historicist eclecticism, partially accepted by her in post-*General Motors* Saarinen; in post-Miesian Johnson; in Rudolph's Wellesley Art Centre, and in the last works of Kahn. In 1964 Moholy-Nagy takes up the subject again:[3]

> The failure of the International Style to stimulate either the creative imagination of the architect, *or* provide identification for the client, *or* answer to the need for historical consciousness in cityscapes, was the immediate cause for the reanimation of the historical corpse. It was a revival that did not start in the most logical place – the schools of architecture, which, at least in America, are servile camp-followers of every trend and not makers of architectural revolutions. The rediscovery of architectural continuity must be credited to practising architects and the most successful ones at that. Saarinen was perhaps the first one with his Lombardising chapel at MIT [the Massachusetts Institute of Technology], followed by Johnson, Rudolph, Kahn, Johansen, Yamasaki – even by Gropius, the celebrated Medicine Man of international Functionalism. They all tried kaleidoscopic combinations of historical and contemporary elements in an attempt to recover architecture from between the teeth of building technology. The results have been rarely successful, and frequently ridiculous.[4]

An exalted role for the historian then, but architectural historicism is seen as an aberrant phenomenon, whose faults are firmly placed on the shoulders of the masters of the Modern Movement.

The theme is taken up again, by Jacobs and Stanford Anderson,[5] and by Reyner Banham in particular, who, already in 1960, saw the Modern Movement merging with the historical tradition as:

> . . . the rediscovery of science as a dynamic force, rather than the humble servant of architecture. The original idea of the early years of the century, of sciences as an unavoidable directive to progress and development, has been reversed by those who cheer for history, and has been watered down to a limited partnership by the mainstream. Those who have re-explored the twenties and read the Futurists for themselves feel once more the compulsions of science, the need to take a firm grip on it, and to stay with it whatever the consequences.[6]

In stating the ideological principles of the Modern Movement, Banham tends to put history back in the realm of the 'tradition of the new'. The anti-historicist tradition is, however, the target of other, recurrent accusations. Zevi writes:

> The architects, glutted with technology and rational objectivism, have turned again to tradition, have mumbled about pre-existing environments, have modelled their buildings on ancient prototypes, but with disarming superficiality. From all this derives the present confusion that mixes together neo-Liberty, so-called 'spontaneous' building, superficial attempts at new environments and even badly modernised revivals. This is the price paid by the middle generation for having embraced, without discussion, the anti-historical ideology of the masters, and then for having suddenly dropped it without any further elaboration.[7]

And again, in his inaugural lecture at Rome University, Zevi stated:

> . . . the masters of modern architecture . . . either sincerely believed in an a-historical architecural methodology, and, therefore, in non-historical teaching: if so, it was their duty to formulate a grammar and syntax for modern architecture, substituting new and more contemporary doctrines for the academic precepts, on the line of Schönberg, Brecht, Eliot, and, in his own way, Van Doesburg; or they believed in a historical methodology of architectural activity (their own activity included), if so it was their duty to formulate this new method, and, instead of removing history from the Bauhaus or placing it in quarantine, they themselves should have become historians, leaving behind the formal, technological and functionalist apodictical

statements, and shaping a criticism able to penetrate architectural reality at all its levels, from territorial planning to the moulding and to the minutest sign of the image.[8]

One could carry on with the quotations, but we think we have shown adequately the diffused attitude of architectural historiography: with the exception of Banham, paladin of technological orthodoxy, the historians are in revolt against the very sources of modern art. The Bauhaus and the masters of the avant-garde have been put in the dock; the new tasks are those left unsolved in the 'roaring twenties'; the anti-historicism of the Modern Movement is judged contingent and surmountable, and what is put forward is the hypothesis of history as a guide for a new type of experience.

It is obvious, then, that we have generations of historians frustrated by the recent adventures of international architecture. What one should rather ask is whether the proposed remedies are not themselves anti-historical. It would not make much sense to accuse a revolutionary movement of having been what it *has* been, and then state one's loyalty to it in every other statement. We must, in other words, test the 'historicity' of the anti-historicism of the avant-gardes, and check to what degree the phenomenon is still adhered to – even if in more evolved forms.

Such an analysis is essential before attempting any methodological incursion into the historical–critical field. To measure the degree of anti-historicism of the time we live in, poses the question of the quality of our commitment, as historians, to the cultural development of the architectural debate. If the salvaging of history, after so many moralising attitudes, has not happened and does not show any sign of happening, in the field of international architecture, then the judgment of the entire process of the modern movement should be modified according to the value given to this theme. And as one of the most widespread prejudices is the one that sees the problem of history arbitrarily censured by the artistic avant-gardes of the twentieth century, we will go back, summarily, to the true origin of the process: to the revolution of modern art carried out by the Tuscan humanists of the Quattrocento.

From the moment in which Brunelleschi institutionalised a linguistic code and a symbolic system based on a superhistorical comparison with the great example of antiquity, to the time when Alberti, feeling dissatisfied with mythical historicism, began to explore rationally the structure of that code and its syntactical and emblematical values: in this period, the first great attempt of modern history to *actualise* historical values as a translation of mythical time into present time, of archaic meanings into revolutionary messages, of ancient 'words' into civil actions, burnt itself out. It may seem paradoxical, but already the Brunelleschian operation had achieved, as a result, not so much the rooting into history of architectural planning, but, rather, its *de-historicisation*. It is important to understand this point because it results in the conditioning of architectural research during the entire historical span from the Quattrocento to the threshold of the contemporary age.

Between Brunelleschi's vocabulary, supported by fragments of the classical world – as rightly perceived by Brandi[9] – and the philological recovery of that classicism (as documented by Alberti's the *De re aedificatoria*, by Giuliano da Sangallo's studies, by Bramante's complex activity in Rome), there is the same distance that exists between those who make use of the evocative power of *quotations* and *allusions* to substantiate an independent discourse in order to *build* a new reality, and those who try to recover the exact meaning of those quotations in order to cover up the disappointments of reality, to re-evoke the substantial structures of an heroic past in order to contrast them, polemically, with contemporary hypocrisies, to defend an artistic revolution that is in danger by locking it up in the ivory tower of an historicism become an end in itself.

The autonomous and absolute architectural *objects* of Brunelleschi were bound to penetrate the structures of the medieval city, upsetting and changing its significance. The symbolic and constructive self-sufficiency of the new three-dimensional spatiality radiated into the urban space a rational order that was the absolute emblem of a strict ethical will. It is sufficient to think of the original project for S. Spirito – in which the continuous articulation of the wall and the almost obsessive unity of the internal and external spaces are clearly the aggressive 'manifesto' of this new figurative language – to realise how much, for Brunelleschi, the structuring of the architectural organisms was consciously connected to the theme of urban space. One of the best lessons to be learnt from Brunelleschi's Humanism is its new conception of the pre-existing town as an available and passing structure, ready to change its global meaning as soon as the introduction of compact architectural *objects* altered the balance of the Romanesque–Gothic 'continuous narrative'.

Urban history and new intervention are, therefore, still complementary, but only in a dialectical sense. One could go further: although S. Maria del Fiore's dome, the two basilicas of S. Lorenzo and S. Spirito and the Rotonda degli Angeli are thought of as architecture on an urban scale, it is clear that Brunelleschi and Alberti did not feel the need to codify any urbanistic utopias. Perspective space as strictly organic is, in fact, stated in the first Humanism as a new and polemical truth, complete in itself. The architecture that is co-ordinated around its rational postulates confronts the pre-existing urban textures and competes with them. There is no need to extend the unifying co-ordination of space to the whole city, because that very same architecture claims to show visibly its capacity to reverberate its rational quality on the multi-stratified medieval textures.

From this one can deduce that in Brunelleschi's thinking there is a conscious historical principle. But it is a connection with history based on the arbitrary selection, from its context, of positive elements to be absorbed – classic antiquity as a background to be left at the state of pure allusion, and the pre-humanistic experiences of the Tuscan Romanesque and Gothic – and negative elements to be overcome: among others, the additive and the empirical in the urban space and the ornamental in the medieval decorative repertoire. In this way Brunelleschi carries on his urbanistic revolution, starting from the architectural objects. He seems to have realised that the rigour in the construction implies in itself the introduction of a new reading code of the town as structure. What before had been the rule – historical superimposition of events and the parataxis of spaces – now becomes the exception, if read in the light of the new humanistic linguistic code. And, inversely, the rational rigour of the organism becomes the norm rather than the exception.

History, according to this conception, cannot be represented by a continuous line, but, rather, by a broken line defined by an arbitrary yardstick that decides, each time, its values and goals.[10] On such 'heroic' caesura of historical time are based almost four centuries of architectural research: even the present experience is considerably influenced by it.

With his leading role in the first artistic 'avant-garde' in the modern sense, Brunelleschi broke the historical continuity of figurative experience, claiming to be independently *building* a *new history*. His allusions to classic antiquity were, then, only a prop – the only one acceptable. And it should be clear that it is an ideological support, better suited to cut off its links with the past than to re-offer it as tradition.[11] It is for this very reason that we have separated Brunelleschi's de-historicisation from the historicist studies of his followers.

Alberti too, in his activity as a 'restorer', quarrels continuously with the pre-existing structures on which he grafts his interventions.[12] But when he leaves the completion of the nave of S. Francesco da Rimini to Matteo de' Pasti, proposing to superimpose on the linguistic *pastiche* of his collaborator the projected but not realised, vast dome, or when he lets the medieval evidence seep through onto the façade of S. Maria Novella, his goals are not as linear and absolute as those in Brunelleschi's work. On the one hand Alberti wants to make tangible the victory of the ideal unity of the classicist language: he therefore leaves breathing space for the pre-existing Gothic elements and for the naïvety of Matteo de' Pasti in order to dramatise, to represent and perpetuate the heroic victory of Humanist *reason* over the medieval or medievalesque 'barbarisms'. On the other hand, he realises that his game is extremely dangerous, because he himself discovers, through it, the contaminated seduction of linguistic pluralism. The exasperated need to specify the classicist code through historical verification is, then, the result of the insecurity reflected in so many pages of *De re aedificatoria*.[13]

The entire culture of the sixteenth century swings between two poles. On one hand, the will to give historical foundation to an *anti-historical code,* like the one of the revived Classicism; on the other, the temptation – repressed but always there – to compromise and dirty one's hands with the very Medieval and Gothic languages that the entire Classicist culture wanted to erase in its apodeictic declarations, because they were guilty of betraying the *true* and the *beautiful* of the *Antique* which had been elected to a *second and truer Nature.* But the exorcism had not been complete: the ghost of the Middle Ages continues to reappear, making the nightmares of Mannerism even more tormented.

History, violently annihilated, seems to revenge itself: a whole range of studies remains to be done on the compromises of the Classicist language with Medievalesque fragments, modulations and even syntactical structures, during the sixteenth century. And we should point out that such commixtures, in a period like the sixteenth century in which Humanism (although betrayed in its ideal aims) had already won its battle, are very different from the, apparently similar, commixtures typical of the provincial circles of fifteenth-century Italy.

It is worthwhile, for the sake of our argument, to stay for a while with these singular mannerist commixtures. First of all we find, since the first part of the sixteenth century, an Anti-Bramante – rather than an anti-Classicist – tendency that takes shape in Raphael's circle, that finds support in the taste for *licence* connected to the discovery of the ancient *grotesques,* that develops into an intentionally *theatrical* architecture – from the Raphaelesque Branconio Palace, to the Villa Imperiale at Pesaro del Genga, to the work by Peruzzi and to the volumes of Serlio. But there exists also a more destructive tendency towards *contaminatio,* towards a polemical deformation of the Classicist lexicon, towards its sadistic perversion by grafting it onto Gothic or Gothic-like systems. Many of the designs for the S. Petronio façade, for example – particularly those by Peruzzi, Giulio Romano and Palladio;[14] in a certain sense Sangallo's design for S. Pietro; the 'restoration' by the same Giulio Romano of S. Benedetto in Polirone; the pre-romantic and hideous mixtures by Dietterlin; the façade by Alessi of S. Maria sopra S. Celso in Milan (a true assembly of casual architectural *things* and perhaps a conscious resumption of the medieval *facciate a vento*), are all examples of putting forward again the *problem of history*: they are all demonstrations *ad absurdum* of the strong need to look again at the 'great void' of the Middle Ages as historical time. But the very technique of *bricolage* of these attempts led to the unavoidable and even more radical destruction of that historical time: unavoidable also because the dream of recovery was only possible by going beyond the limits of Classicist culture.[15]

In the studies of the late sixteenth century one can see two opposite approaches to history. The mannerist contaminations – we will deal with them more specifically later – as desperate self-critical analyses, were multi-valent in order to show the uneasy conscience of the arbitrary culture to which they referred; they tried to squeeze new and deeper meanings from the meeting of the most opposite syntaxes. Against this exasperated experimentalism, typical of the northern groups – Tibaldi, Alessi, Palladio (within certain limits), not to mention the French influence from De l'Orme to Du Cerceau – came the examples of a totally antihistoricist art: the problem of history, stirred up (even though not systematically) by Mannerism, appeared dangerous, full of heretical ferments, frighteningly destructive.

With Vignola and the post-Michelangelo influences in Rome, with Herrera in Spain, Scamozzi in Venice and some tendencies in the architecture of the reformed countries (Germany and Holland), we see the formation, for opposite reasons, of a movement towards a *timeless art*, abstract in the fullest sense of the term. As far as the Catholic countries went, this architecture could not be made to correspond mechanically to a Jesuit style: avoiding any type of compromise with history it hides, mainly, the fear of directly facing the problem of the meanings in architecture. It is clear that an art that does not want to create new meanings, or probe its own interior with merciless self-criticism, but prefers to exalt, beautify and rhetorically enlarge an accepted *truth* without discussion, can only turn away from any temptation to compromise itself with historical verification: especially if that truth is referred to the timeless ideology of the Church of Rome.[16]

Neo-Feudalism and the Counter-Reformation are only, therefore, catalysts in the anti-historicist reaction started at the beginning of the sixteenth century: so much so, that in Milan, the Trentine precepts of Cardinal Borromeo can easily find points of contact with the disquieting poetics of an experimentalist like Pellegrini.

The antithesis between historicist experimentalism and rigorist abstractions is then real, but what matters most is its continuation, under a different cloak, into Baroque Europe. When Bernini accuses Borromini of being a 'good heretic', stating that he would rather have a 'bad Catholic', he catches a vital point of our theme. Borromini, in fact, might well appear 'heretical' in the Rome of Urban VIII, where historical silence was already a fact, and where the master from Bissone imports suddenly and fully the entire wardrobe of the problematic historicism of northern Mannerism. Borromini had been drawing from this source since the time of his collaboration with Maderno.[17]

One of the main features of Borromini's architecture is that he sees himself as the heir of the troubled Mannerist issues, of their uneasy symbolic world, of their ethical criticism. It is for this very reason that Borromini gives first place to the problem of history. For Borromini, architecture must not follow a programme imposed from outside, but has to find its own motives in the independent shaping of its programmes, must fold on itself to show its structure as a renewed instrument of communication, has to stratify itself in a complex system of images and geometric–symbolic matrixes. Therefore the spatial synthesis that will unify such a tangle of problems can only tend to a multi-valence and to a simultaneity of meanings. In the *typological syntheses* constantly adopted by Borromini as a method of configurating space, there always seeps through a *bricolage* of modulations, of memories, of objects derived from Classic Antiquity, from Late Antiquity, from the Paleo-Christian, from Gothic, from Albertian and utopistic-romantic Humanism, from the most varied models of sixteenth-century architecture. They span from the spatial permeations of Peruzzi to the anamorphic contractions of Michelangelo and Montano, to the anthropomorphic decorativism of Pellegrini, to the attempts at linguistic renewal by Vignola and Palladio.

In the geometric matrix of S. Carlino are fused the experiments with ovoidal spaces by Peruzzi, Serlio and Vignola, with the Gothic composition *ad triangulum* (which a Vitruvian of the first Cinquecento, like Cesariano, contrived to find even in Milan Cathedral) and with the anti-naturalistic taste for anamorphosis and for the perspective contraction typical of the mannerist surreal experiments; from Huguet to Montano.[18] And this is not all. The decoration is full of *quotations*: the crowning of the frieze (reminder of Alberti's *Sacellum* of S. Pancrazio) and the Michelangelesque moulding of the entablatures.

The search for *quotations* in Borromini's work could go on for ever. In S. Ivo the meeting and the clashing of the unified space of the Pantheon with Peruzzi's geometrical permeations, with the suggestion, perhaps, of Vitozzi's Chiesa della Trinità in Turin, with the memory of the engravings of Kircher and of the *Iconologia* of Ripa; while the references to Michelangelo are everywhere in the polyphony of decorative structure.[19] But the clearest examples of the historicist mixtilinear language of Borromini are doubtless the funerary altars, conceived as independent perspective *theatres*, in the naves of S. Giovanni in Laterano. Here the elastic and compressed spaces ostentatiously absorb Paleo-Christian, Gothic and fifteenth-century fragments derived from pre-existing monuments. Particularly in the tombs of Cardinal Giussano and of Cardinal De Chiaves, mosaics, gothic mullioned windows with twinlights, sculptures and headstones are used in a wondrous play of allusions. The ancient fragments are inserted – like ready-made objects – in ideal spaces realised through elastic perspective deformations: almost to show, from the inside of those unnatural windows open on to an *autre* universe, the problematics of an existential condition that cannot reject history, but are not yet able to identify its true value.

It has been mentioned, and rightly so, that from a contemporary standpoint, the Borrominian *pastiches* destroy rather than reinforce the historical value of the ancient 'things' inserted in the new contexts. But if we refer to the value that those scattered quotations might have had in the middle of the seventeenth century, we will realise that Borromini's work introduces, in the Classicist world, a genuine *experience of history*. History, like nature, is no longer a one-dimensional value: history may contradict the present, may put in doubt, may impose, with its complexity and its variety, a choice to be motivated each successive time. Late Antiquity, Medieval or Gothic, they all challenge the validity of the Classical codes. In order to carry on using them (as Borromini meant to do, in spite of all his destructive *fury*) it is not enough, as in the fifteenth and sixteenth centuries, to ignore the issue through an act of faith: now one needs to check, to restore by plunging into history, by getting involved with it and soiled by it. Borromini's *realism* could not escape this task, on penalty of eclecticism, and its result is the highest figurative *summa* of pre-Illuminist culture.

With Borromini, then, are we dealing with historicism or anti-historicism? Within the terms of the Baroque dispute, what we have called *experience of history* can only be read as a prophetic anticipation of the attitudes of the twentieth century avant-gardes: the *collage* of *memories* lifted out of their historical contexts finds structure and

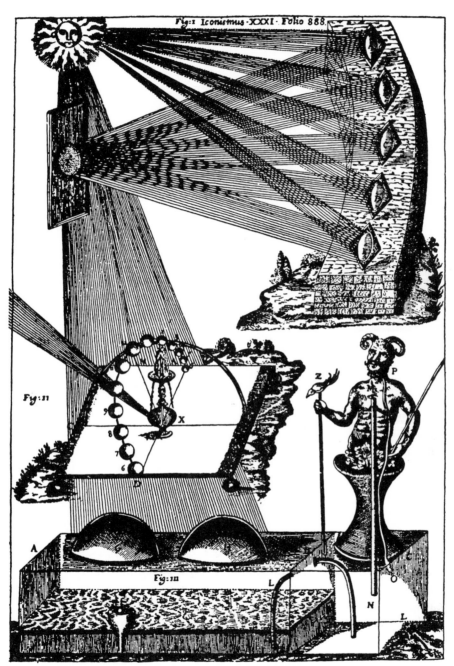

1.   A. Kircher, Magic statue, '*quae ad ortum Solis, et singulis horis consequentibus Sole percussa prodigiosum Sinum excitet*'. From Kircher's *Ars Magna*, Rome 1645. Science, rhetoric and magic are mutually annihilated in the Baroque myth of the 'controlled emotion'

semantic location within the frame of an independently built organic space. It is, in fact, this reorganisation of the historical material that separates Borromini's work from the earlier *pastiches* and from those of his contemporaries like the Elizabethan Prodigy Houses, Sambin's work at Dijon, Inigo Jones's first attempts and Christopher Wren's experimentalism.[20] Borromini, like the architects of the late English sixteenth century and like Wren, uses history in a totally anti-dogmatic way: for him too, as for them, the freedom of quotation and reference acquires a definite semantic value. The difference is in the role given to those quotations and to those references.

Substantially we can identify *three ways* in Baroque historicism:

A. *The critical eclecticism of Carlo Fontana and Fischer von Erlach:* of those, that is, who deliberately ignore the dialectical antithesis between the discontinuity introduced by Borromini into the material inherited from history, and the continuity with the Roman tradition typical of Bernini. The *Entwurf einer historischen Architektur*, by von Erlach, is the most complete document of the tendency to unify in one single system the dramatic dilemma of the Roman dispute during the seventeenth century.[21] For these architects the history of Classicism stretches out like a linear and continuous *corpus*, without any real internal tensions. Their only task, consequently, is its critical arrangement, rationalisation and the elimination of obscure points. Furthermore, we must underline that when we speak (in connection with Fontana and von Erlach) of critical eclectism and intellectualism, we must take these qualifications in their most restrictive sense. In their case to criticise means only to develop and merge different suggestions and compositive methods. Their criticism has to do with Classicist historicism because the very eclectic possibility shown by them, makes illusory any search for the polemic infractions of a linguistic code so obviously and solidly super-historical.

B. *The European Borrominism that develops the problematic relationship with the non-classical and anti-classical historical cultures, in the most varied ways and significances:* from Guarini to Dientzenhofer, to some 'minor' Lombards, to Vittone (particularly his Gothic design for Milan cathedral), to the exceptional Bohemian figure of Johann Santini Aichel.[22] And it is Santini, in the end, who becomes the paradigmatic personality of this second movement. He accepts *a priori* Borromini's historical synthesis of the opposites: for him too the spatial synthesis of antithetical linguistic matrixes and the technique of *bricolage* concur in a unified result. In his work, from the church in Lometz to the one in Kladrau, to S. Giovanni Nepocumeno in Žd'ar, there is a more limited

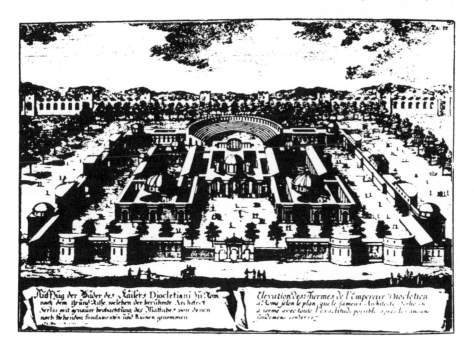

2.   Johann Bernard Fischer von Erlach, Ideal reconstruction of the Diocletian Baths in Rome. From *Entwurff einer historischen Architektur*, Wien 1721, Plate IX

3.   J. B. Fischer von Erlach, Ideal reconstruction of Solomon's Temple, from the descriptions of the prophet Ezekiel and from Villalpando. From *Entwurff*, etc., Plate II

repertoire of salvaged materials: it is in fact the tradition of Bohemian Gothic that Santini Aichel re-proposes in his contaminations, with all their charge of ethnical and craft values, half-way between polemic and irony.[23]

C. *The experimental contamination of different linguistic codes, first by Wren and, then, by Hawksmoor, Thomas Archer and Vanbrugh in a decidedly anti-historicist vein:* one can speak of experimentalism and anti-historicism in this connection, because the introduction of Mannerist, Classicist and Gothic and Borrominian lexical elements, in works like S. Vedast, St Stephen's Walbrook, Tom Tower in Oxford, Seaton Delaval Hall, Blenheim Palace and All Souls College does not contain the least polemical trace, does not propose the historicity of form as an urgent problem (English architecture, traditionally eclectic and synthetic, has never seen history as a dialectical question), but simply uses it to confirm an anti-rhetorical and disenchanted experiment of variations *ad libitum*, with pre-formed historical and geometrical materials.

As we can see, the problem of history is certainly not a central one in Baroque Europe. On the other hand the historicity of art is a decisive factor in the theories of the seventeenth and eighteenth centuries.[24] The Iluminist revolution, however, will justify Baroque historicism in all its forms. On the one hand the archaeological recovery of Antiquity makes clear the ideological value of having recourse to history: the transposition of values is realised through the resonance of the forms as carriers of secular and revolutionary contents; on the other, the elimination of the classic concept of *object* is reflected in the *heroic utopism* of the first generation of neo-Classical architects, for whom the death of traditional symbolism, the desecration of contents, the new civil values as main factors in planning, the break with past history, the anxious turning to a future dominated by reason, become motives for an exasperated search for new linguistic codes, more allusive than those of the late Baroque generations, but equally dominated by experimental contaminations.[25]

The value of the *heroic resurrection* of Antiquity by Illuminist art can therefore be measured outside the 'archaeological cemetery', the main target of so many polemists of the early Modern Movement. On this basis Marx's analysis of revolutionary historicism in *The Eighteenth Brumaire of Louis Bonaparte* seems to us still valid as an explanation of the deeper meaning of the forward movement by exhuming the ancient civil virtues and the figurative culture that went with them:[26]

The tradition of all past generations weighs like an alp upon the brain of

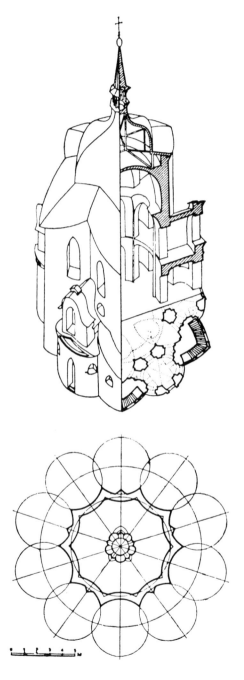

4.   Johann Santini Aichel, Axonometric section of the S. Giovanni Nepocumeno
Sanctuary, near Žd'ar (1719–22) and plan at the level of the drum with geometric
reconstruction

the living. At the very time when men appear engaged in revolutionising things and themselves, in bringing about what never was before . . . they anxiously conjure into their service the spirits of the past, assume their names, their battle cries, their costumes, to enact a new historic scene in such time-honoured disguise and with such borrowed language. Thus did Luther masquerade as the Apostle Paul; thus did the revolution of 1789–1814 drape itself alternately as Roman Republic and as Roman Empire. . . .

   Accordingly, the reviving of the dead in those revolutions served the purpose of glorifying the new struggles, not of parodying the old; it served the purpose of exaggerating to the imagination the given task, not to recoil before its practical solution; it served the purpose of rekindling the revolutionary spirit, not to trot out its ghost.[27]

From a history that quarrels with the organic nature of Classicism, therefore, to a history that tends to become the sole object of expression and exaltation: the accomplished revolution is decisive and irreversible. From then on absolute values no longer rule the symbolic structures of artistic activity; it is the adventure of man that takes on the leading role, and claims the discovery of a new constructive nature of form, directly related to perception, to fruition, to a mundane and contingent symbolism.

   Yet history and nature, unified in the cult of reason, escape analytical inquiry. The 'desacralisation' of artistic activity does not lead to a functional historical criticism; instead, it separates history and architecture, confining to mythology the question of the methodological bases. Neither Cordemoy, nor Laugier, and even less Lodoli, Pino or Milizia, poses the problem of the historicity of the new architecture: on this point a conservative like Blondel is doubtless far more open to critical analysis. The apodictical quality of the new universe of discourse of Illuminist architecture is based on the authority of a history selected in the light of Reason, but the arbitrariness of such selection is kept hidden: Boullée, in his polemic with Perrault, is explicit on this point.[28] And the result is a split: on one side those who try to re-link planning and historico-archaeological analysis; on the other those who discover and emphasise the Illuminist anti-historicism.

   This division had already been prophesied by G. Battista Piranesi, who had caught in its entirety the dialectic inherent in Illuminism. He opens the doors to modern architecture and, at the same time, becomes its most merciless critic. Piranesi's *Parere sull'architettura* is in the form of a dialogue between a rigorist and a proto-romantic, and it is odd that, up to

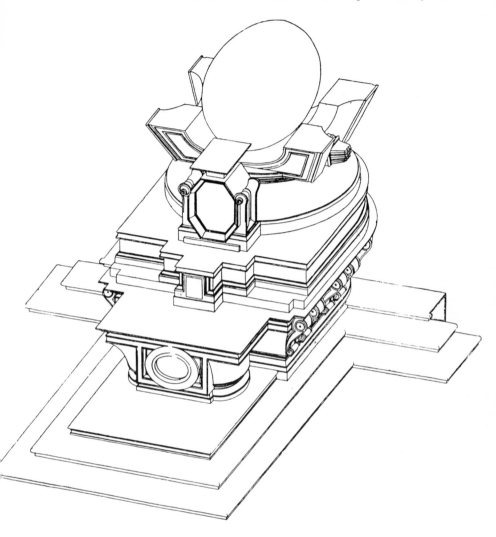

5.   Giovan Battista Piranesi, Structure of the main altar, S. Maria del Priorato in Rome. (Survey by students from the Faculty of Engineering, Rome)

now, no-one has realised that the author does not take sides, but offers instead an agonising dialectic. The altar of S. Maria del Priorato on the Aventino is its explicit architectural realisation, with its double side: narrative, didactic and caustically late-Baroque – facing the public; abstract, anti-descriptive, and of haunting Illuminist symbolism – at the back, where a naked sphere is embraced by a geometrical solid figure, in a sort of allegory of the already achieved *eclipse of the sacred*.[29]

The origin of eclecticism is in Piranesi, while the origin of the combinatory and anti-historical architecture of the nineteenth century is in the anti-symbolism of Robert Morris first, and of Durand and Dubut later. Both movements postulate the crisis of historicism: the first in a pitiless and self-destructive self-criticism, the second by simply ignoring the question. The end of the *object* is tied to the eclipse of history: as bear witness the sphere of Piranesi and the paradoxical mechanics of his fantastic architecture, the utopism of Ledoux, Boullée, Lequeu and Sobre, the realism of Quarenghi, Valadier and Chalgrin.

What Garroni has discerningly called the 'semantic crisis of the arts' finds its sources in the Illuminist hiccups and in the relativist historicism of positivism. The very concept of *art* begins to decline with the decline of history: when Hegel, between 1817 and 1826, decrees the *death of art*, rather than a prophecy he makes a lucid diagnosis.

> . . . In the presentations of romantic art, therefore, everything has a place, every sphere of life, all phenomena, the greatest and the least, the supreme and the trivial, the moral, immoral, and evil; and, in particular, the more art becomes secular, the more it makes itself at home in the finite things of the world, is satisfied with them, and grants them complete validity, and the artist does well when he portrays them as they are. . . . Within this contingency of the objects which come to be portrayed partly as a mere environment for an inherently more important subject-matter, but partly also as independent on their own accord, there is presented the collapse of romantic art. . . . On one side, in other words, there stands the real world in, from the point of view of the ideal, its prosaic *objectivity*: the contents of ordinary daily life which is not apprehended in its substance (in which it has an element of the ethical and divine), but in its mutability and finite transitoriness. On the other side, it is the *subjectivity* of the artist, which, with its feeling and insight, with the right and power of its wit, can rise to mastery of the whole of reality; it leaves nothing in its usual context and in the validity which it has for our usual way of looking at things.[30]

This quotation from Hegel can be read in two ways. Seen in its contemporary historical situation, it shows how clearly the German philosopher saw the end of the traditional concept of art: as, for Hegel, the universality, the objectivity, the organicity, the congruity of subjective expression with the content of the work, are essential values to the very concept of art, he had to prophesy its death. The Romantic world dissolves into the particular, the contingent, the mundane, an ideal organicity that must by now be transmitted to a new objectivation of the Idea. Art dies to make room for a higher form of knowledge. But at the same time Hegel's words can be referred directly to the present situation. In this second reading – completely arbitrary, of course – they are not only very close to those of the avant-gardes of the beginning of the century, but also manage to explain, at least partially, the *Romantic* origin of so much recent neo-avant-garde. ('Updated' readings of Hegel aesthetic have been tried by Lukács, Morpurgo-Tagliabue and Sabatini.[31]) What, in fact, dies, for Hegel, is art as super-individual institution and as immediate communion with the universe: the release from its contents, the autonomy from its formal processes, its desecration, make Hegel see subjective humour and irony as the final stage of this form of knowledge.

> In our day, in the case of almost all peoples, criticism, the cultivation of reflection, and, in our German case, freedom of thought have mastered the artists too, and have made them, so to say, a *tabula rasa* in respect of the material and the form of their productions, after the necessary particular stages of the romantic art-form have been traversed. Bondage to a particular subject-matter and a mode of portrayal suitable for this material alone are for artists today something past, and art therefore has become a free instrument which the artist can wield in proportion to his subjective skill in relation to any material of whatever kind.[32]

In Hegel's analysis we find a clear explanation of the questions of eclecticism, anti-symbolism and the de-mythologising typical of the entire cycle of contemporary art.[33] His prophecy touches the main reasons for the semantic crisis of the arts – to quote Garroni – and links, in particular, the *crisis of the object* to the crisis of the historicity of modern art. It is in this sense that the death of art and the death of history coincide in Hegel and in Mondrian, in Van Doesburg, in Dada and in Sant'Elia. To the dissolution of art as the realm of intuition, Hegel contraposes self-consciousness, criticism, and the rationalisation of creative processes. It is in the boiling magma of historical recollections that one can see the true subject of the eclectic research. As Garroni has rightly said, 'it is its non-institutionality that constitutes the institutionality of nineteenth century art'.[34]

What the Romantics would like to achieve is the impossible fusion of a present that is feared in the very moment in which one takes stable roots in it, and a past that one refuses to read as such, whose sense one is frightened of: because an exact reading of the past would necessarily lead to the discovery of the sense of *the today* that the Romantic eclectic artist tries desperately not to see. Therefore 'the real inability to put order into such an intricate, chaotic, even sordid, *incurable*, almost *irrational* matter, becomes pathos, becomes frantic need to speak, to tell, to symbolise and institutionalise. It is an art at the same time desperate and hopeful (that of the nineteenth century), impotent but very powerful in its irresistible impulse to give voice to its impotence.'[35]

The alliance between eclecticism and new technologies seems to lead to a way out, the only possible and legitimate way: to the definitive killing of history, carried out after the hopes placed in it had been betrayed; this is fairly obvious in the work of Frank Furness and even of Berlage. In reacting against the indiscriminate identification of historical research with architectural research, against the instrumentalisation and the unproductivity of history, the artistic avant-gardes of the twentieth century have pushed aside history in order to *build* a new history. Their nihilism and totalitarianism take, therefore, the form of operations directed to the recovery of the only type of historicity still possible after the crepuscular flares of Parnassian Symbolism in Art Nouveau: the one founded on the *tabula rasa,* totally independent from the past.

In this way, the neat cut with preceding traditions becomes, paradoxically, the symbol of an authentic historical continuity. In founding anti-history and presenting their work not so much as anti-historical, but rather as above the very concept of historicity, the avant-gardes perform the only historically legitimate act of the time. Hitting back at history is nothing more than a revenge – a painful revenge – of the present: what one wants to be revenged of is the burning disappointment caused by the unkept promises of historicism.

In their way Ruskin and Morris also negated history. And the same negation can be found, still because of a terrible disillusion, in the *Illuminations* by Rimbaud or in Gauguin, who tried to find in Tahiti a purity of myths not yet corrupted by the 'barbarity' of modern man.

The anti-historicism of modern avant-gardes is not, therefore, the result of an arbitrary choice, but, rather, the logical end of a change that has its

*epicentre in the Brunelleschian revolution, and its basis in the debate carried
on for more than five centuries by European culture.*

The anti-historicism of Art Nouveau and of Futurism – linked by the
common original ideal and by the common expectation of a cathartic
future[36] – is still uneasy, as it is also the annihilation of Expressionist
language. In order to explode towards the future, one drowns in a sea of
empty and disposable symbols, pure fragments of a decomposed order,
only usable in absurd *collages.*

A passage of exceptional importance by Benjamin, on the ability of the
cinematographic techniques to create a new relationship with things and
nature, might help us to interpret the phenomena under analysis.
Benjamin studies film techniques as a generalisable example in which the
reproduction techniques put the artist, the public and the *media* of
production into a new condition: in the case of the film-actors and the
mechanical apparatus. If, as a general phenomenon, the reproduction
quality of the work of art causes the 'destruction of the aura' traditionally
connected to it (with the fall of the fetishistic myth of the artistic *thing*
valid in its apparition *hic et nunc*),[37] for Benjamin – and those are concepts
that date back to 1936 – any complaint or apocalyptical diagnosis of the
alienated condition of the actor or of the predominance of the artificial
over the natural become meaningless through a brave act of conscious
realism: the same realism – we note in passing – as that of Gropius, Léger
and Le Corbusier. He writes:[38]

The magician keeps a distance between himself and the patient; more
precisely he slightly reduces it, through the application of his hands,
and considerably increases it through his authority. The surgeon, on
the contrary, reduces his distance considerably from the patient, by
entering his inside, and slightly increases it with the cautious
movement of the hand among his organs. In brief: unlike the
magician. . .the surgeon renounces facing the patient man-to-man;
instead he penetrates his body operatively. The magician and the
surgeon behave respectively like the painter and the operator. The
painter keeps, in his work, a natural distance from what he is given,
while the operator penetrates deeply into the texture of the data. . . .
[The image] of the painter is total, that of the operator is multi-
fragmented, and *its parts are rearranged according to a new law.*
Therefore the cinematic representation of reality is vastly more
meaningful for the modern man, *because, precisely on the base of its
intense penetration through the equipment, it offers him that aspect, free
from the equipment, that he can legitimately ask from the work of art.*[39]

Here you have stated with exceptional lucidity – a lucidity, we must emphasise, that contemporary criticism of visual arts and architecture hardly ever had, even when it presented itself as an ally of the Modern Movements – a principle for the identification of the distinctive features of the avant-gardes of the twentieth century.

A. On one side there are those who tend to perpetuate the figure of the artist-magician: those who, apparently, get close to the new world of industrial production but then withdraw immediately because of the use they make of it. Italian Futurism, particularly in its least 'European' manifestations, in part Dada, the more dogmatic sections of the Russian Constructivism are all 'breakaway' movements, because they no longer hide the new productive, social and moral reality created by the *universe of precision* behind aesthetic pretext. But, faced by this *new nature of artificial 'things'*, used as basic material for their artistic work, they still behave with a mentality anchored to the principle of *mimesis*.

Industrial *things* take the place of Classical Nature, of the Illuminist cult of man, and even of Reason: they are the result of the pitiless logic of Capital that has destroyed, paradoxically, the faith in anthropocentrism. In this sense they are *new nature*. And it is in this sense that Marinetti, Sant'Elia, Picabia, Marcel Duchamp, Ladovsky and Melnikov look at it for new emotional occasions, trying to *reproduce* it in a completely new way.[40] Their work is typical – to use Benjamin's words – of those who are not yet *free from the equipment*, of those who look at it excitedly, rather than go behind it and use it.

B. On the opposite side are Gropius, Le Corbusier and Mies van der Rohe. They identify the *new laws of the equipment*, and solve, by entering into it, its irrationalities and contradictions. They do not accept the industrial *new nature* as an external factor and claim to enter into it as producers and not as interpreters: their work shows how empty are the Jeremiads of the inevitability of alienation or the apocalyptical *Verlust der Mitte* ('loss of centre').[41]

C. In between are the undecided, those who feel the difficulties of such courageous and radical realism: Bonatz, Tessenow and Fahrenkamp.

We will therefore jointly analyse the phenomenon of the *eclipse of history* and that of the *crisis of the object* in contemporary avant-gardes, in the light of the observations already made.

The intuition of the value of *new nature* assumed by technological reality, in opposition and antithesis to Nature as a source of stable and permanent values, can be clearly seen in Sant'Elia's *Messaggio*:

In the same way as the ancients took inspiration for their art from the elements of nature, we - materially and spiritually artificial - must take inspiration from the elements of the brand new mechanical world we have created.[42]

There is no need to mention the well-known prophecies contained in Sant'Elia's *Messaggio* about the new urban space, seen as a changing and contingent field, cause and consequence of the death of architecture as immutable *object*. They are, in fact, prophecies common to the Expressionist culture, to the futurist writings of Paul Scheerbart, to the intuitions of Bruno Taut, of the *Gläserne Kette* and the *Arbeitsrat für Kunst* after 1918.[43]

How complex was the attitude of the Futurists towards the technological reality and how much Futurism itself tended to go beyond the energetic myth is demonstrated in that it itself had introduced, in favour of a new objectivity, in a letter from Boccioni to Barbarini of February 1912, on the occasion of the exhibition of the triptych *Moods (Stati d'animo),* in Paris:

> This synthesis – given the increasingly accentuated tendency of the human spirit to render the concrete through the abstract – can only be expressed through objective and spiritualised elements. This spiritualisation will be achieved by pure mathematical values, by pure geometrical dimensions, *instead of traditional reproduction,* by now defeated by the mechanical media. . . . Which are the subjects of this *superior objectivity?* If the objects are mathematical values then their setting itself will give a particular rhythm to the emotion surrounding them.[44]

Art becomes then a sort of prototype of the technological processes: or better, a mediation between world of quantity – perceived in its abstract values – and world of quality – resolved in the mirroring of subjective emotions towards machines.

In our opinion Calvesi has caught exactly the link between Lombard Futurism and some instances of the European avant-gardes. Boccioni's passage can easily be related to Hans Richter's experimental film *Rythmus 21* of 1921, in which abstract figures are articulated in a dynamism of syncopated cinematic tempos, and also to Léger's work, after 1918.[45] What seems particularly important for the purpose of our analysis in such studies is the leaving behind by so many European avant-gardes of what we could call the *machine naturalism*. The problem is no more the renewal of the mechanical means, nor the fidelity to the principle of *mimesis* by passing from the imitation of nature to the imitation of the *new* technological *nature*.

In Boccioni's words there is already the atmosphere that dominates the first work by Oud, the experimental projects of Rietveld and Cor van Eesteren and, a little later, the courses run by Albers and Moholy-Nagy at the Bauhaus. We are, that is, in the middle of an experiment that rationalises the co-ordinates of planning, and that separates itself, temporarily, from the *mechanical mean*, in order to go back to it equipped with an autonomous critical capacity. Let us compare this complex Futurist attitude to the most radical negation of the historicity of Art by the Modern Movement: the one by Dada. Already in the manifesto of 1918 one can appreciate the flow, into the Dada revolt, of a highly ethical concept – and, one could add, in spite of the appearances of the last echoes of a deeply *European* bourgeois ethic[46] – of a discovery of new means of communications intentionally left in the bud and of a sharp awareness of the need to go back to a *zero degree* visual communication:

The new painter creates a world, the elements of which are also its implements, a sober, definite work without argument. The new artist protests: he no longer paints (symbolic and illusionist reproduction) but creates – directly in stone, wood, iron, tin, boulders – locomotive organisms capable of being turned in all directions by the limpid wind of momentary sensation. All pictorial or plastic work is useless: let it then be a monstrosity that frightens servile minds, and sweetening to decorate the refectories of animals in human costume, illustrating the sad fable of mankind.[47]

We have here the identification between the materials of the image and the images themselves, and the destruction of every linguistic code, but mainly the radical destruction of the historicity of the artistic processes.

Dada's *tabula rasa* did not only start from the *necessary disorder* already mentioned by Rimbaud, but was, in a way, the sign of the birth of a new code of values: a code, at the same time, of human behaviour and aesthetic construction. And it should not be surprising that we speak of construction in respect of the Dada movement. In spite of all the Dadaist polemic against Cubist constructivism,[48] the desperate need of eversion typical of the movement amounts to a clear, and only apparently sceptical, realism.

For Tzara and his companions Dada is somehow a reflection of reality. To give back the tangle of the opposites and the incongruence of daily life, the apocalyptic floundering of the European rationalist tradition – not only as regards the 1914–18 war, but in a more absolute sense – this is the exact meaning of the Dadaist 'shrill scream'. But this is not all. It is clear that what Dada wants to institutionalise is exactly the ambiguity of the daily experience, the already accomplished victory of *things* over man, the clash of absurdities. In this sense, its absolute *disorder* is not only denunciation but also a test of the foundations of the pre-existing disorder that could not any longer be ignored: in particular the disorder of the urban condition.

Let us now turn our attention towards the problems of the international architecture that was contemporary with Dada, and let us try to answer the question: why is it not possible to discover any substantial Dadaist contribution to the development of modern architecture? The first and immediate answer that comes to mind is the impossibility of translating such a radical formal destruction into a – of necessity – constructive language such as architecture. But it is not a fully convincing answer. The Futurist and Expressionist poetics also implied the destruction of the traditional concept of form: and we all know how this did not prevent the acceptance of their eversive instances into architectural languages, even if only at the level of formal utopia, such as in the case of Sant'Elia.

Let us, first of all, clear the field of the occasional meeting points between Dada and modern architecture, discernible through a careful philological analysis. The only architects that seem to have been in touch with the Dada movement are Bruno Taut and Loos. Loos knew Georges Besson and Paul Dermée, both active in Dada and other avant-garde movements. Besson and Dermée both translated some of Loos's writings: the first was responsible for the French edition of 'Ornament und Verbrechen' in *Les Cahiers d'aujourd'hui* in 1913, while the second republished the same essay in *L'Esprit nouveau* in 1920.[49]

But the Dadaist's interest in Loos does not mean much. Clearly, the Loosian causticity and desecration sound akin to the Dada revolt: but it is significant that Dermée belonged both to Dada and to the *Esprit nouveau*, while Loos's essay had also been accepted in *Der Sturm*, by Herwarth Walden in 1912.

We can see something more in the relationship of Loos and Tzara: but the Swiss poet was in Paris only in 1925, and his influence can only be seen in some marginal episodes.

Again, one could quote Schwitters's *Merz-Bau* as an example of Dada architecture, but the exception does not prove the rule and, also, with the isolated example of the *Merz-Bau*, we are dealing with a highly subjective experiment.

The answer to our initial question begins to take shape: Dada did not influence architecture because Dada is, essentially, *urban art*, or, better, destructive criticism of urban art. Dada resolves itself into action, and recognises that the only place for action is the city. In the end, its search for a new link between things tends to become a search for a new way of action, within an a-logical space, empty of *things*: empty, also, of architectural things.

With this we have not only confirmed the coincidence of the *death of history* and the *crisis of the object*, but we have also found the thin link that joins the most anti-constructive to the most constructive movements in contemporary art: Dada and De Stijl. They fully coincide in their negation of any validity of the *object* and in their prophecy of the coming of collective action, that will result in the new city.

Already in the first Mondrian there is the intuition of the possibility of the disappearance of art because of the elimination of irrationality: if it is the tragic, the struggle of the opposites, the exasperation of oppositions, that generate expression, then the sublimation of the tragic in a dynamic balance, at first formal, and then of life, of costume, of daily behaviour, can only outdate the need itself of *expression* and, in particular, of artistic expression.

In the meantime, though, art has still the task of messianically announcing the realm of reason translated into style of existence: 'The purely plastic is not imitation of life but its opposite. It is the immutable and the absolute as opposed to the changing and the capricious.'[50] The changeable and the transient aspects of existence are therefore not accepted as such, but exorcised by the contact with the opposite values of order and permanence, they too are inherent in existence as part of human intellect.

> Art advances where religion once did. Religion's basic content was to *transform the natural*; in practice, however, religion always sought to harmonise man *with nature*, that is, with *untransformed* nature....Art, on the other hand, sought this *in practice*. It increasingly *interiorised* natural externality in its plastic until, in Neo-plasticism, nature *actually* no longer dominates. Its expression of equivalence prepares the way for full-humanity and for the end of 'art'.[51]

The aporia of Neo-plasticism is entirely contained in these words of Mondrian written in 1922. The visual arts' means of communication are reduced to a mere perceptual organisation. But this radical destruction of the traditional symbolism of art is, in its turn, symbol and image: even if symbol and image of the expectation of a Theosophically flavoured final redemption; and we know how much both Mondrian and Van Doesburg were influenced by the theosophical metaphysics of Schoenmaekers.[52]

Beyond this contradiction one can perceive the Hegelian flavour in the substitution of art for religion as a prelude of the definitive *death of art*. Mondrian writes:

> A day will come when we shall do without all the forms of art as we know them today: only then will architecture reach maturity, in a concrete reality. The humanity will not be lost. . . .When the new man will have transformed nature into what he is himself – nature and non-nature in equal proportion – then man. . .will have found in the new man heaven on earth.[53]

And again:

> The real artist sees the metropolis as abstract and imagined life: he feels it nearer than nature and will receive more of an aesthetic emotion from it than from the latter. Because in the metropolis the 'natural' is always tightened and regulated by the human spirit. . . .In the metropolis the beautiful is expressed more mathematically: therefore it is the place of the future development of the mathematic artistic temperament: the birth-place of the new style.[54]

From which we can draw some very important conclusions. First of all it is clear that, for Mondrian, art, as a transient phenomenon, has still to make for itself the objective of the integral transformation of every natural datum into culture. *Heaven on earth* will be realised when the 'danger' inherent in Nature will be definitely overcome by its total transformation into *culture*, with the clear implication of the faith in a possible future *death of history*.

Art's suicide should, in fact, be carried out in successive steps. First of all should die painting, absorbed (after having performed to the end its role as carrier of avant-garde methodology) by architecture, as concrete existential space: but only temporarily, because architecture itself will have to dissolve in the city, in the *ordered* metropolis, in which the rhythm of life that has gone beyond the dissensions of history – for Mondrian the dissensions of the *tragic* – has become the rule of rational behaviour, in point of fact, of a kind of *Stijl*.[55]

Diffused artistic quality takes the place, then, of the artistic *unicum*, architecture cancels itself out in its dispersal into the urban project, history's contradictions find peace in the *Nirvana* of the final struggle of man against nature: Mondrian's propositions are in many ways prophetic and full of hidden meanings.

Isn't modern *design* based on the theoretical principle of the diffusion of artistic quality into the world of life?[56] And hasn't the *way beyond architecture* through *planning*, meant as an open project of changeable topological conditions (no longer of *space*, at least in its Classical sense), been, up to now, a continually repeated slogan as a last act of faith in the *design* itself, in spite of the fact that its price is, obviously, the death of architecture?[57]

And again: doesn't the reduction of all nature to culture, introduce (paradoxically, as far as the anti-historicism of the Neo-plastic poetics goes) a historicist code for the reading of the landscape, not yet used coherently to solve the old question of the preservation and transformation of its *cultural values?*

These prophecies apart, let us note Mondrian's rigour in carrying out his anti-historicism to the last:

> . . . we must not forget that life, in its continuous growth, is free from time and space and that it creates through destruction and construction. The great art of antiquity appears to the modern man more or less like darkness, even when it is not obscure or tragic. . . . In general all the particularities of the past are oppressive like darkness. The past has a *tyrannical* influence, difficult to escape. And the trouble is that there always is something of the past *in us*. We have memories, dreams . . . we go into old museums and churches; we are surrounded by old buildings. Luckily we can also enjoy modern constructions, scientific wonders, all sort of techniques, and also modern art. We can enjoy real jazz and its dance; we see the electric lights of luxury and utility; a window is opened. Just the thought of all this satisfies. We realise then the great difference between the modern times and the past. Modern art and life are *removing the oppression of the past*.[58]

History is considered a danger to the present and, as such, must be 'suppressed': the blasphemous statements of Marinetti and Tzara seem to be re-echoing here. But the meaning given by Mondrian to the *tyranny* of the past is nearer to that expressed by Gropius or Wright. 'Certainly the art of the past is superfluous to the new spirit – Mondrian writes in *Plastic Art and Pure Plastic Art*[59] – and harmful to its progress: its very beauty keeps many away from the new conception.' On this point there is considerable common ground between Neo-plasticism and the tendencies of Russian Constructivism.

It has been noted – both by a contemporary of Malevich, such as Gan, and in more recent times[60] – that between the Suprematism of Malevich and the Constructivist symbolism of Ladovsky there is a large gap. For Malevich, formal research consists of methodological experimentation towards an architecture conceived as 'enormous social object': the 'supremacy of colour founded on calculation' is akin, but with a decisive ideological deviation, to Van Doesburg's researches on form. For Ladovsky formal research is full of utopic intentions: it lands on the symbol in order not to sink completely into everyday reality; while about the group ASNOVA, Gan speaks of 'atavistic nostalgias'.[61] A repetition, then, of already known opposites. Those who seem to negate history produce historically motivated work, those who try not to cut their links with it, run into the shoals of ambiguity: the contrast between Le Corbusier and Hugo Häring changes face but remains substantially the same in Constructivist Russia:

> Today we proclaim our words to you people. In the squares and on the streets we are placing our work, convinced that art must not remain a sanctuary for the idle, a consolation for the weary, and a justification for the lazy. Art should attend us everywhere that life flows and acts... at the bench, at the table, at work, at rest, at play; on working days and holidays ... at home and on the road ... in order that the flame of life should not be extinguished in mankind.
>
> We do not look for justification, neither in the past nor in the future ... Today is the deed.
> We will account for it tomorrow.
> The past we are leaving behind as carrion.
> The future we leave to the fortune-tellers.
> We take the present day.[62]

Let us measure the distance between the 'Realism-Constructivism' of Gabo and Pevsner and the Manifesto of the Productivist Group, signed by Rodchenko and Varvara Stepanova a few months later (certainly with the approbation, if not the collaboration, of Tatlin):

> ... The Constructivist maxims are:/1. Down with art and up with technology/2. Religion is a lie, art is a lie/3. Even the last remnants of human thought die when you tie it to art/4. Down with the maintenance of artistic traditions, up with the constructivist technician/5. Down with art, that is only masking humanity's impotence/6. The collective art of the present is the constructive life![63]

This reduction of artistic production to the production of *objects*, this crisis of the Classical objects, of the *things* endowed with autonomous emblematic charge, or, if you like, with a romantic historical meaningfulness, may even try to salvage its relationship with history, by going beyond the Dadaist and Suprematist nihilism: this is the line, for example, of the magazine *Vešč* ('the object'):

'VEŠČ' is for the constructive art, that does not beautify life, but organises it.

We have called our magazine 'VEŠČ' because for us art means creation of new objects. . . . But we do not want to limit artistic production to functional objects. Any organised product – the house, the poem or the painting is an object with a purpose, that does not remove men from life, but helps them to organise it. Therefore we separate ourselves from the poets who propose in their verses to renounce poetry, and from the painters who foretell in their work the renunciation of painting. The utilitarianism of the productive type is not for us.[64]

Vešč came out in 1922, in Berlin, edited by El Lissitzky and Ilya Ehrenburg, with the declared task of bridging the gap between Russian art and western culture. We are not interested, here, in following the Russian polemic against *Vešč* (well documented in an article by Arvatov in 1922),[65] except for one relevant point: whereas for the editors of *Vešč* it is possible to introduce a new historicity of the object, Arvatov, accusing them of aestheticism and opportunism, re-emphasised the absolute identification 'of industrial and artistic work'. The bourgeois myth of art is answered by the, still bourgeois, myth of productive work as the new 'value'.

Let us try to sum up what we have schematically analysed up to now. First of all we think we have proved that Gropius's choice, in refusing to provide a history course within the Bauhaus, belongs to a vast movement, whose historical and conceptual roots we have outlined. It is, therefore, a strongly motivated choice, that finds resonance in the cult of the empirical method and in alliance with the technological world, typical of the greater *workshop* of European Constructivism.

What is the significance, for the artistic object, of the loss of its traditional value as thing subject to ageing, and of its renunciation to a life in time analogous to that of man, to an intrinsic, meaningful historicity? Obviously, an object without historic value lives only in the present. And the present, with its contingent and transient laws, completely dominates its life cycle: the rapid consumability of the object is built-in from the very first stage of planning.

Art [Argan writes] moving through a changeable and limitless life, where everything escapes definition, is left without stable reference points: not nature, that, being now considered a representation of the human mind, falls within the history of human thoughts and actions; and not history, that, no more a theological construction, presents itself as a congeries of events, a *so-sein*, a maze where one is never certain of one's position, so that distant things may appear suddenly terribly near, and the near ones distant and almost ungraspable . . . historical information is doubtless immensely greater than in the past, but history is no longer a construction based on judgment values and, instead of supplying models, keeps posing urgent problems.[66]

If architecture must model itself on technological reality, so intimately as to become an *epistemological metaphor*, if it reduces to pure perception the structures of visual communication, if it tends to become pure object, and, even, pure industrial object, it is clear that one cannot even begin to question its historicity.

Here we are, in fact, in a quite different situation from that of the first avant-gardes. We have seen that for Marinetti, Boccioni and Sant'Elia, there still exists a distance (the one typical of traditional art) from technological reality: the new work must relate to this reality or sense its intimate structure, but it does not yet identify with it. Similarly for De Stijl the use of a language as a method of structural analysis and research, implies a very mediated relationship with the world of production. As one of the most absolutist movements of our century, Neo-plasticism tries to take on the function of model – and, not by chance, of a model rich in symbolic and semantic values – for industrial reality, on all its levels.

In other words, both Futurism and De Stijl were trying to give autonomy, often full of traditional nuances, to the expressive range proper to art. A semantic autonomy, capable of providing a leading role to the values of industrial reality, to make them its own, to exalt them, even – but remaining proudly locked in its own, jealously guarded, context.

These are the conceptual *materials* that Bauhaus tried to organise: for the purpose of our analysis, there is no need to show the internal contradictions of Gropius's attitude. We would rather point out that the radical anti-historicism of the Bauhaus, its free cult of the *present*, justifies the late-Romanticism of the movements of *expectation*: of the generous but unproductive utopism of the *Gläserne Kette* and of Russian symbolism. To use Benjamin's metaphor again: Gropius chose to *place himself behind the equipment* in order to free himself from it. Today we can see Wright's anti-historicism as richer than Gropius's because of its capacity to absorb fragments of *anti-European* historical memories: the Mayan, Aztec and Toltec architecture of the Barnsdall and Ennis houses, or the North-American Indian tepees in the *Tahoe* huts and floats.[67]

But Wright too is anti-historicistic: his main tool is still the *bricolage*. What links, however, Wright and Le Corbusier – apart, of course, from all the differences that separate their methods and their poetics – is their recognition of the historicity of their anti-historicism. For Wright the search for the autochthonous forms of the Usonian myth, and for Le Corbusier the fidelity to Illuminist dialectic, are guarantees of a multivalent structure of language, able to accept, at the right moment, all the instances of 'memory' and of new critical (even self-critical) symbolism. Referring to the paradoxical quality of the work of the sixteenth-century masters, in the pre-constituted urban structure of Venice, Le Corbusier writes in *When the Cathedrals Were White*:

> But those of us who live intensely in the present moment of modern times, have broken through the boundaries of such limited and poverty-stricken curiosity. We have extended our *sympathy* to all the world and to all times. We have rediscovered life and the axis of all human marvels and agonies. We are far from the theatrical stage which tries to place events of qualitative interest above and outside of human labours.[68]

The anti-Renaissance polemic of Le Corbusier (so different from that of Wright's) has far less interest than his declaration of *sympathy* for the past, of fondness for the entire arch of history as a signal of human presence, so that we can, legitimately, place the Swiss master next to the other great friend of history, and for this very reason, as great a radical innovator – Pablo Picasso. This is perhaps the reason why Louis Kahn recognised Le Corbusier as his master.

Let us check now the effects of modern historicism on critical activity, and on the relationship between the old town and contemporary architecture. How intricate the problem of history seemed, even to those few critics that had completely embraced the cause of 'modern' architecture, can be fully appreciated in the statements of a scholar like Alexander Dorner:

> ... I had continually to focus my thought on the role of the historical art work in the context of our present-day life and on its value and legitimacy as a life-improving factor. Which of the two was more important: the better functioning of a street, bringing about an elimination of accidents, or the preservation of a medieval building? Was it not a sign of our clinging to a rather primitive cult of relics allegedly containing timeless values that we were still basing our culture on the concrete maintenance of a maximum of historical

buildings, while everything around us furnished mounting proof that the value of life consisted in the act of transformation? Were we not driven towards a deeper and more intense evaluation of historical art products, an evaluation that would make us preserve only those monuments which represented such an act?[69]

Dorner wrote his famous book *The Way beyond 'Art'* between 1946 and '47, but the interest of this work is all in its being a symptom of the European culture of the twenties. It was in those years that Dorner was in close touch with the Bauhaus and that his cycle of lectures at the architectural college and his activity as director from 1923 onwards, of the Landes Museum, influenced the artistic circle of Hanover.[70]

In Dorner's thought the pragmatic components of Gropius didactics enter into singular contact with the problem of history, in favour of a direct commitment to museographic activity. What would be the meaning, in fact, of conserving ancient artistic documents, if they didn't act on the present, if the very concept of 'art' is left behind in favour of *design*, as a continuous process of transformation,[71] if modern art and architecture move towards the construction of a purely 'energetic' world, freeing us from 'the rigid tyranny of the preordained principle'?[72]

And how is one to fill the dramatic gap between the modern 'Way beyond Art' and its historical acknowledgment?

> The expression 'the way beyond "art"' still suggests a change on the surface that does not reach the essence of the matter in question. But in our case it should mean an explosive transformation of the very idea of *art*. We have set *art* in quotation marks to indicate that even our conception *art* is but a temporary fact in human history. This semantic problem is part of a universal problem: the transition from thinking in terms of eternal basic conditions to thinking in terms of a self-changing basis.[73]

The concept of *art* is then placed beyond the vicissitudes, the dynamism, the transformative and transient value of action. The Modern Movement, in its unconditional identification with the constructive action of the world, can only refuse, for itself, the artistic attribute. In fact, it must declare that art is without meaning as a concept related to old values.

It has been noted that Dorner, critic and theorist, takes the same standpoint as the artist.[74] In fact, Dorner goes much further. The *death of art*, diagnosed by him, though, maybe related to the one prophesied by Hegel, and, much more so, to that of the Russian Constructivists, is in absolute contrast with the theories of Loos, Gropius and Taut.

In spite of the fact that Dorner's criticism tried to be a true and proper *operative criticism*, already at that time the total elimination of the distance from the creative process had become clearly impossible. The anachronistic considerations on art by many modern architects (with Loos they take on even decadent and crepuscular nuances, when he speaks of music or literature), are due to the intentional 'putting into parenthesis' of historical time, and to the involuntary result of all this: to the mythologisation – although it may seem paradoxical – of what had been thought left well behind in an apocalyptical reduction to *tabula rasa*.

It is for this reason that Dorner can theorise the pragmatism of the modern movement, proclaiming its alliance with the ideas of James, Dewey, Joseph Ratner, and it is still for this reason that his *death of art* doesn't spring from a totalitarian anti-historicism, but from an attempt of historicisation, however *engagé* and partial.

Dorner's efforts to explain historically the fracture with the history of contemporary *design* could not help running into difficulties. He knew the irreversibility of the already accomplished revolution, but, writing after the war, he warned of the threats contained in it.[75] The main difficulty is in the problem of the inevitable contact between the historical presences – whether urbanistic, painting or sculpture – and the products of the Modern Movement: a difficulty he met first hand in his activity as a museum curator. Dorner's solution is brilliant but contains, at the same time, all the contradictions in which post-war *design* and urban planning were gradually involved:

First, the museum must finally bridge the gulf between art and our industrial life. This it can only do by participating in all the struggles of the present. It must show that the most recent evolution is determined to bring about a new integration, and that modern design is no longer self-sufficient art – produced by dreamers withdrawn from life – but an active component of the new economy and society which it will help to unify. Second it must show that the modern movement is inseparable from the whole evolution of historical art and that that evolution has been driving with tremendous momentum from the remote past into the immediate present. . . . The only warrant of the art museum and of the esthetics and art history behind it is the present moment with its particular exigencies. But the 'present moment' of yore is no longer that of our own epoch. Past exigencies craved the confirmation of an immutable truth, and the museum in its present form is still a valuable caterer to such needs. Yet our own needs are not served but rather frustrated by it. In order to serve us it must learn to distil a new progressive energy from the objects of art history.[76]

Which means a deformation of history in the search for the reasons of a present, seen illuministically as the final stage of a long process: even though in the effort of finding historical analogies, Dorner recognises in prehistorical art a counterpart, or at least a direct antecedent, of the Modern Movement.[77]

The historicisation of the 'recourse to the primitive', and the concept of *Way beyond Art* had already found a deeper analyst in Walter Benjamin. It is not by chance – especially from the ideological point of view – that Benjamin sought support in the theories of Brecht, in his postulate on the absolute weight assumed by what he calls the *Exhibitionable value* 'of the work of art, because of its technical reproducibility'.[78]

> If the concept of art [Brecht writes in the *Dreigroschenprozess*] can no longer be used to define the result obtained when the work of art has been transformed into merchandise, then we must let this concept go, carefully but without any fear, so as not to lose the function of the thing obtained, because, anyway, it must go through this phase without reserve. It is not a question of deviating from the right path; but, rather *this event will modify it radically, and will destroy its past* to such an extent that, in the event of the old concept being taken up again – why not? – this will no longer suggest the thing that it used to designate.[79]

What is happening now cancels out its own past: the new functions of art, of *design*, of architecture, cancel out the historical quality and character of the artistic processes, revolutionise their meanings and compromise their values, involve them in the dynamics of the continuous construction of the world. This is the link between the architectural avant-gardes and the thought of Dorner, Benjamin and Brecht: history does not condition activity, rather it will be the case of the latter transforming the functions of the former. But trying to define such functions meets with obstacles rather difficult to overcome.

Can there really be an interdependent relationship between an architecture that has destroyed every residue of the Classical *object*, that poses itself as pure active presence in the process *in fieri* of the town (itself a process *in fieri*), that becomes an instrument of action and an endlessly reproducible object in a radical 'annihilation of the *aura*' (to use Benjamin's words), that allows its direct insertion into daily life and the presence of historical environments, with their mythical and cultural values or their static and contemplative fruitions? Dorner, in his own way, has already answered this question.

Between the permanent values of *art* and the continually changing values of contemporary *design,* there can be only one type of relationship: the historical products and values conditioned, subdued, even cancelled by being read in the code of the modern movement. If in Dorner's ideal museum, the ancient remains must be revitalised in order to enter the positive flux of the present, then the ancient remains of town and territory cannot, also, simply remain objects of contemplation. These are no more self-justifying: without a new vital context recharging their values, making them *present,* they are empty, or, even worse, useless *things.* The *extinction of the past* by a present raised to the status of new value, is merciless. Artistic production is not, then, *consumed* by the inevitable adjustment of the public to the forms,[80] but it is born with the precise purpose of being rapidly consumed: the condition necessary to reach this objective is the contemporary consumption of the entire past, whose presence carries the memory of an extinct way of producing *values,* a disturbing and dangerous memory because of the illusion of the possible return to a sacral conception of artistic activity. This is the reason why all avant-garde movements see in history a *danger* for modern art.

In fact, both these movements and Brecht were right in their prophecies. When J. J. P. Oud with his Shell building at The Hague, opened the long and not yet concluded series of nostalgic salvages of an extinct reality, he showed how appropriate had been the radicalism of Dorner and Brecht.

We don't think it is at all by chance that Le Corbusier and Wright essentially agreed with Dorner on the destiny of the historical remains of the towns: and it is a kind of destiny that implies, as the only alternative to radical destruction, their museographic mummification. In one of his lectures at the RIBA in 1939 Wright stated:

... London is only seriously in danger from this thing we call Life, life itself, because, let us face it, my lords, ladies and gentlemen, Architectural London is senile. London is senile. How can we deny it any longer? Now had you a grandmother hopelessly senile, what would be your attitude toward her? It would be one of amelioration and of mitigation, wouldn't it? That should be your human attitude, and you probably would not embalm her and preserve her in a glass case if she died. As I see it something like that should be your attitude toward London – amelioration, mitigation, honouring old London and leaving it at that, but at last and soon preserving the best of it as memorial in a great green park.[81]

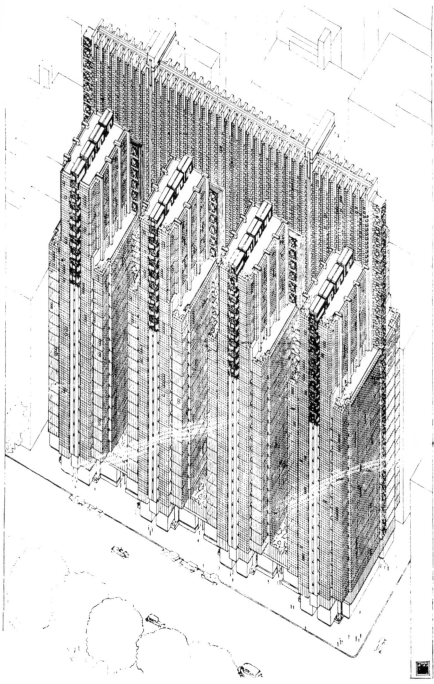

6.   Frank Lloyd Wright, Project for the National Life Insurance Building in Chicago (1920–25)

Let us compare Wright's passage to Le Corbusier's guide-lines for the Voisin scheme in Paris, as described in *Urbanisme*, in 1925:

> In this scheme the historical past, our common inheritance, is respected. More than that, it is *rescued*. The persistence of the present state of crisis must otherwise leap rapidly to the destruction of the past.
>
> First of all I must make a distinction, of a sentimental nature, but one of great importance; in these days the past has lost something of its fragrance, for its enforced mingling with the life of today has set it in a false environment. My dream is to see the Place de la Concorde empty once more, silent and lonely, and the Champs Élysées a quiet place to walk in. The 'Voisin' scheme would isolate the whole of the ancient city and bring back peace and calm from Saint-Gervais to the Étoile.[82]
>
> ... The 'Voisin' scheme covers 5% only of the ground with buildings, it safeguards the relics of the past and enshrines them harmoniously in a framework of trees and woods. For material things too must die, and these green parks with their relics are in some sort cemeteries, carefully tended, in which people may breathe, dream and learn. In this way the past becomes no longer dangerous to life, but finds instead its true place within it.[83]

Both Le Corbusier and Wright – leaving aside, for the moment, the obvious differences that separate their global conceptions of the modern city [84] – take a phenomenon for granted: the historical centres, if used as 'pieces' of the contemporary city, *are dangerous to life.* Such a concept may seem odd to those who live the daily struggle between consumer civilisation and historical urban and territorial survivals. But Wright's and Le Corbusier's positions are of an iron consistency, rather rare in the polemists of the fifties and sixties.

When Loos theorised on the lack of quality in *utilitarian architecture* and reserved aesthetic qualities to graves and monuments, he was extremely near to the positions of the two great masters of the Modern Movement, in spite of the incongruities that seem apparent from a strictly theorical point of view.[85] Where the form shapes itself in absolute adherence to the needs of life, one can no longer accept the criterion of the permanence of values (and of the forms themselves), typical of pre-industrial art. (A return to Dorner's theme, but in a different cultural context.)

Now, if for Loos the choice, at least on the theoretical level, is apocalyptical (a homage to the psychological exasperation of the Viennese intellectuals of the beginning of the century), for Wright and for Le Corbusier the problem was far more complex. For them, the opposition is between two structures in their real sense. The entire historical texture is a structure, quite apart from its stratifications. Or, rather, it is a structure that somehow is defined, *negatively*, by contraposition to another structure: the, even though only hypothesised, structure of the modern city. (But even the disorganised and bankrupt sketches of a new urban space, at the outskirts of the main cities, might do, if only for their potential suggestions.)

It is for this reason that the old town centre, in order to become again *structure*, must expel from itself the post-industrial alterations that compromise its readability, and all the conditions of fruition incompatible with its primary function. And since the historical textures are relegated by the new towns (appointed places of the changeable, transient and non-representational) to the appointed places of permanent values, of representation, of organicity, there follows a double attitude towards them:

A. In a certain light they are considered models, in the sense of figurative values that, although unrecoverable as such today, can show the contemporary urbanist the need to translate into a coherent linguistic system the confused, though vital, indications offered by the ephemeral worlds of the non-representational and consumable objects of technological reality: Le Corbusier's continuous references to the ancient urban spaces in his self-publicity, are clearly to the point.

B. As, however, the poetic of the changeable – directly related to the incessant and rapid mobility of the new structure of the capitalist production cycle – is at the base of the hypothesis of new urban structures, it is the values of permanence, immutability, a-temporality of the ancient towns that are seen as dangerous challenges to modern urban planning and as a dangerous opponent. (This *danger* has a concrete meaning, beyond its merely ideal one; both Wright and Le Corbusier refer to the invisible chaos resulting from the forced injection of modern mobility into the old textures.)

The emphasis placed on the representative static nature of the historical structures by turning them into silent museums, has then the purpose of consolidating their values: Paris or London are artificially regarded as unified organisms, but this simplification answers to a need for schematism that, today, we may consider legitimate. Reducing the historical centres to museums meant also accepting a dialectic with them and going beyond a vulgar anti-historicism.[86]

We now face a historicity made into a fetish because of the inability to grasp it concretely – the historical centres are considered organisms outside the dialectics of their development – but it is important to note that in such a way (it becomes obvious and readable by everyone and at every level of the daily function of the town) the opposition between modern history and architecture may slot back (*as the clash of different 'structures'*) into the universe of discourse codified by the new techniques of visual communication.

When the Italian architectural culture of the fifties picked up again the question of the historical centres, it did not link it directly with the great tradition of the Modern Movement, but, with the excuse of introducing *new valencies*, turned its back on the *Charte d'Athènes* and picked up again Giovannoni: a process all the more serious because it was carried out without a clear understanding of what it was postulating.[87]

We have seen anyway how the tendency to go back to a *sacral*, artisan, historicist conception of architecture, is recurring throughout the history of the Modern Movement. It is not only a question of resistance from outdated circles, but also of the constant temptation to go back, to go over the old road again, enriching it with values initially left behind. Scandinavian neo-empiricism, English and Italian populisms, 'enrichments' and dialogues with the old, are all in the brief-case of post-war architecture.[88] The dialogue with history seems to weigh obsessively on the conscience of modern architects. Besides, the Modern Movement seemed to have failed in its attempt to dominate the future through the means of pure reason: technology seemed to show, only then, its ideal emptiness and its alienating power; the anti-historicism of the avant-gardes, ignored in its deeper implications, was seen as a contingent and resolvable, if not already solved, phenomenon.

Nature becomes the new substitute myth, and history is reproposed as a secondary myth. What escapes is the exact relation between the value of the continuity of the process inevitably grafted on the avant-gardes of the twenties, and the value of the newly introduced critical valencies. Under the flag of this myth, the rescue of history is reduced to farce, while Wright and Le Corbusier proposed, with varying fortunes, a re-mythicisation and an ambiguous 'historicity' of architectural images. 'Neo-Liberty' is the most garish of these processes: but we must add that it amounts to nothing more than to a precipitation of tendencies already present (just more cautious) in the kaleidoscopic ferment of intentions typical of post-war Italy.

It is right and proper to acknowledge, as Portoghesi has done, the various cultural sources of the many neo-Liberty tendencies and their deeper and even polemical intentions.[89] And it is certainly not difficult to see, underneath an immediately fashionable phenomenon, made evasive by those who appropriated it for snobbish reasons, a frustrated revolt against a modern tradition which, often with sincere despair, one saw fail.

For the young Milan and Turin architects the salvage of history could not happen in the wake of the enrichment of the *tradition of the new*, even if the 'recovery of the valencies left free' by the avant-gardes – a symptomatic statement by Rogers that well suited the post war activity of BPR – might have supplied a background for their experiences.

It is for this reason that, in the polemic triggered off by Banham's famous article in the *Architectural Review*, there is an error of judgment. The English critic sees the studies on neo-Classical, Romantic and Liberty architecture published so frequently in Italian magazines (*Metron, Architettura cronache e storia, Casabella continuità*) as responsible for the move towards 'the childish withdrawal from the Modern Movement'.[90] All this frantic probing into the origins of contemporary architecture coincided with the need to firmly anchor the present experiences in the wake of the modern tradition. Neo-Liberty architecture tried to challenge this tradition, and if one could call it revisionist, it would be a revisionism on the fringe of the most total challenge.

Only on the fringe, though. In the end, the real drama of neo-Liberty is in its lack of courage: the return of the phenomenon depends in equal measure on the enthusiastic adhesion to it by the middle and high Italian bourgeoisie that sees in the equivocal quality of that architecture a resonance of its own evasive costume, and on the realisation of not having changed the dimension of the architectural problems in the least by codifying ambiguity, but of having simply opened the way to the most suffocating narcissisms.

Neo-Liberty has not rescued history, but only the arbitrary right to flirt with it, in the most hidden corners of its 'familiar lexicons'. As an expression of uneasiness, neo-Liberty had been too cautious; as a symptom of the will to sound the dialectic of contemporary architecture, it has left its task unfinished, running only calculated risks on the lines of provincial polemics. The failure of neo-Liberty has then a symptomatic value: it expresses the impossibility of returning the *objects* into fetishism, within the universe of discourse of contemporary architecture. It must be noted, in particular, that when Gabetti, D'Isola, Canella and Gregotti, on one side, and Portoghesi on the other, tried to *recover the values of memory*,[91] they injected into their work – from the 'Bottega d'Erasmo' to Casa Baldi – recollections that did not historify their architecture, but, if anything, made it even more rootless. The salvaged sources, in fact, in spite of their statements to the contrary,[92] were easily recognisable: it was not history that was being salvaged, but the emotions, the nostalgias, the incidental interests of the autobiographical kind that gave an ambiguous structure to their linguistic choices.

Wendingen, the various, major or provincial, Art Nouveau schools, and Baroque modulations alternated in a sort of Fellinian memory lane: too realistic to take on the misty irony of the dream; too abstract to cut with real critical depth.

The young neo-Liberty designers had not realised that their escapades into autobiography were permissible only on condition of remaining within the *structures of enrichment* of the linguistic codes, and not as a search for a new language.

We must mention, though, that in the case of neo-Liberty, the critics played a negative role. They rose in defence of a mythical Modern Movement, instead of trying to understand the intimate reasons for a symptom of distress; they opposed an orthodoxy without trying to historify the phenomenon and see its less short-lived elements. They left it free, after all, to get involved, to become deformed and to die, wasting, in this way, a good chance of clarification.

In fact, one could have opposed the anachronism of neo-Liberty by pointing out:

A. That its polemic did not rescue the sense of history, but was anti-historicist and Romantic, almost in the Hegelian sense.

B. That the very same polemic had chosen too simple a target and too late: the International Style, while the rest of the world was building Chandigarh, La Tourette, Ronchamp and the Price Tower.

C. That the linguistic analysis proposed as a need, in a time in which Italian architecture was drowning in an empty and sterile ideologism, did not become a 'self-critical tool' because the parameters used for it received their only justification in the 'folds of history', while 'history' itself, as an organic system in constant revolution, remained the great incognito.

The value of neo-Liberty has, then, been mainly as a symptom of the urgency of the new, but not yet clearly defined, problems.

Italian neo-Liberty goes hand-in-hand with the anti-Mies revolt of Philip Johnson, with the scores of American eclectisms, and with the many other naïve, or shrewd, false salvages, devoid of the morality of the young Italians. It is significant, though, that within the international polemic, the return to history as a compromise of history with the present, as a reduction of the historical dialectic to the dimensions of the present, remained only at the budding state.

It is worth while spending some time on a recent work that proposes with great insight, and on a new level, the notion of history as 'instrument' of planning. In his *Territorio dell'Architettura*, Vittorio Gregotti, well supplied with arguments ranging from phenomenology to structuralism, takes the pulse of this tendency, bringing to light many of the main factors that have influenced the best and more cultured Italian architectural praxis, particularly that of the northern circles.[93]

Gregotti accepts *a priori* a perspective within the *tradition of the new* and within 'modernity' as a central historical reference point and as an inevitable existential condition. Such a tradition, he states, turns historical attention on itself, moving backwards towards a 'radical revision of the historical time' contained in 'phenomena flattened into a formal concreteness, which one digs into and waits until the tunnel has reached, through the thick layers of things and events, a new condition of knowledge.'[94]

> The revision [he continues] seems to be confirmed by the attention paid by anthropology, linguistics and art (through the studies on the mythical aspects of the various cultures, particularly of primitive cultures) to the conditions of a quasi-suspension of historical time. Historical research seems to be moving towards models of interpretation of history, conceived as a series of successive and discontinued configurations, consciously placed, by us, on different levels of values.

If we read Gregotti's statements as a reticent declaration of a poetic (reticent because it is hiding in a context presented as objective and generalisable) rather than as a historiographical survey, we might then see it as a clear analysis of the most disquieting difficulties facing the work of the architect.

The Modern Movement tradition of continually asking itself tragic questions; the insecurity of the *tradition of the new* itself, revealed by the need to dig in the 'thick layer' of historical things; the frustrations caused by this uneven exploration in those who discover, through it, the lability of the present; the *quasi-suspension of the historical time* as an absurd result of a sincere will of historical verification: isn't all this the condition, or, if one prefers, the mood, typical of the new architectural eclecticism? Why then, raise to historiographical method what is after all only a particular situation of planning? Gregotti himself answers, in a way, this question:[95]

This task, in which history and planning merge, could be defined as the search for the essence of architecture. A search that doesn't lead to the discovery in itself of the object, but to the realisation that it is (for us) changing in a certain direction. In a way one can rediscover such an essence by conceiving history itself as a project . . .

Not so much, then, the research of cause and effect of that historical fact, but the research of the relation structures of the entire system in which the events take place . . . implies the concept of an historical space that is no longer in perspective, in which time cannot be conceived as a uniform succession, and the placing of the values is not permanently tied to some immovable fact, but rather to the fact that the phenomenon is being defined not only by a particular historical location, but also by the memory of having been, and by the possibility of next being. Furthermore we must acknowledge the determined interest in the present (related to today's architecture in its open problems) that commits us to make use (but not by falsifying it) of our knowledge of history.[96]

In this passage there is a terrifying swing from history as a test for the present, history – paradoxically – as the source of insecurity, history as a store of memories to be revitalised, to history as a prop for autobiographical comment.

We are not interested here in picking up possible inconsistencies on a strictly historiographical level. What matters is that Gregotti's words are the faithful mirror of a condition typical of the contemporary architect: unsure of the tradition of the Modern Movement, because of its obvious daily failure and the decline of revolutionary pride, unable – because it is objectively impossible – to overcome the *impasse* by breaking away from it, turning in despair towards a past without any idea of how to use it – because still within a culture that compels him to *make use* of any cultural acquisition – given to eclecticism and to the *pastiche*: but without excessive drama, almost as a vocation.

All this is again confirmed by Gregotti:

. . . we *clash* with the problem of history, and we must say immediately that one must be careful of the illusion that it might provide us with elements for deducing the forms of architecture, that it might show us some safety rules before we carry out our first move. Any real advancement is always discontinuous and disarticulated, but it too is defined as such, against something else, against, that is, the historical sediments of the present.[97]

Then, after quoting a famous passage from Wittgenstein, he continues:

> . . . history, then, presents itself as a curious instrument whose knowledge seems indispensable, but that, once acquired, can't be used; a sort of passage one has to walk through, but that doesn't teach us anything on the art of walking.[98]

Gregotti surely had in mind Rosenberg's analysis of Gorky's poetic with regard to Picasso's particular historicism. The analogy is too obvious to be ignored: Gregotti's statements are so similar to those of the *battle with time*, as it is presented by Rosenberg, to justify the supposition that between the architecture of the Milanese scholar and the paintings of Gorky and Picasso, there exists an analogy, at least of principle.[99]

If this doesn't actually happen it is because of the instrumental treatment of history, of laying history down on the drawing board, next to the other working 'materials' (from the drafting pencil to representational techniques), that helps to create, for Gregotti and for so much 'cultured' contemporary architecture, the conditions for an even greater insecurity, or, if you prefer, the sense of transience and chance of the tradition into which one tries desperately to merge. Compared to that of Marston Fitch and Stephen Jacobs, Gregotti's instrumentalisation of history is doubtless more legitimate and on a higher level.[100] At the same time we think that his words express perfectly the guilt-complex towards history that dominates the present architectural debate. A guilt-complex that we have already seen in the neo-Liberty and that is fully and with rare clarity recognised as such in the more advanced American research of the last decade, particularly in the work of Louis Kahn.

The subtle ambiguity of Kahn's historicism has been outlined by Aldo Rossi in his study of the critical contributions that seemed to be contained in Kahn's work:

> Let us note how Louis Kahn's formal and surface research on classicism and on the architecture of the eighteenth century, becomes in his works a widely used model; in fact Louis Kahn's *Roman-ness* is all played on half stylistical and half functional elements and references, and the result is certainly not systematic, nor does it offer itself as a meditation on the persisting forms of architecture.[101]

In other words, Kahn's complex cultural operation diffuses and vulgarises a problem – that of the ambiguous link between contemporary architecture and its historical sources – rather than producing a concrete, motivated and to the point analysis of the values of the contaminated architectural *systems*.

At this point one can well ask whether Kahn has not already achieved his task through the transience of his historiographical data. In effect, as Kahn is certainly not trying to accentuate, polemically, the de-historicisation of modern art through the *pastiche*, or (against all appearances) to fix, unequivocally, a new code, or, again, to sieve critically the historical material he, successively, refers and alludes to, one begins to suspect that the misty and variable inconsistency of the Kahnian poetic, might be, after all, entirely coherent with its purposes. If we look at Kahn's work in the light of American architectural history, we see that it had a precedent in the City Beautiful movement, and that its ambiguity is a sort of denunciation, a way of coldly observing an unsolved dilemma of the modern American tradition and immediately loading it with a suggestive theoretical luggage.[102]

Kahn's is indeed a *new objectivity*. The kind of objectivity that presents with detachment the terms of a problem difficult to solve, lining them up in an abstract series: the high didactic quality of Kahn's architecture – or, rather, of his designs and methods, more than of his, often disappointing, realisations – is in the ability of making objective and verifiable the path that leads to architectural communication, throughout its complex structures. We can say, therefore, that for Kahn too, history is only an *ingredient* to be manipulated. He uses it to justify choices already made or to shed semantic light, through the open allusion of the references, on values that aspire towards the symbol and the institution, but that, at the same time, try to be open and readable without betraying the code that rejects myths, symbols and permanent institutions.

The critical activity of Kahn's work is not, then, directed towards the historical material, but towards the manipulation of its forms carried out by the less advanced groups of the Modern Movement. With all this we mean to say that Kahn is not more advanced, but, in fact, lagging behind someone like Le Corbusier, for example, at least as far as the methods of dealing with the form go, even if Kahn is perhaps more *up-to-date* than the Swiss-French master because of his combinatory analysis of *composition* materials, that answers to a particularly contemporary felt need for verifiability.[103] The fact that the Kahnian rigorist school, with the exception of some work by Giurgola, Vreeland, Kallmann, Knowles and McKinnell and of the latest Pei, falls into an uncontrolled praise of the 'Master's' criticism, is something else altogether.

It is significant, though, that the analytical method of these *rigorists* (at least before it too became a consumer phenomenon) was found provocative by American and international circles. The historicism of the Kahnian school harks back to the European myth of Reason: as such it becomes a phenomenon opposed to the pragmatist American tradition, balanced, by now, between a fun-fair irrationality and a guilty cynicism.

How much can we accept, then, of Robin Middleton's statement that Gropius's negation of history serves, now, only as a pretext for an architectural *game*? Middleton writes about Rudolph, Kahn and Johnson:

> Historical study had not served to enlarge their perceptions or strengthen their powers, it had prompted them to make a number of adaptations of the most limited and limiting kind. They are composing with fragmentary rubbish. It would seem that they are no longer prepared to accept engagement in the architectural struggle. They have turned it down. But are they daunted or dismayed? Not at all. Flourishing. It seems almost mean-minded and petulant to cavil at their success.[104]

Like some Italian authors, Middleton does not accept the reading of the meanings underlying the apparent historicism of the new American schools.[105] Further on, we shall examine the *critical* value of this group of experiences. For the moment it is enough to observe that the most obvious element introduced by them is a new rigour in checking the architectural configuration, that might be echoed in a renewed relationship between architecture and historical pre-existences.

We have mentioned, polemically, the 'rediscovery' of Giovannoni and the rejection of the *Chartre d'Athènes* by Italian culture, engaged, in the post-war years, in the defence of the historical centres. By reducing, in fact, the semantic poly-valency of the ancient textures to the generic concept of *organism*, by substituting the myth of the figurative unity of the historical centres to the study of the dialectic within the urban structures, by producing a neat cut between the ancient and the new, the modern architects were expressing their guilt complexes towards history and their renunciation of an objective and analytical study. The historical centres were conceptually enclosed in an abstract dimension: they were, in fact, reduced to unusable *fetishes*. Modern architecture was pushed into 'game reserves' to enjoy a freedom that was not made use of when the moment came.

The sectorialisation of the urban problem has been the constant theme of Italian culture, afflicted by incurable amateurishness, in spite of Benevolo's acute historical study that saw urban history as a vital necessity for our culture, in spite of the critical attempts by Rogers and Samonà, that took up again Pagano's pre-war theme on the value of the indigenous traditions, in spite of the widening, on all levels, of the architectural debate.[106]

Having rejected the dialectical clash predicted by Le Corbusier, the ancient town became an *object* to be defended: in this way it was reduced to myth, and the right of the outsiders to ignore its values was sanctioned. Brandi's theory on the split between ancient towns and new architecture was coherent because of his rejection of modern architecture. Less coherent were the modern architects who accepted in their work what they would not have accepted in their theory, showing their deep inhibitions towards both history and modern architecture. What was missing was a clearly structured new *code*, through which one could decipher and renew the *corpus* of urban and territorial environments with their complex historical dialectics. By remaining half-way, one only created ambiguous and fascinating *contaminations*, that instead of renewing their context, commented lyrically on it: the typical position of the BPR, that has its monument in the brilliant invention of a Milan that doesn't exist (or exists only as ineffable atmosphere, like in the Torre Velasca).

This kind of operation could be justified in Albini's Bianco e Rosso (White and Red) buildings and in the Tesoro of S. Lorenzo in Genoa, or in Scarpa, 'restorer' of the Palazzo Abatellis in Palermo, of the Castelvecchio in Verona and of the Querini Stampalia in Venice. Some of the best Italian architects showed – on the level of a careful reflection active in a very particular historical context – the possibility of using a deeply critical even if not yet historicised architectural meta-language. But on the level of the city such exceptional operations showed their cultural sterility, because their taking refuge in the myth of the *city as organism*, of the 'non-historicity' of modern architecture from 1800 to the present, of the impossible re-configuration of the urban environments, has led to the uncontrolled plunder of the historical centres, to the silence of architecture towards historical pre-existences, to the inability to see critically the historical environments as meaningful structures.

In other words, it has not been understood that to give up reconfiguring the city means to give up understanding it critically. Conservation has been reduced to a problem of urban stage-designing, overlaid on a functional re-structuring process that is arbitrary in its premises and purposes, because it is not substantiated by an organic historical consideration of the problem.

The historicism of Italian architecture is there, then, only in appearance. As far as the formulations of the avant-gardes went, there has not been an effective salvaging of history (if this has any meaning within an ideological superstructure), but rather a gutless and indecisive attempt to get free from the *tradition of the new*. Here too, the *end of the avant-garde* is something quite different from going beyond it.[107]

With the appearance in 1959 of Samonà's *Urbanistica e l'avvenire della città* a new chapter opens in the history of our problem. A structural reading takes the place on one side, of a purely visual and romantic conception of the historical towns and on the other, of their being a battle field for the building industry. In this book the problem of the urban form is considered in its totality, as a dynamic organisation of the perpetual dialectic between structural permanences and morphological changes. Samonà leaves behind the concept of historical centre in favour of an historical reading stretched into space and time; he places the problem of the continuity with morphological structures in its proper dimension, in spite of a strong problematic tension about the new analytical methods and their alternatives. Compared to other studies, more analytical but less valid in their research methodologies,[108] or to the work of Kepes and Lynch that would enjoy, a little later, a short lived mundane success, Samonà's volume opened the doors to an analytical field not yet tried but surely, if seen in the right perspective, among the most valid.[109]

> During the growth of the city [Samonà writes][110] along the course of the centuries, there is a vital sense that shapes everything contained in it, and a coherence recognisable in the custom as well as in the spaces; so that every part of the city, or, at least, every essential part, has meaning because it belongs to the continuity of extension of the urban texture according to unmistakable characteristics. . . .
> Any effort towards saving the historico-artistic heritage of our towns must dissolve its negative charge, and allow the old texture to enter the process of reshaping urban life, and where this process has not yet started, must create the right conditions to bring it about.[111]

The interest in Samonà's propositions is increased by the problematic expressed in his ideological interpretations. The third edition of his volume must be a fundamental text for anyone who wants a complete documentation on the tension between historicism and anti-historicism in the present debate. He seems to start a dialogue with himself taking, in turn, opposite sides:

> if . . . the reasons that would, in the name of historical coherence, take away every discrimination between traditional and potential environments, in order to consider operative one environment only,

that is, the total environment in which man lives, appear to us rather schematical, in the same way appear dangerous the opposite reasons that try to historify the utopia of the ancient environment, presenting it as a need to be satisfied after the defeat of the rationalist utopia.[112]

Samonà's conclusion is then still problematic in its polemical extremism:

I think that a norm inspired by the strictest preservation could be efficient, if it were inserted in the programmatic lines of a complete plan of the city; this plan, more than just sounding out the extension of the old areas to be preserved, preparing the gradual insertion of regenerating economical activities that would not alter it, should bravely propose the preservation of the *entire form of the city*.[113]

Samonà, more recently, has further defined his position, moving on to operative considerations, without, however, lifting his suspension of judgment:

The only possible planning within the historical centre must first try to discover all the relationships within its physical configuration; these should then become the determining factors in defining its character and organising its restoration, according to a project of future stabilisation completely independent from factors extraneous to the centre itself. This implies giving the historical centre a finiteness with maximum expressivity through the use of coherent formal elements, according to a still undiscovered figurability.[114]

For Samonà, then, the figurative isolation of the historical centre, and its value as a single organism, are each the consequence of the other: but one can read more into it. The 'need to give, as far as possible, a clear vision of the ancient town detached from the present vicissitudes',[115] recognised by Samonà, sounds similar to the proposals of the masters of the thirties.

The figurative facts [Samonà continues] are not only formal, but are saturated with permanent values, with forms that qualify exactly the figurability of the monuments and of their structures. . . . This brings us to the conclusion that the more or less distant destiny of the historical towns will be to be used as areas of pure and simple contemplation.[116]

This doesn't mean that modern architecture cannot act within the choices dictated by the evolution of the urban structures, cannot clarify the meaning of the historical textures, make perceptible their internal valencies and re-establish their meanings. It might be a somehow violent operation; but its results will be conditioned by its capacity to bring out from the clash between old and new, the dialectical link between historicity and the permanence of the ancient textures and the values of the present, the changeable, the arbitrary, the energetic, typical of contemporary life and architecture.

The project for the new Parliament buildings by Giuseppe and Alberto Samonà is a particularly meaningful example of this concept. The transparency of the ancient behind the filigree of wiry iron structures – seemingly a reminder of Paul Klee's irony – and the upwards explosion of an unbalanced dynamism of geometrical forms: the dialogue is made possible by accepting the terms of the problem as they are, in sharp opposition with each other.

This means, also, that architecture helps to clarify a historical situation by charging itself with critical values.

While Samonà was able to carry on such an operation – unfortunately only at the level of proposal – on a small scale and in an exceptional case, the lesson from the project for the new Venice hospital by Le Corbusier insists on the same range of problems, showing, at the same time, the most suitable way to face them.

Le Corbusier creates a definite link between the structure of Venice and that of the new intervention: the dialogue between the structures is carried out at the level of their respective organisms, emphasising, in the new hospital, the continuity and the seriality of the various nuclei. A specific environment, then, undergoes a reorganisation imposed by the articulated hospital *machine*. While the urban structure takes on a completely new character through the critical clarification of Le Corbusier's work and its definition of a still unrealised 'fringe'.

His relationship with a town like Venice, so particularly 'finished' and organic in its historicity, allows Le Corbusier to single out the articulation of the architectural organism as the mediating element between new intervention and consolidated history: as in the previous projects for Algiers and the South American towns, he was able to set up a new code of values and a new frame of reference, absorbing natural, geographical, historical elements into articulated organisms, as if they were *ready-made objects* open to the revolution of their semantic attributes.

Historical dialogue and revolution of the meanings: the binomial – Le Corbusier shows – is inseparable. It is the same operation tried by Quaroni in his competition project for CEP at the Barene of San Giuliano, by Kahn in his projects for Philadelphia, by Tange in the Yamanashi Building. These and some experiments of the younger generation have widened it to the point where it is seen as the pivot of the new urban framework. And it is the attempt to involve the entire urban system, as a dialectical group of meanings consolidated in their primary features, open to new semantic charges in their secondary features and in their territorial lay-out, that seems to be saving the historical towns from the fetishist museification predicted by Dorfles.[117]

At the same time the historical structure can be read on a second level: the equivocal concept of *environment* offered by academic culture as an alternative to the seriality of the new configuration processes, must, in this context, take on a new character.

Aldo Rossi's and Carlo Aymonimo's studies in this field clear the ground of many misunderstandings and prepare it for the new themes of the debate. The reconsideration of the *architecture of the town* is placed against the dissolution of architecture in the town and in the anthropogeographical territory predicted by Argan, Benevolo, Brandi and Gregotti: on one side the re-proposal of a constructivist postulate, on the other the jump towards an apparently new dimension.[118]

When Aldo Rossi compares the town to a great architectural manufactured product and looks for the elements able to verify its meanings,[119] or when Aymonimo sets the basis for a planning in which typology and morphology are confronted,[120] the dissolving of the phenomenon *architecture* in its context is rejected in favour of the recovery of the specific meanings of the town *place*.

Between *L'architettura della città* (The architecture of the town) and *Progetto e destino* (Project and destiny) there is a radical opposition. Theoretically it can be bridged by bringing back Aldo Rossi's analysis within the architectural phenomena and Argan's within the phenomena specific to territorial planning, but it opens the door, anyway, to two ways of tackling the problem of urban structure. Placed against the *absent-minded perception* of super-structural images, we have the symbolic and historical meaning of the urban places: this is, to us, the most interesting and, at the same time the most equivocal, side of Aldo Rossi's and Carlo Aymonimo's studies.[121]

The character (or meaning) of a city [Aymonimo writes] is related to the degree of over-laying of spatial and interpretative elements, to the point in which they become indispensable to each other. This indispensability may only result in a 'judgment' if one reinterprets each time all the elements in the game; and to reinterpret means to plan. In this sense the old centre must be planned in its general form, according to the idea one has of it and the form that one means to give to the contemporary city in its entirety.

From this view point, the problems of 'insertion' and the more generic one of the 'environment' do not exist any more. What remains is the problem of more or less formally completed architectural complexes and urban sectors.[122]

The themes singled out by Aymonimo and Aldo Rossi, Le Corbusier's project for the Venice hospital, Quaroni's for the CEP in Mestre and the Parliament buildings in Rome, Aymonimo's for the Paganini Theatre in Parma, Copcutt's for the urban and territorial system in Glasgow, some *intentions* hidden in the studies of Lynch and Kepes, and in those by De Carlo for Urbino, seem to change the problem considerably by widening it and articulating it from within. We must mention, however, that this dimensional widening still leads either to a considerable embarrassment in the move to architectural scale or to a considerable chance-factor in the planning phase.

Between the intuitive criticism of Scarpa and the study of objective control systems, there is still a gap bridged only (but in the negative sense) by Le Corbusier's 'silences'.

The great task facing the ideology of the Modern Movement seems to be, then, definitely renouncing history as a source of prospects and values for the future: not a rejection of history but finding its right place in planning. The avant-gardes had begun to consider the problem in a new light in the only historically possible way: they already carried the seed of failure, but one should not discard off-hand those who thought possible an equivocal relation with the past.

To consider history as an *event* and not as a value to be offered, unchanged, to the present, required, obviously, an uncommon courage and clarity of ideas: the indecisiveness towards such a jump has led, and still leads, to ambiguous and unproductive situations that make understandable the suggestion of a new jump into the dark, of a new, but more radical (and this time completely ambiguous), murder of history.[123]

On the other hand the banal a-historicism that rules the, more or less cunning, products of the International Style, leads the opposite way: to an equally a-historical compromise, like that of the worst American eclecticism, from Yamasaki to Stone, for example.

Still, it is not impossible to accept fully the two poles of the dialectic, to ask from history something else besides an instrumental function, and to stop oneself from turning bitterly against it, seeing in it faults that are only in the observer who wants to remain in an equivocal position towards it.

There is still no better lesson on the subject than Le Corbusier's, because it comes from one who has accepted, without late-Romantic second thoughts, the dissolving of the traditional function of history, of the artistic object, of the concept itself of art, recovering, from a radically new starting point, the values of memory, of history, of the indefinite: the very operation (the only historically legitimate one) predicted by Brecht in the passage from the *Dreigroschenprozess* quoted earlier.

In spite of Le Corbusier and in spite of the still disconnected and confused attempts to open new ways, there remains an insuperable contradiction in contemporary architecture: the destruction of the *object*, the destruction of the 'aura', the death of history, still present themselves not as transient conditions of a stage left behind, but as essential elements of that code of values conventionally referred to as the Modern Movement.

To predict, in the abstract, its historicisation has, therefore, little meaning. Besides the fact that the choice of the Bauhaus was the only legitimate choice, that the 'abstinence from history' had its own historical reason, that all the attempts to redefine a historical dimension were frustrated, we find that among the de-historicisations carried out by the avant-gardes, the one (unintentional) of neo-Liberty, of the present neo-Illuminism, and the existing differences, leads to the single thread that explains them all. [124]

It is even too easy to explain why it has been up to the historians to denounce, after having unconsciously supported it, the crisis of historicism. Less justifiable is the attempt by many of them to re-insert, in a rather simplicistic fashion, the historical thematic in such a complex operative process, without accepting the fact that, once the dreamt-of historification is realised, the result won't be a modern movement rooted in history – it is already rooted in it because of its anti-historicism – but, rather, something completely new, that still escapes any prediction.

It would be better, then, to accept reality as it really is, and give the historian a dialectical role in respect of the architect; almost to the point of constant opposition. But before outlining the new dimensions of historical criticism, we must investigate the conceptual dimensions that contemporary architecture has introduced at all levels of critical study and of the daily fruition of the form.

Notes to chapter 1

[1] Nikolaus Pevsner, 'Modern Architecture and the Historian, or the Return of Historicism', in the *Journal of the RIBA*, 3rd series, LXVIII (April 1961), pp.230–40.

Stephen W. Jacobs, commenting favourably on Pevsner's essay, wrote in 1964 that the substitution of 'neo-De Stijl' for neo-Classicism, and of 'neo-German Expressionism' for the 'Gothic Revival' means that 'significant numbers of contemporary architects have the same attitudes and failings as their Victorian forebears. In my opinion we architectural historians are largely to blame.' Stephen W. Jacobs, 'History: an Orientation for the Architect' in *The History, Theory and Criticism of Architecture*, Papers from the 1964 AIA-ACSA Teacher Seminar, Cranbrook, MIT Press, Cambridge 1965, p. 66.

[2] Sibyl Moholy-Nagy, Lecture in Pittsburgh Conference, in *Charette*, April 1963.

[3] S. Moholy-Nagy, 'The Canon of Architectural History', in *The History, Theory*, etc., p. 40.

[4] 'The artless ingenuity with which earlier times enriched themselves on the perfect solution is lost for ever because architects today are the product of the anti-stylistic revolt, whether they participated in it or not. Whatever re-adaptation they try is done with bad conscience. It is old sin poorly rationalised as new virtue.

'It is here that architectural theory reveals its total futility for learning or practising architects. . . . The danger of the new historical wave is not, as Gropius naïvely assumed at the Bauhaus, the inhibition of budding, architectural self-expression by past genius. . . . The danger is the theoretical justification of the stylistic crutch.' S. Moholy-Nagy, ibid. pp. 40–1. But one should mention that when the author moves on to outline a coherent use of history, she ends up by stating abstract categories of classification and interpretation (cf. pp. 42–6).

[5] Cf. Stephen W. Jacobs, *History*, etc. and Stanford Anderson, 'Architecture and Tradition that isn't "Trad, Dad"', lecture at the Architectural Association, London, Feb. 1963, and pub. in *The History, Theory, etc.* pp. 71–89. Cf. also: Robin Boyd, *The Puzzle of Architecture*, Melbourne University Press, London and New York 1965.

[6] Reyner Banham, in the *Architectural Review*, May 1960, p. 332. But for a comprehensive study of Banham's thought on the relations between history and planning see: 'The History of the Immediate Future', in *RIBA Journal*, 3rd series, LXVIII (May 1961), pp. 250–60, 269, and 'Convenient Benches and Handy Hooks, Functional Considerations in the Criticism of the Art of Architecture', in *The History*, etc. p. 91.

[7] Bruno Zevi, 'Il futuro del passato in architettura', in *L'architettura cronache e storia*, 1963, IX, no. 98, pp. 578–9.

[8] B. Zevi, 'La storia come metodologia del fare architettonico', opening lecture at Rome University, 18-12-63, p. 7. This text is the most comprehensive of the

many produced by Zevi on the methodological problems of history of architecture: its premises are to be found in *Architettura e storiografia*, Tamburini, Milan 1951; 'Benedetto Croce e la riforma della storia architettonica' in *Metron* and in *Pretesti di critica architettonica*, Einaudi, Turin 1960, pp. 3–19; 'Il rinnovamento della storiografia architettonica', in *Annali della Scuola normale superiore di Pisa*, II, vol. XXII (1954) part I–II; *Il futuro del passato in architettura; Il linguaggio moderno dell'architettura. Guida al codice anticlassico*, Einaudi, Turin 1973.

[9] Cf. Cesare Brandi, *Arcadio o della Scultura, Eliante o dell'architettura*, Einaudi, Turin 1956, p. 140. We refer with particular pleasure to this passage by Brandi, as we think it challenges, by itself, the non-linguistic nature of art and architecture, forcefully defended, as is well known, by the Siena scholar.

[10] The arbitrary choice in the context of history is identified therefore with the arbitrary choice of a reference linguistic code: the Classicist balance between historicism and anti-historicism is completely founded on this identification.

[11] 'One of the essential features of the European spirit,' Panofsky and Saxl wrote, 'seems to be the way in which it destroys and reintegrates on new bases, breaking with tradition only in order to go back to it from a brand new standpoint – and this is what produces "rebirths", in the true sense of the term . . . So we can say that what can be called the problem of the "rebirth phenomena" is a central problem to the history of European culture.' Erwin Panofsky and Fritz Saxl, 'Classical Mythology in Medieval Art', in *Metropolitan Museum Studies*, 1933 (IV), n. 2, pp. 228–80. This explanation of the *persistence of Classicism* in European rationalism coincides, in part, with Jaspers' identification of an 'axial period' in the history of the world. Cf. Karl Jaspers, *Vom Ursprung und Ziel der Geschichte*, 1959.

[12] On Alberti the 'restorer' the contributions by Zevi are noteworthy, see: 'Alberti' in the *Enciclopedia Universale dell'Arte*, and in *Pretesti di critica*, etc. pp. 26–31; and also Paolo Portoghesi *Introduzione al De re aedificatoria*, Il Polifilo, Milan 1966.

[13] Cf. L. B. Alberti *De re aedificatoria*, 1. X.

[14] On the S. Petronio 'affair', basic to the understanding of our study, there is a vast bibliography, but the most important text still remains: E. Panofsky, 'Das erste Blatt aus dem "Libro" Giorgio Vasaris, eine Studie über der Beurteilung der Gotik in der italienischen Renaissance mit einem Excursus über zwei Fassaden projecte Domenico Beccafumis' in *Städel-Jahrbuch*, 1930, VI, pp. 25–72; and in *Meaning in the Visual Arts*, 1955. See also Hartt's interpretation (with which we disagree): Frederick Hartt, *Giulio Romano*, vol. I, pp. 246–7. On the neo-medieval phenomenon in the architecture of the second Cinquecento, cf. Federico Zeri, *Pittura e Controriforma: L'arte senza tempo di Scipione da Gaeta*, Einaudi, Turin 1957, and Manfredo Tafuri 'Jacopo Barozzi da Vignola e la crisi del Manierismo a Roma', in *Bollettino del Centro Studi di architettura Andrea Palladio*, Vicenza 1967, IX, pp. 385–98.

[15] Cf. note 28.

[16] Cf. F. Zeri, op. cit.

[17] Cf. Howard Hibbard, *Maderno and Borromini*, lecture at the Borrominian Studies conference, Rome, Acc. di S. Luca, Oct. 1967; and Borromini's studies for the bottega of Maderno in Heinrich Thelen, *Francesco Borromini, Die Handzeichnungen*. 1.-Abteilung-Zeitraum von 1620/1632, Akademische Druck- u. Verlagsanstalt, Graz 1967.

[18] Hocke has particularly insisted on the value of anamorphosis in the art of the *Cinquecento*. Cf. Gustav René Hocke, *Die Welt als Labyrinth, Manier und Manie in der europäischen Kunst*, Hamburg 1957. The relations between Mannerist anamorphosis and Borromini's irrealism were first identified by Pollack, Panofsky and by Sedlmayr, although without precisely historicising the phenomenon (cf. O. Pollak, 'Die Decken des Palazzo Falconieri in Rom und Zeichnungen von B.' in *Der Weiner Hofbibliothek, Jahrb. d. Kunsthis. Inst. der K.K. Zentralkommission*, v. 3, 1911, p. 111 ff; E. Panofsky, 'Die Scala Regia in Vatikan und die Kunstanschauungen Berninis', in *Jahrb. d. Preussischen Kunstsammlungen* 1919, XL, p. 241 ff; H. Sedlmayr, 'Die Arch. Borrominis', Berlin 1930; München 1939); more recently this fundamental link has been analysed by Argan in his small volume of 'BMM' (1951), and in other papers; by M. Tafuri, 'La poetica borrominiana: mito, simbolo e ragione', in *Palatino*, 1966, nn. 3–4, and by P. Portoghesi, *Borromini: analisi di un linguaggio*, Electa ed, Rome, Milan 1967.

[19] On the interpretation of S. Ivo geometry as pure spatial construction, see the fundamental study by Leonardo Benevolo: 'Il tema geometrico di S. Ivo alla Sapienza', in *Quaderni dell'Istituto di Storia dell'Architettura dell'Università di Roma*, 1953, III, n. 1; while on the iconological interpretation see: Hans Ost, 'Borrominis roemische Universitätskirch, S. Ivo alla Sapienza', in *Zeit. fur Kunstg.*, 1967, n. 2, and: Eugenio Battisti, *Simboli e allegorie in Borromini* (paper at the Borromini conf. 1967); Portoghesi has tried to fuse the two types of readings in *Borromini: analisi di un linguaggio*, op. cit.

[20] For the Elizabethan precedents of Inigo Jones's figurative revolution, see: Mark Girouard, *Robert Smythson and the Architecture of the Elizabethan Era*, Country Life Ltd., London 1966, a complete study with considerable critical depth. On the contaminations of the early Jones cf. John Summerson, *Inigo Jones*, Penguin Books, Harmondsworth 1966. Fürst's and Sekler's monographs on Wren provide a useful contribution to our analysis, but Pevsner's study still remains the best critical work on the subject.

[21] Cf. J. B. Fischer von Erlach, *Entwurff einer historischen Architektur*, Wien 1721; and: G. Kunoth, *Die historische Architektur Fischer von Erlach*, Düsseldorf 1956, a good philological research on the sources of Von Erlach's *Entwurff*; and: H. Sedlmayr, *Johann Bernard Fischer von Erlach*, Wien 1956.

[22] On the 'Gothic' projects for Milan cathedral cf. Nino Carboneri, 'Filippo Juvara e il problema della facciata gotica del Duomo di Milano', in *Arte Lombarda*, 1962, VII, pp. 94–104.

[23] We still have no up to date critical studies on Santini Aichel, in spite of the fact that he is one of the most important and original protagonists of Bohemian Baroque. Cf. anyway: H. G. Franz, 'Gotik und Barock im Werk des Johann

Santini Aichel', in *Wiener Jahrbuch der bildenden Kunst,* 1927, N.F. IV, n. 99; id., *Bauten und Baumeister der Barockzeit in Böhmen,* Leipzig 1962; E. Hempel, *Baroque Art and Architecture in Central Europe,* Penguin Books, Harmondsworth 1965. Cf. also the recent: Christian Norberg-Schulz, *Kilian Ignaz Dientzenhofer e il Barocco boemo,* Officina, Rome 1968.

[24] Cf. G. C. Argan, *L'Europa delle capitali,* Skira, Geneva, 1964.

[25] Experimentalism, anti-symbolism and scientism are the three constants of English architecture, from late-Gothic to the present. In spite of the gaps (in the history of the English artistic movements) in the period we are dealing with, there is no doubt, as stated by Pevsner, about an *Englishness* of English architecture that has continued to the present time, considerably lessening the historical jump in respect of pre-existing traditions caused, on the Continent, by the avant-gardes. The fact that so much of contemporary English architecture fits so easily within the historical textures, is due to this totally exceptional *continuity* of British culture (cf. N. Pevsner, *The Englishness of English Art,* Penguin, Harmondsworth 1956).

[26] Karl Marx, *The Eighteenth Brumaire of Louis Bonaparte,* Intern Publishing, New York, 1898. p. 5.

[27] This passage should make one reflect on some recent reshuffling of the perhaps too *à la page* historical problem of Illumistic architecture. In this sense, though conscious of the hagiographic quality of many fashionable exaltations of neo-Classicism, we have to disagree with its unjust (because a-historical) condemnation.

See, in particular, Paolo Portoghesi, *Roma barocca,* Laterza, Rome-Bari 1973, and id., *Bernardo Vittone, un architetto fra Rococò e illuminismo,* L'Elefante, Rome 1966.

[28] The ideal polemic between Perrault and Boullée is about the arbitrariness of architectural language: to the eighteenth-century amateur the language of the classical orders is arbitrary (a proposition of surprising modernity), while Boullée confirms its adherence to naturalistic laws. Cf. Charles Perrault, *Parallèle des Anciens et des Modernes,* Paris 1693, p. 75 ff. (already criticised, in the XVII century, by François Blondel); L. E. Boullée, 'Architecture, Essai sur l'art' (Bibl. Nat. Paris, ms 9153) in: Helen Rosenau, *Boullée's Treatise on Architecture,* London, Alec Tiranti, 1953. (Rosenau does not seem to us to have caught the modernity of Perrault's propositions in respect of the a-critical naturalism of Boullée.)

[29] Cf. G. B. Piranesi, *Parere su l'architettura,* Roma 1765; see Rudolf Wittkower, 'Piranesi's "Parere su l'architettura"', in *Journal of the Warburg Institute,* 1938, vol. II, n. 2, pp. 147–58, the first to compare it with *Magnificenza e Architettura de'Romani* (1861) and to note the tension existing between the two studies; Emil Kaufmann, in *Architecture in the Age of Reason,* does not realise the complexity of Piranesi's position, seeing the *Parere* as a backward step in respect of the *Magnificenza.* Cf. also: Lorenza Cochetti, 'L'opera teorica del Piranesi', in *Commentari* 1955, n. 1, pp. 35–49.

[30] G. W. Fr. Hegel, *Aesthetik,* Aufbau-Verlag, Berlin 1965. Translated by M. Knox, Oxford: Clarendon Press, 1975. pp. 594–5.

[31] Cf. György Lukács, 'L'estetica di Hegel', in *Contributi alla storia dell'estetica*, Feltrinelli, Milan 1957; Guido Morpurgo-Tagliabue, 'Attualità dell'estetica hegeliana', in *Il Pensiero*, 1962, n. 1–2; and id. 'L'estetica di Hegel, oggi', in *De Homine*, 1963, nn. 5–6, p. 463 ff; Lia Formigari, 'Hegel e l'estetica dell'Illuminismo', ibid., p. 473 ff; Angelo Sabatini, 'La "morte dell'arte" in Hegel e la critica come momento costitutivo della poesia contemporanea', ibid. p. 482 ff. Cf. also: Cesare Brandi, *Le due vie*, Laterza, Bari 1966, and Piero Raffa, 'Studi sulla "morte dell'arte"', in *Nuova Corrente*, 1962, n. 27.

[32] G. W. Fr. Hegel, op. cit.

[33] Ibid.

[34] *Emilio Garroni, La crisi semantica dell arti,* Officina, Rome 1964, p. 308.

[35] E. Garroni, op. cit., p. 309.

[36] The Art Nouveau origin of the great part of Sant'Elia's linguistic repertoire has been noted, first by Giedion and then by Tentori, Ragghianti and Rykwert. It might be useful to document further the phenomenon (understandable through the shared sense of expectation that both Art Nouveau and Futurism resolve into messianic tones), by comparing Sant'Elia's drawings (in collaboration with Italo Paternostro) for Monza's cemetery of 1912, and Emile Hoppe's (a student of the *Wagnerschule*) projects on academic themes, at the beginning of the century. Cf. note 42 and Ragghianti's essay, ibid.

[37] For this aspect of Benjamin's work see the following chapter, where it is related to the new means of visual communciations.

[38] Walter Benjamin, 'Das Kunstwerk im Zeialter seiner technischen Reproduzien-barkeit', in *Zeitschrift für Sozialforschung*, Paris 1936, and in *Schriften*, Frankfurt a.M., Suhrkamp, 1955.

[39] Our italics.

[40] Very significant are the attempts at a *cubist* architecture, through the deformation of totally traditional elements, according to elementary laws of geometrical disconnection. Raymond Duchamp-Villon's project for a Cubist Villa (1912) is a typical example of this impatience dominated by a voyeuristic attitude toward the *civilisation machiniste*. Duchamp-Villon's project was published in: Guillaume Apollinaire, *Les Peintres Cubistes*, Paris 1913, mentioned by Reyner Banham in *Theory and Design in the First Machine Age*, London, Arch. Press, 1962, p. 203 ff. The work of some Czech architects, between 1912 and 1914 – Otakar Novotny, Josef Gočár and Pavel Janák, whose project for a monument at Jan Zizka is the most interesting of this group – are very near to the naïve research of Duchamp-Villon. Cf. *Architektura ČSSR*, 1966, n. 3; *Casabella*, 1967, n. 314, and Brian Knox, 'Czech cubist architecture', in *Architectural Design*, vol. XXXVII, 1967, n. 10, p. 113.

[41] Cf. Hans Sedlmayr, *Verlust der Mitte*, Otto Müller Verlag, Salzburg 1948; id. *Die Revolution der modernen Kunst*, Rheinbek-Hamburg, Rowohlt Taschenbuch, 1955; see also review of Italian ed. of *Verlust der Mitte* by Umberto Eco, 'Il "cogito interruptus"', in *Quindici*, 1967, n. 5.

[42] On the question of the paternity of the *Manifesto dell'architettura futurista* as regards the *Messaggio*, cf. R. Banham, *Theory and Design* op. cit. p. 127 ff. and

bibliography. Cf. also, for a different interpretation of Sant'Elia's work: Carlo-Ludovico Ragghianti 'Sant'Elia, il Bibbiena del Duemila' in *Critica d'Arte*, 1963, X, n. 56, pp. 1–22.

[43] Cf. also other futurist architectural manifestos, like Chiattone's and Marchi's, Fani's (in *L'Italia Futurista*, 15 Jan. 1914) and Prampolini's 'L' "atmosferostruttura" futurista. Basi per un' architettura', in *Noi* 1918, nn. 2, 3, 4 (but already in *Giornale d'Italia*, 28 Feb. 1914); see also: Enrico Crispolti 'Dada e Roma. Contributo alla partecipazione italiana al Dadaismo' (n. 2), in *Palatino*, 1967, n. 1, p. 42 ff.

[44] Letter from U. Boccioni to Barbantini published in *Catalogo della mostra dei Primi Espositori di Ca'Pesaro*, Venezia, 28 Aug. 1958, and cit. in: Maurizio Calvesi 'Primi espositori di Ca'Pesaro. Postilla a Boccioni', in *Arte antica e moderna*, 1958, n. 4 and in *Le due avanguardie*, Laterza, Bari 1971.

[45] Cf. M. Calvesi *Le due avanguardie* op. cit. p. 130 ff. (chapter 'Il futurismo e le avanguardie', in *La Biennale*, 1959, nn. 36-7). On Richter's film shown in Rome (Dec. 1958), at the Galleria d'Arte Moderna together with other experimental films by the artist, during his exhibition, see the notes by Richter himself, in the catalogue of the exhibition.

Quite rightly Calvesi notes the substantial affinity between Mondrian's texts (in particular *L'Effort Moderne* of 1921) and some passages of Sant'Elia's *Messaggio* and Marinetti's *Lo splendore geometrico e meccanico e la sensibilità numerica* of 1914.

[46] 'Dada – Tzara wrote later on – sprang from a moral need, from an implacable will to reach a moral absolute, from the deep conviction that man, at the centre of all the creations of the spirit, stated his pre-eminence on the impoverished notions of human substance, on the dead things and the badly acquired goods. Dada sprang from a revolt common to all adolescences, that required a complete adhesion of the individual to the profound needs of his nature, regardless of history, logic and the morals of his environment . . . we wanted to look at the world with new eyes . . . we wanted to re-examine the notions imposed by our predecessors from their foundations and check their accuracy.' Sandro Volta's Introduction to: Tristan Tzara, *Manifesti del dadaismo e Lampysterie*, Einaudi, Turin 1964, p. 18.

We must add, though, that the humanistic key used by Tzara in re-reading, at a distance of time, the Dada phenomenon, seems to reduce the fundamental contribution of the movement to the discovery of *things* as having independent communicative value, and to the destruction of a mummified consideration of history.

[47] Dada Manifesto of 1918. In: *Dada on Art*, Prentice-Hall, N. J., 1971, p. 16.

[48] Cf. T. Tzara, 'Pittori e poeti dada', in op. cit. p. 124.

[49] The relations between Loos and the European avant-garde movements have been studied, in particular, by Banham. Cf. Reyner Banham, 'Crime and Ornament', first in *Architectural Review* and then in the chapter 'Adolf Loos and the Problem of Ornament', in *Theory and Design in the First Machine Age* op. cit.

[50] Piet Mondrian, 'Is Painting Secondary to Architecture?' Paris 1923, in Hans

L. C. Jaffé *De Stijl* Thames and Hudson, London, 1970, Cf. Mondrian's passage with van Doesburg's and Schoenmaekers's writings widely quoted in Jaffé's *De Stijl* op. cit.

[51] P. Mondrian 'The Realization of Neo-plasticism in the Distant Future and in Architecture Today', ibid. p. 167.

[52] It is odd that such radical movements as De Stijl, the ideological utopianism of the Arbeitsrat für Kunst, of the Gläserne Kette and later of the magazine *Frühlicht*, felt the need to rely on two mystics like the theosophist Dr Schoenmaekers and the late-romantic utopist Scheerbart. It is also important to note that Mondrian poses the alternative 'art or revolution' with extreme clarity. Like most of the constructivist avant-gardes, De Stijl choses art, ascribing to it all the characteristics and tasks typical of a politically revolutionary movement. In this way the European avant-gardes camouflage ideologically their ambiguous relation with political reality.

[53] *De Stijl*, III.

[54] *De Stijl*, I.

[55] Cf. P. Mondrian, *Casa, strada, città*, 1927, p. 111 ff.

[56] On the problem posed by the *diffusion of artisticity* as a substitution for the concept of *art*, cf. Rosario Assunto, *L'integrazione estetica*, Comunità, Milan 1959 (Chapters I, II, III); and the previous: Herbert Read, *Art and Industry*, Faber & Faber, London 1934; W. Benjamin, op cit.; G. C. Argan, *Walter Gropius e la Bauhaus*, Einaudi, Turin 1951; Luigi Pareyson, 'I teorici dell'Ersatz' in *De Homine*, nn. 5–6; id. *Estetica, teoria della formatività*, Zanichelli, Bologna 1960; Renato De Fusco *Architettura come mass-medium*, Dedalo libri, Bari 1967, p. 59 ff.

[57] Cf. Following chapter.

[58] P. Mondrian, 'Liberazione dall'oppressione dell'arte e nella vita', 1941, in Morisani op. cit. p. 161.

[59] P. Mondrian, *Plastic Art and Pure Plastic Art*, 1941, ibid. p. 151.

[60] Cf. Aleksej Gan, 'Note su Kazimir Malevič', in *SA*, 1927, no. 3; Italian translation in *Rassegna Sovietica*, 1965, no. 1, pp. 158–63.

[61] A. Gan, op. cit., p. 161.

[62] N. Gabo and N. Pevsner, 'The Realistic Manifesto', 1920. On the Russian avant-gardes' manifestos cf. Mario De Micheli, *Le avanguardie artistiche del '900*, Schwarz, Milan 1959, and the works by Gray, V. De Feo, Quilici, A. Kopp on Russian art and architecture, in particular *Rassegna Sovietica* (nos. 1, 2, 1965; 1, 2, 4, 1966; 1, 3, 1967) where G. Kraiski and V. Quilici have patiently collected, translated and commented a vast quantity of original material. Cf. G. Kraiski, *Le poetiche russe del '900*, Laterza, Bari 1968 and V. Quilici, *L'architettura del Costruttivismo*, ibid. 1969.

Canella has perceptively related the theme of the Constructivist *death of art* to the messianic and nihilist premises of Russian art of the nineteenth century (this aspect was identified also by C. Gray), in particular to a passage of N. G. Černyševskij of 1855. Cf. Guido Canella 'Attesa per l'architettura sovietica', in *Casabella continuità*, 1962, n. 262.

72 Theories and History of Architecture

⁶³ A. Rodchenko and V. Stepanova, 'Programma del gruppo produttivista', 1920 (in De Micheli op. cit.). Cf. K. Malavič, 'L'architettura quale schiaffo al cemento armato', in *Iskusstvo Kommuny* 1918, no. 1, and in *Rassegna Sovietica* 1966, no. 4, pp. 120-3 (under many aspects tragically prophetic) with B. Arvatov, 'Utopia realizzata' in *Lef*, 1923, no. 1, and in *Rassegna Sovietica* op. cit., that may supply many motives for a direct comparison with architectural Italian futurism, the *ideological utopism* of the Gläserne Kette and the present neo-utopist movements.

⁶⁴ From *Vešč*, 1922, nn. 1-2. The third paragraph of Vešč's programmatic manifesto is explicitly directed against the dadaist 'negative tactic', taken as an anachronistic return to the first pre-war Futurism.

⁶⁵ B. Arvatov, 'Critica a "Vešč"' in *Pecat i Revolutsija*, 1922, no. 7; in *Rassegna Sovietica* op. cit. pp. 173-5. On Ehrenburg's position cf. *Eppur si muove* 1922 (I. Ehrenburg, 'La costruzione' in *Rassegna Sovietica*, 1965, no. 2, pp. 102-3).

⁶⁶ G. C. Argan, *Progetto e destino*, Il Saggiatore, Milan 1965, p. 11.

⁶⁷ The insertion of Mayan and ancient American cultural *memories* in the context of his architecture of the twenties, has for Wright an explicit anti-European meaning. It expresses an ostentatious search for autochthonous roots, but at the same time is a sign of an elliptical process of historicisation: Wright's *bricolage*, either of his Californian houses or of the Imperial Hotel in Tokyo, dips, not by chance, into mythical sources difficult to historicise. The phenomenon had happened before in America, in, for example, work by Frank Furness.

⁶⁸ Le Corbusier, *When the Cathedrals were White*, Routledge, London 1947, p. 8.

⁶⁹ Alexander Dorner, *The Way beyond 'Art'*, New York 1947, p. 17.

⁷⁰ On Dorner's museum activity see: Samuel Cauman, *The Living Museum Experiences of an Art Historian and Museum Director, Alexander Dorner*, New York University Press 1958.

⁷¹ Cf. A. Dorner op. cit.

⁷² Ibid.

⁷³ Ibid. p. 15.

⁷⁴ Cf. Charles L. Kuhn, Preface to op. cit.

⁷⁵ 'As long as we ignore the fact that the "art work" and the concept of reality it expressed were only passing historical solutions of a much profounder problem, we shall be unable to understand the scope of the revolution through which we are passing. . . . The red danger signal of absolutistic thought is still up. . . .' A. Dorner, op. cit. p. 134.

⁷⁶ Ibid. p. 147.

⁷⁷ Ibid.

⁷⁸ '. . . just as in primitive time, through the absolute weight of its cultural value, the work of art had become an instrument of magic, and only later recognised as a work of art as such, so today through its exhibitionable value, the work of art becomes a formation with completely new functions, of which the one we are aware of, i.e. the artistic function, looks as if it may, in the future, become only marginal.' W. Benjamin, op. cit.

[79] Bertolt Brecht, 'Die Dreigroschenprozess', in *Versuche 1-4*, Berlin and Frankfurt am. M. 1959, p. 295.

[80] The *consumption* of the modern aesthetic product is conditioned by reasons within its formative process: Benevolo's comments on the inability of buildings such as the Bauhaus or the Dessau-Törten Siedlung to age seem to us far more to the point than Dorfles's. Cf. Gillo Dorfles, *Simbolo, comunicazione, consumo*, Einaudi, Turin 1962 and Leonardo Benevolo, *Storia dell'architettura moderna*, Bari, 1960, vol. II.

[81] Frank Lloyd Wright, *An Organic Architecture, the Architecture of Democracy*, Lund Humphries, London 1939. See also some of Wright's answers to the public, where he states: '. . . The better parts of London, like so many of our great cities, constitutes now the greatest museum-piece in the world. . . . London, its insignificant parts and slums removed to make room for trees or grass, would make a wonderful park. . . . We occasionally go to the graveyards of our ancestors, so why not to the remains of their cities?'

[82] Le Corbusier, *The City of Tomorrow*, Arch. Press, London, p. 287.

[83] Ibid.

[84] We think it is extremely important to underline the fact that the opposition between Broadacre City and the Plan Voisin model, as far as the destiny of the historical centres is concerned, is considerably lessened.

[85] Cf. Guido Morpurgo-Tagliabue, *L'esthetique contemporaine. Une enquête*, Marzorati, Milan 1960. We are left with the doubt, though, that a rigorously philosophical criticism might be an inadequate yardstick for the analysis of a 'poetic' such as that of Loos. Some interesting notes on the theme are contained in Aldo Rossi's Introduction to Boullée's treatise (op. cit.).

[86] It seems important to underline this aspect, consciously pointed out by Le Corbusier in one of the notes to *The City of Tomorrow* (p. 193): 'It bores me more than I can say to describe, like some minor prophet, this future City of the Blest. [He is referring to the literary description of the principles of the Plan Voisin.] It makes me imagine I have become a Futurist, a sensation I do not at all appreciate. I feel as though I were leaving on one side the crude realities of existence for the pleasures of automatic lucubrations! On the other hand, how thrilling it is, before one sets pen to paper, to work out on a drawing-board this world which is almost upon us, for then there are no words to ring false and facts count.'

[87] Cf. the high value given, in the *Charte d'Athènes*, to the meaning of the historical remains within the new city: *La Charte d'Athènes*, Paris, 1942.

[88] According to Banham there are surprising similarities between English and Italian architectural vicissitudes in the immediate post-war years: from a populist empiricism to the anxious recovery of a lost rigour. It is also interesting to note how a rigorously historical treatise like *Principles of the Age of Humanism* by Wittkower, could help, in that sense, architects like the Smithsons. Cf. Reyner Banham, *The New Brutalism*, Documents of modern arch., edited by J. Joedicke, Karl Krämer, Stuttgart-Bern 1966, pp. 9–20.

[89] Cf. P. Portoghesi, 'Dal neorealismo al neoliberty' in *Comunità*, 1958, N. 65, but mainly 'L'impegno delle nuove generazioni' in *Aspetti dell'arte contemporanea*,

catalogue of the 'Rassegna internazionale di architettura, pittura, scultura e grafica', L'Aquila 1963 (Edizioni dell'Ateneo, Rome 1963). Cf. also, in the same catalogue, Francesco Tentori's article: 'D'où venons nous? Qui sommes nous? Où allons nous?' (p. 264) with the autobiographical and self-critical contributions of many protagonists of the 'neo-Liberty'.

[90] Cf. No. 215 of Casabella continuità with Gabetti's and D'Isola's presentation of the 'Bottega d'Erasmo' and the debate with E. N. Rogers.

[91] Of valuable documentary interest, in order to understand fully the situation that spawned neo-Liberty, are the contributions by V. Gregotti, A. Rossi, Gabetti e D'Isola, G. Canella, in the catalogue of the exhibition Nuovi disegni per il mobile italiano (Milan, March 14–27, 1960).

[92] Cf. 'Revivals e storicismo nell'architettura italiana contemporanea' (open discussion with R. Gabetti and P. Portoghesi) in Casabella, 1967, n. 318, p. 14. On Portoghesi's text see the author's corrections in n. 319 of the same magazine.

[93] Vittorio Gregotti, Il territorio dell'architettura, Feltrinelli, Milan 1966, chapter: Architettura e storia (pp. 101–41). Extracts from this chapter appeared in the volume of AA.VV. Utopia della realtà, Leonardo da Vinci, Bari 1965, p. 110 ff. and in Edilizia Moderna, 1965, n. 86, p. 3 f (La ricerca storica in architettura).

[94] V. Gregotti, op. cit. p. 136.

[95] Ibid. p. 137.

[96] Ibid. p. 139.

[97] Ibid. p. 132.

[98] Ibid. p. 133. Wittgenstein's passage is from Tractatus logico-philosophicus.

[99] 'This master [Rosenberg wrote] showed by his example that today the artist must be a living embodiment of the whole history of art. In our time every new work must represent a choice between what is dead and what is alive in the painting of the past. Therefore the artist's meditation on the history of art is, at the same time, meditation on himself, on his own taste, on his intellectual interests, on the social concepts and on the symbols that push him forward. The spring of really significant creations, in this epoch of historical self-awareness, is not the individual genius, but rather the double meditation of the artist on his aesthetic inheritance and on his assimilation of that inheritance.'

[100] Cf. James Marston Fitch, Architecture and the Aesthetics of Plenty, Columbia University Press, New York and London 1961, and Stephen W. Jacobs, 'History: an Orientation for the Architect', in The History, etc. op. cit. pp. 47–69.

[101] Aldo Rossi, Introduction to Boullée's Architecture op. cit.

[102] The relation between Kahn's architecture and the City Beautiful movement has not yet been assessed. Cf. M. Manieri-Elia 'Per una "città imperiale"', in La Città americana op. cit., and Thomas S. Hines, Burnham of Chicago, Oxford Univ. Press, New York 1974.

[103] About the verifiability of Kahn's architecture Manieri-Elia has used the phrase 'formal logic': a perhaps too literary hypothesis, but that confirms the logical and critical character of this architect. Cf. Mario Manieri-Elia

L'architettura dell dopoguerra in USA, Cappelli, Bologna 1966, p. 131 ff.

[104] Robin Middleton, 'Disintegration' in *Architectural Design*, 1967, vol. XXXVII, n. 7, p. 204.

[105] There are many ways of deforming the meaning of American rigorism: interpreting it as a rescue of qualitative values that renounce urbanistic commitment and look nostalgically to the question of form; reducing it to a generic historicism, or, even worse, inserting it in abstract and arbitrary hypothesis based on unverifiable premises. As an example of the first attitude see: Carlo Melograni, 'Due culture anche in architettura?' in *Rinascita*, 6 Jan. 1967, n. 1, pp. 17-19. See also:Marcello Angrisani, 'Louis Kahn e la storia' in *Edilizia moderna*, 1965, n. 86, p. 83 ff; Maria Bottero 'Louis Kahn e l'incontro fra morfologia organica e razionale' in *Zodiac*, n. 17, 1967, p. 47 ff. An interesting statement on Kahn by Romualdo Giurgola is to be found in 'On Louis Kahn' (in *Zodiac* op. cit. p. 119): 'L.K. has used the fragment of the Euclidean geometry, as probably a new geometry will be formulated in order to translate those simple postulates he proposed – postulates which became lost both in the stylistic sterility and in the avant-garde ventures as well. But in those broken crystals are the signs of our reality, of a contradictory world where the contradictions give the time measure of our situation but where a coherent architectural dimension is indeed obtained.' Cf. chapter on Kahn in M. Manieri-Elia, *L'architettura del dopoguerra in USA* op. cit.

[106] Benevolo has written much on the problem of historical centres but the most complete of his essays is the winner of the A. Della Rocca Prize: Leonardo Benevolo 'La conservazione dell'abitato antico a Roma' in *L'Architettura cronache e storia* 1956, n. 6. Benevolo stated the operative deductions from his theorical positions at the Venice Conference of 1966, in his study on the *potential voids* of the city of Rome; a study taken up again by Italo Insolera in his competition project for the new Parliament buildings. Although we agree with most of Benevolo's premises we must note that the exclusion of the architectural theme from the general framework of his propositions is an element of considerable weakness, because it leads to choices that cannot be automatically deduced from the urbanistic structure.

[107] Cf. the clear synthesis of the historical problem of Italian avant-gardes, and the consequences of the attempts by Italian architects to keep an undefined 'continuity' with tradition in Leonardo Benevolo 'Continuità e conservazione' in *Casabella continuità*, 1960, n. 236, pp. 52-3 (Part of the debate opened by Luigi Cosenza in n. 230 of the same magazine.) Compare the lucid, even though intentionally limited, diagnosis of Benevolo with the article by Marco Dezzi-Bardeschi 'Il problema della storia nell'architettura italiana ultima', in *Comunità*, 1965, n. 130.

Among the many essays on the continuity of architectural avant-gardes in recent years, worth mentioning because of his expository method, is Douglas Haskell, '75 Years of Change – Mostly Unpredicted' in *Architectural Forum* 1964, vol. 121, n. 2, p. 73 ff.

[108] We are referring to the analyses of the structures of Venice and Rome by

Saverio Muratori and his school. They have the merit of being among the few based on concrete study and description of the urban organisms and of the dynamic of their morphological structures. They have also the demerit of starting from a-historical methodological premises that often falsify the analytical process and the choice of samples. Cf. Saverio Muratori, *Studi per un' operante storia urbana di Venezia*, Ist. Pol. dello Stato, Rome 1960, vols. 1–2; S. Muratori, R. and S. Bollati, G. Marinucci, *Studi per un'operante storia urbana di Roma*, CNR, Rome 1963. But cf., now, C. Aymonino, *Il significato della città*, Laterza, Rome-Bari 1975.

[109] There has been an attempt to extend and make operative Samonà's intuitions in the studies for the *Conferenz a nazionale dell' edilizia residenziale a Roma*, in the Atti del Convegno INARCH, Rome 1965.

[110] Giuseppe Samonà *L'urbanistica e l'avvenire della città negli Stati europei*, Laterza, Bari 1959, 1963. We are quoting from the completely revised third edition, p. 129.

[111] Ibid. p. 250.

[112] Ibid. p. 251.

[113] Ibid. p. 252.

[114] Giuseppe Samonà 'Il problema urbanistico dell'intervento nei centri storici' in *Sipra-Uno*, 1966, n. 6, p. 77.

[115] Ibid.

[116] Ibid. pp. 77–8. 'But [Samonà continues] until we feel that the ancient town has a public content that belongs to us, as a stimulating force for our meetings, these should not be opposed within the ancient structure, they should, rather, be gradually identified. We shall fight all those that want to destroy this use' (p. 78). Cf. also: Alberto and G. Samonà *Relazione al progetto di concorso per i nuovi uffici del Parlamento a Roma*.

[117] 'If . . . we will realise that it is us, with our own hands, who mummify our past, then we may become qualified to do it. It would be, anyway, a kind of "operation Museum", not unlike the reconstruction, on the hill overlooking the Hudson estuary, of the complex of Romanesque Cloisters and Abbeys – the famous "Cloisters" of the Metropolitan Museum.' Gillo Dorfles *Nuovi riti, nuovi miti*, Einaudi, Turin 1965, p. 98. (But cf. the chapter: Mummificazione e feticizzazione dell' architettura, pp. 97–100). Note that here Dorfles seems to contradict what he had previously stated: cf. G. Dorfles *Il divenire delle arti*, Einaudi, Turin 1967, pp. 148–9.

[118] The total absorption of the phenomenon architecture into the urban dynamic, prophesied by such a variety of authors, is due, in our opinion, to a historiographical misunderstanding for some, and to an extreme 'rationalist' orthodoxy for others.

[119] Cf. Aldo Rossi, *L'architettura della città*, Marsilio, Padua 1966, chaps. I and III.

[120] Cf. note 122.

[121] The difference between the two scholars is in the weight they give to the urban 'dimension'. Aymonino sees it as a determining factor of urban qualitative

changes while Rossi rejects it. Cf. A. Rossi, op cit. pp. 184–7 and C. Aymonino and P. L. Giordani *Il centri direzionali*, Leonardo da Vinci, Bari 1967.

[122] Carlo Aymonino, *L'edificio e L'ambiente; premesse alla progettazione*, lectures at the Corso di Composizione dell' IUAV, Venezia, 1967, pp. 20–1 of the proofs. Cf. by the same author: 'Il significato delle città' in *Sipra-Uno* op. cit. and 'Tre esemplificazioni sulla città di Roma' in *Rapporti tra la morfologia urbana e la tipologia edilizia*. Documenti del corso di carattere degli edifici, IUAV, Ac. year 1966–67, Cluva, Venice 1966, p. 123 ff.

It is interesting to see the application of these theoretical premises in Aymonino's competition project for Parma's Teatro Paganini in the context of Palazzo della Pilotta, as compared with the proposals by Aldo Rossi and Luigi Pellegrin (cf. special ed. Cluva, Venice 1966, with introduction by G. U. Polesello), and in the project for the new Parliament buildings in Rome.

[123] 'From the very beginning [Guglielmi writes] man has realised himself in history, has found in it the meaning of his actions and of his life. There was a direct link between his life and history, and to fight for life meant to fight for history. To be, meant to be in history. . . . All this has gone. Today history doesn't pay any more. True, it is still man that builds history and lends it his gestures. But history doesn't pay back a penny. . . . History is by now a lost value. No more a meaning – only a happening.' Angelo Guglielmo, *Avanguardia e sperimentalismo*, Feltrinelli, Milan 1964, p. 78. Guglielmi's passage is typical of a vast neo-avant-garde movement that draws its a-historicism from the history of the Modern Movement: 'The central line of contemporary culture is a-ideological, uncommitted and a-historical; it does not contain messages nor does it produce general meanings. . . . Its task is to recover reality intact: it can do this by removing it from History, revealing it in its most neuter sense, at zero degree.' p. 69.

[124] Obviously when we speak of *legitimacy* about the choices of the avant-gardes or of the Bauhaus, we pass a totally relative judgment within the dialectic of the avant-garde concept. Quite different is the 'political' judgment implicit in note 52, this needs to be made quite clear in order not to appear too generic. Cf. anyway, as positions similar to ours, the *pars destruens* of Franco Fortini's essay 'Due avanguardie' in *Avanguardia e neo-avanguardia*, Sugar, Milan, 1966 p. 9 ff. and the answer by Alberto Asor Rosa 'L'uomo, il poeta' in *Angelus Novus* 1965, n. 5–6, pp. 1–30 to Fortini's *Verifica dei poteri*, Il Saggiatore, Milan 1965, 1969.

2

Architecture as 'Indifferent Object' and the Crisis of Critical Attention

The uncertain attitude of present day architecture towards history is the main difficulty facing criticism, but we must add immediately that it is not the only one. Criticism is in fact linked to a further aporia of contemporary art: the swing between a communication that tends to absorb the critical dimension within the artistic structures, and figurative formulations more and more determined to expose pure images to the rigorous 'shaping of the form', that had been the starting point of the avant-garde movements. In the end we are left with the problem of the mere size of the assumptions imposed by the acceptance of the form, from the eclipse of Classicism onwards.

Such an analysis cannot be started without considering the problem of the relation between the architectural product and the user, closely linked to the vast phenomenon of the crisis of history, the crisis of the object, and of the 'way beyond art', as dealt with in the previous pages. Criticism is deeply involved in these processes because the revolution of the conditions of reception and of visual communication imposes the following choice: either to read the new perceptive processes from the inside (giving up then even the relative possibility of objectivity) or to analyse them, as far as possible, from the outside (but, then, without perceiving their specific qualities). Not a very obvious alternative!

What we are dealing with is the entire universe of meanings of modern architecture: it is not by chance that from the first half of the eighteenth century onwards, it has been the very concept of *architecture* that changed its attributes. (We are referring to Europe, but the American case is even more symptomatic because of its extremism.) The *archaeology of the human sciences*, tried by Foucault, can then be checked against the history of architecture.

Between the end of the sixteenth and the end of the next century, we moved from a state of fusion of architectural code and collective functions (practical and symbolic at the same time) to a *general grammar* – we are referring to the great linguistic systems of Blondel and Perrault and, later, of Campbell and Lord Burlington – to arrive, within the eighteenth century, at an inquiry into what makes architecture possible: that is, into its system of meanings as related to those who pose them.

Psychology, society, *man*, enter into the discourse on architecture. The treatises by Alberti, Francesco di Giorgio, Cataneo, Cornaro and Borromini's *Opus*, in many ways foretell this event, but it is certain that the arrival of the interest in man as a concrete and determining factor in the structuring of figurative language dates from the cultural revolution of eighteenth-century empiricism, sensism and criticism. The radical revolution of the systems of meaning is already explicit in Winckelmann's work, in the very passage that Croce said he didn't quite understand the meaning of: 'those that up to now have dealt with the beautiful [Winckelmann writes in 1767][1] through laziness rather than lack of knowledge have eaten metaphysical food', referring, immediately afterwards to the *Iconografia* of Cesare Ripa. Remember that a great part of baroque decoration comes from Ripa's volume, a true and proper symbological lexicon, published several times from 1593 onwards; from Sacchi to Borromini, the symbolic figures of *Iconografia* are used to translate into pictorial, architectural or simply decorative figurations, the *narratives* saturated with intellectualistic or hermetic concepts.

In the seventeenth and eighteenth centuries, allegory and symbolism were ways to hold back a residue of universality in the meaning of artistic images; in order, on one side, to stop the total undoing of the classicist figurative system compromised in its last ideal movements; on the other to escape – through rhetorical amplification – a genuine critical introspection. But an art that accepts only directly programmed content, that rejects the communication of transcendental dogmas in order to speak to man of the history of humanity, and deals directly with his psyche, must also reject the entirely mundane universalism of symbolism and conceptism because it exploits, with the single purpose of persuasion, the emotional reactions generated by ambiguous and esoteric images.

It is at this point that architecture realises the impossibility of finding

7.   William Chambers, Through sections of the 'Mosque' at Kew Gardens. From:
W. Chambers, *Gardens and Buildings at Kew*, London 1763

its own reasons exclusively in itself. From Addison's and Pope's polemics in the *Spectator* in favour of the landscape (perhaps we should say *psychologistic*) garden, to Burke's *Inquiry*, to the contraposition of 'Picturesque' and 'Sublime' aesthetics to Ledoux's *Architecture*, up to the anticipation of *Pure visibilism* (if not of *Gestalt* psychology) in Robert Morris's study,[2] the fruition of the building becomes a decisive factor of the productive and critical process.

Sedlmayr has spoken of the late Rococo as *architecture that describes itself*.[3] But it is clear that one can describe, tell and speak only by presupposing a willingness to talk on the part of the interlocutor. With Capability Brown, William Kent, Chambers, Soane and the supporters of the *architecture parlante* – Camus, Mézières, Speeth, Lequeu – the interlocutor does not simply receive the messages, but he is asked to complete them, even to change their meaning while they are being deciphered. Chiswick, Blenheim and Kew Gardens are not simply the translation of the concept of *picturesque* into landscaped vistas: as Argan has said, they are microcosms that reflect not (as in the case of the sixteenth-century and Baroque villas) the divine cosmos, but the world of human experiences.[4] As didactical instruments they are turned towards man, awakening his senses and injecting into them, immediately afterwards, a critical stimulus: Nature, by now not a reflection of the divine Idea but a structure shared by man, can merge with the history of the entire human species, showing that the rational course of civilisation is *natural*, because it moves (Gian Battista Vico) from the realm of the senses to that of the intellect.[5]

Architecture, from absolute object, becomes in the landscaped context, relative value: it becomes a medium for the description of an edifying play. The Gothic, Chinese, Classical and eclectic pavilions inserted in the texture of a 'nature trained to be natural', are ambiguous objects. They allude to something other than themselves, losing their semantic autonomy. It is the same phenomenon that, a little later, will move into *major* architecture, that will explode in the period of eclecticism and be recovered in the expressionist (or quasi-expressionist) *bricolages* of Gaudi, Poelzig, and the *Wendingen* group, that touches the first Wright and the Californian school of Maybeck and Greene & Greene, and that the Bauhaus and *l 'Esprit Nouveau*, from opposite sides, will try to contain. But it is also the same phenomenon in which we are again immersed.

The division between *clear perception* and *confused perception* sees lined up on one side Boullée, Durand, Dubut, Schinkel and, later, Garnier, Loos, Le Corbusier, Gropius, European Constructivism, Louis Kahn;

8. J. Muntz, Plan and elevation of the 'Gothic Cathedral' at Kew. From: W. Chambers, *Gardens*, etc.

on the other Lequeu, Romantic and Expressionist movements, and, then, Dada, Action-Painting, Pop Art and the architectural neo-eclectic and neo-expressionist movements.

What joins together the entire Modern Movement is, however, the concept of architecture as *ambiguous object*. The Doric column planned by Loos for the *Chicago Tribune* competition, as a first and violent experiment in extracting a linguistic element from its context and transferring it to an abnormally sized second context, is the anticipation of a caustic and ambiguous Pop Architecture. It offers – apparently tied down to an established code, but in reality available to a maximum degree – an almost excessively open reading to the observer, or, rather, to the absent-minded user of the city. But the same could be said about Wright's Barnsdall and Ennis houses, and, perhaps, even about Le Corbusier's Ronchamp and Church of Firminy. Hilberseimer's project for the same *Chicago Tribune* competition realised what Loos simply 'represented': as in Mies' houses and in the work of the early Breuer, the availability of architecture to the user finds here the greatest possible efficiency.[6]

Different objectives, but identical tools. The observer becomes more and more the user who gives meaning to the *object* or to the *series*, and who is more and more caught and absorbed in this ambiguous collocation. At once inside and outside the architectural work, he is confronted by the alternative of active or passive participation (but even the latter is a form of participation that changes the meaning of the work).

What is being compromised is the critical detachment. The phenomenon is seen very clearly by Mondrian, who carries his exploration to the end:

> The Neoplastic conception of utilitarian objects, etc., merging into the whole and neutralising one another, is in complete conflict with certain modern tendencies which set furnishings apart as 'decorative art'. Their aim is to make art 'social', to bring it 'into life'. In fact, it is nothing other than the making of 'paintings' or 'sculptures' – but in an impure way, for 'art' demands freedom. Such tendencies can never 'renew' our environment. The attention it receives is dispersed on details.[7]

One has the impression of facing a contradiction: if the *things*, the *objects*, must completely lose their symbolic charge in order to be perceived in their pure relational values, what kind of attention should one ask of the observer – the concentration required by traditional art, or mere daily perception? In this second case, what is the use of speaking of *attention* as

Mondrian does? Is it not the rhythm of life itself, transformed into rational behaviour and already saturated with artistic value, that must produce and consume, at the same time, its own meanings?

Absorbing art into behaviour excludes the possibility of speaking of painting or architecture as *objects*: they are, rather, *happenings*, and in this sense the crisis of historicity of art is linked to the *crisis of the object*. Historical links and architectural phenomena are reduced to pure *events*, to 'splashes of pure matter', as Rosenquist says.[8]

The new values resulting from the crisis of introducing reproduction in the processes of architecture and of the visual arts have been best acknowledged by Walter Benjamin:[9]

> The circumstances in which the product of technical reproduction may find itself might leave intact the intrinsic consistency of the work of art but, anyway, they cause the devaluation of its *hic et nunc* . . . this process invests a nerve-centre of the artistic object that is far more vulnerable than in any natural object. That is to say its authenticity. The authenticity of something is the quintessence of everything that can be transmitted from its origin, and goes from its material duration to its value as an historical remain.
>
> As the latter is based on the former, in reproduction, where the first is taken away from man, the second – its value as remain – begins to falter also. Nothing else, but with it, begins to falter precisely the authority of the thing itself.[10]

It is, then, the technique of reproduction itself (rather than the objects submitted to it) that for Benjamin becomes communicative, significant and charged with messages. And as the technical reproducibility presents itself with all the characteristics of a *mass medium*, the expressive range that was once a prerogative of the single artistic event, flows directly into the productive process, charging it with independent meanings and independent communicative values. The result is clear: the reproductive technique takes on the features of a symbolic system, and, as such, issues communications and finds, within itself, linguistic articulations. What before was the absolute repository of communicative values – the single product, with all its 'authority as thing' – is now emptied of meanings, and lies, if taken *in se*, outside the process of which it has become a mute and inert element.

Benjamin could have well quoted, as confirmation of his perceptive phenomenology of the artistic production permeated with new reproductive techniques, the 'objects' of Picasso's, or Braque's, paintings, or, even better, Le Corbusier's canvases and the details of the architecture of Gropius, Corbu and Mies.

The loss of 'authority' suffered by the 'things' in the new artistic process touches also what presents itself as *pièce unique*, as single object. In these cases we witness a conceptual extension of the perceptive and symbolic phenomenon linked to the reproducibility of the work of art. As has been noted,[11] both the houses that Gropius built for the Bauhaus lecturers and those of Le Corbusier for the rich Parisian bourgeoisie, between 1920 and 1930, are only ideal cells of a larger aggregate: the former presuppose the idea of *Siedlung*, the latter presuppose complex structures like the *Immeubles-villas*, and all the series of researches that lead to the *Unités d'habitation*. This is exactly the case where *the code conditions the product*: where a new way of relating to the artistic structure conditions the single *events* of that structure. And as now the *structure* is a series, an indefinite process, an open formal and productive organisation, the artistic *event* is measured against its role in that process *in fieri*.

Transience and repeatability free, then, the object from its sheath, 'from the slavery of unicity and duration'. In this way:

> The destruction of the aura (traditionally connected to the work of art) is the sign of a perception whose sensibility towards *what in the world is akin to it*, has grown to such an extent that, through reproduction, it achieves equality of *genre* even with what is unique. So that, in the field of intuition is announced what in the field of theory is shown as the increase of the importance of statistics. Taking the masses to reality and reality to the masses is a process of unlimited import for intuition and for thought. . .
>
> Those who stand in front of the work of art will sink into it; they enter it; as in the legend of the Chinese painter at the sight of the finished work, on the contrary the absent-minded mass absorbs the work of art in itself.[12]

The process of appropriation of the artistic process is then recognised by Benjamin no longer or not so much in its communicative value, but, rather, in its characteristics as a model or instrument for action.

Now, as architecture has always related to the general public through an *absent-minded reading*, a superficial if not transient contact, a collective approach without depth (at least in the daily experience of the average user of the town), 'the laws of its reception are most instructive' for the study of an artistic structure that presents itself as a process open to free use and to free appropriation on the part of the public.

So, for Benjamin, architecture, because of its nature, already allows the kind of collective consciousness requested by Brecht: a use that permits relaxation and reflection in those involved in the theatrical achievement.[13] Architecture, town and epic theatre, all claim an extreme clarity through the processes that led to their realisation. These processes can therefore be seen by all those that follow the narrative with detachment.

It is worthwhile quoting in its entirety Benjamin's passage on architecture and its relation to the cinema:

> Architecture has never paused. Its history goes back further than any other art; and in any attempt to understand the relation between the masses and the work of art, one must not ignore its influence. Buildings can be used in two ways: through use and through perception. Or, more precisely: in a tactile or in an optical way.... There is nothing, on the tactile side, that would make a counterpart of what, on the optical side, is represented by contemplation. The tactile function is performed more on the level of habit than on that of attention. With architecture the former greatly determines even the optical reception. This latter also, is far more realised through occasional looks than through a careful observation. This kind of reception in respect of architecture can have, nevertheless, a canonic value. Because the tasks that in times of historical change are offered to the human perception cannot be resolved through purely optical, that is, contemplative, ways. All this is realised gradually, thanks to the intervention of the tactile reception, and to the habit.
>
> Even the absent-minded can form a habit. Furthermore, the fact of being able to perform certain tasks absent-mindedly shows that their performance has become a habit. Through the absent-mindedness, such as it is offered by art, one can check in what measure the perception will be able to perform the new tasks. And as the individual will be always tempted to avoid these tasks, art will face the more difficult and more important task of mobilising the masses.[14]

Benjamin's analysis is not only typical of a culture or of an era, it is exemplary for the scientific quality of the method used in dealing with an anything but clear and straightforward concept. It has been noted, in fact, that for Benjamin the transformation of the traditional arts into instruments for mass-communication, in their turn stimulated and realised through the absorption of the technological *media*, is not automatic or taken for granted.[15] On the contrary, a good part of Benjamin's early work underlines the possible dangers to the values of the Western cultural tradition and to the democratic praxis itself, because of the uncontrolled 'mass' processes that go with the extension of technology, with morality and with ideas.

Renato Solmi, commenting on the *Angelus Novus*, has rightly pointed out the contrast between the early and late Benjamin.[16] He swings between the two extremes of rejection and acceptance of the new global meanings of mass and technological civilisation. His tragedy is shared by all the most sensitive European intellectuals since the beginning of the century – Max Weber, Husserl, Brecht, Klee, Le Corbusier.

Benjamin's choice becomes clear from 1931 onwards. The intellectual that investigates without prejudices the new means of reception and communication, rather than spreading Jeremiads on the alienation of technological culture, is already starting the rescue of *man* so much invoked by the apocalyptical culture. The biographical elements are witness to the degree of tension reached by this criticism. Positivity and alienation are both terms of the same process: Benjamin committed suicide in 1940, Weber pays with neurosis for his ideological realism, Adorno, first, and then Marcuse, having reached the most explosive centre of *mass media* – America – chose the most radical and somehow nostalgic line of opposition.[17] Brecht himself had to admit that 'from the new aerials' may come 'old rubbish'.[18]

The same state of tension is shared by architecture. When Lukács criticises the idea of the disappearance of the 'aura' as a consequence of a 'romantic-anticapitalist position',[19] he shows a deep misunderstanding of the structural characteristics of the *mass media*. With its many points in common with the claims of the architects of the Zehnering group in the Berlin of the twenties, and of Hugo Häring in particular, we might call it late-Romantic.

We do not think we are forcing the hand of historical reality too much by stating that the present diffusion of complex and multi-valent architectural structures can be traced back to obvious, though few, tendencies already present in the avant-gardes of the twenties. The organicism of Häring and of what we can call the *Berlin school* (from Taut to Erwin Gutkind), the entire work by Le Corbusier from 1919 to 1938, Asplund after the Stockholm Library and pre-war Aalto, all worked on a complex and multi-valent structuration of architectural images, with the many possible planes of reading and use in mind.

We have quoted these architects, and not the others with whom they are normally associated, for a very precise reason. It is, in fact, illogical and wrong to lump together the work of some members of the *Ring* like Bruno Taut and the Luckhardt Brothers with those of Mendelsohn or Mies, who belong, for political or polemical reasons, to the same groups;

in the same way one can trace links between Häring (and the *Ring* group in general) and Le Corbusier, in spite of their violent clashes within CIAM.[20]

This distinction is justified by keeping in mind the different position of the spectator in front of architecture, as postulated, for example, by Taut or Mendelsohn. Although on the plane of visionary abstraction the sketches of *Alpine Architektur*, of *Auflösung der Städte*, or the scenario for *Weltbaumeister* burst towards an imaginary collectivity in which *things* have ceased to exist, the self-advertising monuments of Mendelsohn still require concentration, they still ask the observer to *merge* with the work of art.[21]

Now, if perception doesn't even assume a value and a meaning in itself, but remains only the means for the use of a *process* or a *series* (with no need to have this series already translated into an industrial series, because of the 'model' value of artistic behaviour) we have the confirmation that what is in great crisis is the Classical concept of *object*, its institutional attributes and the sacrality connected to it.

In the next chapter we will point out, in some exceptional architectural experiences, a few historical precedents of the *crisis of the object* and of the restructuration of artistic production into an independently structured process. But we must emphasise the fact that, in spite of all the historical precedents, the phenomenon is completely new and constitutes the kind of jump typical not only of the Modern Movement but also of the human condition. This accounts for the present impossibility of using the same interpretative yardsticks for Michelangelo's architecture or Titian's painting and for a product of Le Corbusier or Calder's mobiles.

When we spoke of the death of sacrality in connection with artistic activity, we touched a theme closely linked to the *death of art* dealt with in the preceding chapter. The desecration of art happens in two ways: through the crisis of the artist's direct contact with his work, and through the intentional insertion of the artistic product into the cycle of daily life, open to transformation, interpretation and even misunderstanding on the part of the observer.[22]

Argan's classic essay on *Gropius and the Bauhaus* has been criticised for having forced the historical meaning of the *Constructive* phase of the German architectural avant-garde. But Argan only behaved as, with all due distinction, Vasari did when, by introducing careful deformations in the *Vite*, he aimed at a more communicable and workable *historical truth*. Argan's analysis, in fact, threw light (in a time dominated by naturalistic misunderstanding) both on the perceptive utopism of the *architecture as didactics* of Gropius and on the historical inevitability of utopianism. So much so that, in reading the poetics of *Action painting* as anti-Constructivist eversions, he did not forget that Constructivism and anti-Constructivism are at two opposite dialectical poles that perhaps only Klee (and Le Corbusier, we add, consciously forcing Argan's thought) had been able to merge within a single and stratified vision of the world.

It is not surprising, then, to find within *Tachisme* itself a faith in the value of the reception of the work, not so very far from that of the Constructivist avant-gardes. Here too the painter 'merges' into the canvas, dragging the observer with him into a risky adventure, while the canvas itself is projected towards the surrounding world, releasing its energetic charge. For Gombrich such 'merging' into the canvas is not necessarily in contradiction with a detached appreciation of the work. On the contrary, for him the energetic cosmos of the Abstract is able to supply information (and at a critical level) on industrial and urban reality.

> [The 'action painter'] wants to achieve an identification of the beholder with his Platonic frenzy of creation, or rather with his creation of a Platonic frenzy. It is quite consistent that these painters must counteract all semblance of familiar objects or even of patterns in space. But few of them appear to realise that they can drive into the desired identification only those who know how to apply the various traditional consistency tests and thereby discover the absence of any meaning except the highly ambiguous meaning of traces. If this game has a function in our society, it may be that it helps us to 'humanise' the intricate and ugly shapes with which industrial civilisation surrounds us. We even learn to see twisted wires or complex machinery as the product of human action. We are trained in a new visual classification. The deserts of city and factory are turned into tangle-woods. Making results in matching.[23]

The connection seen by Gombrich between *Action painting* and industrial reality is certainly not new. Pollock, asked explicitly by Selden Rodman, denied any direct links between his painting and the urban condition, but he could not deny, though, a wider connection.[24] Here is a typical *invariance* of modern art, or, at least, of its most radical wing.

Duchamp's *ready-made* objects have been defined by Hans Platschek as 'signals of doubt about real facts'. They offer the spectator an unsolved dilemma, as if saying 'art is unsuitable as an institution, while, perhaps, the spectator is suitable for the dialogue'. Like Duchamp, Willi Baumeister also asks for a provocative participation in the decoding; and when Masson speaks of an art that must 'blow up reality' he states a theme common to pop painters like Jasper Johns and Warhol, to aleatory music, to Meyerhold Theatre, to the *Total Theatre* of Gropius, and to the involvement of the user in the process of planning and consumption of *industrial design*.[25] The model of *open work* divulged by Eco finds a structural equivalent in the revolution of the reception systems introduced by the various avant-garde movements.[26]

Modern architecture can involve the spectator in two ways: by reducing the image to a pure, empty and available form, reducing every morphology to the invariance of *types*, cancelling the *object* in the repetitive process of the series; or by presenting itself as permanent *Total Theatre*, as a new object able to make reality explode into an *espace indicible*. On one side Mies, on the other the late works of Le Corbusier. Nor can we say that the distance beween these two conceptions is due to the complete abstraction of the first and to the neo-symbolism of the second. Even the empty spaces of Mies are symbols: as ghosts of European intellectualism they have, in fact, become emblems.

The simultaneous presence of these two different ways of reception should not lead to confusion: they are, in fact, complementary. They both try to stimulate in the observer acts of conscious freedom, placing him at the centre of an almost endless net of outlined but not yet completed relationships. What changes is the degree of consciousness of the architect in either accepting the completion of the work on the part of the user, or choosing it as his own programme.

In dealing with extremes, there are, as we know, two objective limitations: the *noise* created by a work so open as to destroy itself as a finished and recognisable structure; and the *noise*, conversely, created by a work so closed as to reduce itself to totally *empty* object.

In the first case – that of the late Scharoun, of the late Michelucci, of Lubicz-Nyz and of *technological utopianism* – one betrays, by excess, the dialectics between *work and apertura*, between structure recognisable as such and its availability; in the second case – that of the post-Miesians, of the French and German *modern style* academism – one betrays, by default, one of the main values of our culture: that of sensing, seeing, building the world, substituting the category of possibility for that of rigid casuality.[27] To suddenly free the observer from custom by teaching that there is always the possibility of a jump towards new dimensions, that the present order can and must be upset, that everyone must take part, simply by their daily actions, in this permanent revolution of the order of things: these were the objectives of architectural avant-gardes, the objectives of a bourgeoisie desperately trying to unite *Kultur* and *Civilisation*.

But since nothing happens without some reason, the *décalage* of such an ideology must, necessarily, spring from internal contradictions. One can well say that many of the most forward experiences of the architecture of the last fifteen years have intentionally deepened the contradictions within the historical avant-gardes. The recovery of compositive rigorism, in its strictest sense (within the sphere of the North American schools and in the *new* Japanese *school*, from Mayekawa to Tange, to Kikutake, and in some Italian experiences, from Aldo Rossi to the neo-Constructivism of Samonà, to the new proposals of the younger generations) corresponds to a deepening of the dichotomy, present from 1920 to 1930, between *absent-minded perception* and images of high intellectual content.

Architecture like that of the Yamanashi Building in Tokyo, the Government Service Center in Boston, or the Capitol, Dacca, cannot possibly become part of an *absent-minded observation* of the town. The way in which they force, with the intensity and allusivity of the images, the usual rhythms of daily life; their emphatic reference to a space different from, if not opposed to, the one of common existence; their closing themselves within their own forms, all express the intention to protect themselves from any action of the outside world, by wrapping themselves in the *hortus conclusus* of a self-sufficient mechanic of forms. It is useless hiding the truth: one can hail these, and other similar works, as genuine masterpieces, but there is no doubt that at their base is the fear of taking part in a process directed towards use and consumption.[28]

This is an architecture that does not want to be *consumed*, that wants to prevent an absent-minded usage, and that, consequently, does not accept its disappearance as *object*: on the contrary, it means to reconstitute the 'aura' round itself. All the same, in spite of the intentions, it is not able to renew the condition of *concentration* in front of the complex dynamic of its images: it is not able to make the observer *merge* with its core (as Benjamin says). Kahn, Rudolph, Giurgola, Tange and Stirling remain half-way: like their followers and successors. On one side, then, the city as field of images, as a system of super-structures, as an a-logic sequence of surreal and casual forms to be recovered in an a-syntactic visual re-organisation. On the other the city as structure, as container of 'values' connected by urban history, rather than by perceptive continuity, as permanence of 'places' in constant dialogue among themselves.

By proceeding schematically, one could recognise in the first ideal model the result of the continued 'destruction of the aura', in the second

9. Le Corbusier, Interior of the Bata Pavilion for the Paris International Exposition, 1937.

an attempt to replace the permanent, unrepeatable, even mythical values of architectural *objects*.

The problem is in reality more complex. We are dealing, in fact, with a phenomenon parallel to the theme of history examined in the last chapter. The dissolving of *attention* into the immediate use changes every structure into a super-structure. The town, after having absorbed every architectural object, disguises itself as structure, and offers itself to the absent-minded perception as an a-syntactic and a-logic field of pure *images*, to be consumed daily, creating a new dimension of collective behaviour.

The symbolic values attached to typology – the new codified structure of the *perception of the genre* replacing *the perception of the unicum* – are destroyed too by their hiding behind the vast sea of images superimposed on, and in consequence dominating, the formal explicit nature of typology itself. The schematic identification of the *type* with the structure of the form (a characterisation of the second neo-Classicism and of the Middle European experiences between the wars, from the *Siedlungen* in Frankfurt and Berlin to the theoretical studies of Gropius and Meyer), is not replaced by a return to the *unicum*, but by the rhetorical vacuum of the typological structures.[29]

On these bases, we can compare the perception and use of the city to a true and proper 'banquet of nausea'.[30] But there is more. The end of 'rationalism' has brought with it the end of the illusion about the possibility of dissolving critical activity in the use of the city. Because it is this, in the end, that Benjamin, on one side, and the early Le Corbusier, on the other, had dreamt of, just as the Futurist painters had tried to place the spectator *in the middle of the painting*, just as Duchamp, Masson and the *Action painting* had tried to establish with the observer a sense of participation with the work, and just as the 'Total Theatre' of Gropius, or, today, aleatory music, phonetic poetry and other neo-avant-garde forms, also architecture, drowning in the city, *explode* towards the user, involve him in its processes, make him co-author of a formal event *in fieri*.

But it doesn't make him co-planner. The Constructivist utopia, that saw in the *project* an artistic activity coinciding with the blue-print of collective co-planning, did not materialise. The consumption of the city as an unstable tank of images undermines the meaning of *project* (in the Gropiusian sense of the term), while showing, at the same time, that the disappearance of the *object* hasn't been replaced by a critical behaviour, but by an extension of the heterodirectional means of choice and behaviour, that finds its right place in the chaos of the contemporary city.

The search for a new order within the chaos separates itself, then, from

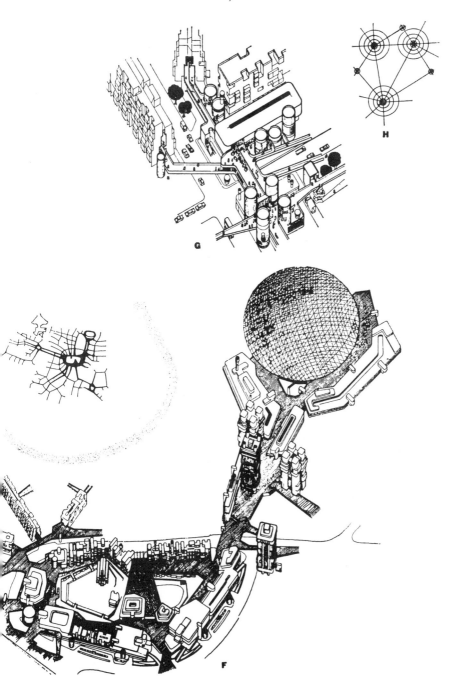

10.   ARCHIGRAM, Project for a commercial centre in Montreal, 1964

the critical opposition to it. The critical attention is absorbed by involving the observer in a sort of mere game, *divertissement, imagerie*: the city as a non-functioning fun-fair, full of persuasive images, replete with signs and more and more empty of meaning, that has as its symbolic monuments the Lincoln Center and New York World Fair, on one side; the Scandinavian *new-town centres* (from Vällingby to Farsta), and the projects for the restructuration of Paris on the other. The *emphasis on the void* is the recurring structure of this new urban rhetoric. We know very well, however, that even this attempt of a persuasive use of form – persuasion of the inevitability of disorder, offered as a new *iconic sign* of experience – can be defeated by a critical or even 'mistaken' decoding on the part of the user. Even the *conditioned consumption* town can be analysed outside the rhetorical code offered by it as a unique and uni-dimensional value.

At this point the circle is completed. The city as such does not educate to a *critical use* by 'relaxing the attention', but exploits that relaxation to condition the choices of use: nor do we get from any other quarters stimuli and influences leading to a public request for new structures. The great task that contemporary utopianism does not fulfil, and so shows itself more and more inadequate, is precisely that of stimulating experiment-ally, by constantly verifying on a reduced scale, the request for a new urban structure.[31]

The availability of the town allows, however, some contradictions, allows the *realisation* of utopias, allows criticism from within: this is what Kahn and Tange seemed to say, in spite of the different yardsticks of their propositions. We can of course judge their architecture as a renunciation designed to control the multiformity of processes in too rapid evolution: in this sense, we can speak of *Action architecture*, quoting from Kallmann's acute study of a few years ago.[32] The fact remains though that in their desperate need to found new planning methods and to find new public symbols, these architects express two complementary values. Their work is charged with critical content, refusing to nullify in the *absent-minded use* the stimuli that are now ineffective for a *critical behaviour*. At the same time they substantiate the fact that the maximum of aesthetical information does not coincide with the maximum of entropy, but that in a highly organised system, the reproposal of finite values causes destructive and contrary effects in all the *critical* senses.

The absurdity of the situation is that, having asked for a 'dilution of the attention' and for a 'relaxed participation' to the constitutive process of the city, architecture should, today, see a new value in withdrawing from the world that, for better or worse, it has helped to shape. (And do note that the Seagram Building does withdraw from the urban context, in the same way as the Guggenheim Museum).

Works like the Boston Government Service Center, the centre of Cumbernauld and the Dacca Capitol Buildings have to fold in on themselves, have to become a critical discourse on architecture, have to inquire into what makes them architecture. The same work that reveals the unsolved relationship tying its anti-historicist origin to a present that no longer justifies that very anti-historicism, uses the metalanguage of criticism, announcing loudly the crisis of the tradition that allows it to exist as new symbolic object. As such, it has to remain a readable diagram of an intolerable situation.

The parallel between Picasso and Schwitters, between Schönberg and Stravinsky, between Gropius and Häring does not disappear, but closes itself in an elliptical presence of opposites. In such a *mixture* the role of the observer becomes ambiguous. Involved and rejected at the same time, he takes part in the drama performed by architecture: but he is simultaneously launched outside architecture, into a dimension that doesn't even touch the limbo of utopia. And as the critic, in the tradition of contemporary art, is nothing but a privileged observer, his position enjoys an even more accentuated ambiguity: from the position of committed collaborator he is pushed into the front row to witness, as a silent accomplice, the show offered by an architecture continuously splitting itself in an exhausting mirror game.

Notes to chapter 2

[1] Johan J. Winckelmann, *Monumenti antichi inediti*, 1767. Croce mentions Winckelmann in *Estetica*, Laterza, Bari 1966, pp. 291–4, and, again, expressing a different opinion, in *Storia dell'Estetica per saggi*, Laterza, Bari 1967, pp. 171–80; the quoted passage is at p. 179.

[2] Cf. Nicolas Le Camus de Mézierès, *Le Génie de l'Architecture*, Paris 1780, and also: Robert Morris, *Lectures on Architecture*, London 1734–36, and *Rural Architecture*, London 1750. The relations between architecture and eighteenth-century sensualist and empiricist aesthetics have not yet been adequately analysed.

[3] Hans Sedlmayr and Hermann Bauer, item 'Rococo' in *Enciclopedia Universale dell'Arte*, XI, 1963, coll. 665–6.

[4] G. C. Argan, *La pittura dell'Illuminismo in Inghilterra*, Bulzoni, Rome 1965, cf. p. 25 ff. 'It may be that (the English garden) reproduces some "wild" aspects of the landscape because the paintings of, let us say, Salvator Rosa have taught us to see in those aspects the more genuine face of nature: but it is an illusion, totally similar to the illuministic illusion of the "noble savage". It is not an image of uncorrupted barbarity, but of cultured civilisation. It is a re-acquired spontaneity and happiness, a paradise regained, after having lost it in the social affectations. In fact this garden is not made of "values" like the Italian garden ... but of "things".' (p. 32.)

[5] Rosario Assunto has perceived the analogy between the eighteenth- and nineteenth-century (for example) recognition of the Alpine landscape as 'aesthetical object'; and the process of recognition of aesthetical objects as such, beyond their practical consumability: 'process whose direction, in the consumer objects, goes from a function with inherent aestheticity to an aestheticity that has re-absorbed in itself the function, offering itself as its artistic image – from real function to possible function. In the landscape, on the contrary ... the process is in the opposite direction to aesthetic *discovery*, that is, the shaping of the landscape as aesthetic object follows in fact ... a transformation of the landscape into an object of immediate consumption'. R. Assunto 'Introduzione alla critica del paesaggio' in *De Homine*, 1963, nn. 5–6, p. 260. Worth mentioning is Assunto's reference, in his analysis of the landscape as figurative object (that finds a correspondence in the landscaped garden and in the modern attitude towards the urban and territorial context) to Hartmann: 'the observer behaves ... like the artist (in the use of the landscape), first discoverer, then creator' (op. cit. n. p. 261). Cf. Nicolai Hartmann, *Aesthetik*, Berlin 1953, pp. 147–51. Also important on the theme in question: R. Assunto *Stagioni e ragioni nell' estetica del '700*, Mursia, Milan 1967 (chaps. I and II).

[6] The fundamental analyses on these themes are by B. Zevi *Poetica dell'architettura neoplastica*, Tamburini, Milan 1953, and by G. C. Argan *Marcel Breuer*, Görlich, Milan 1957. Cf. also G. C. Argan 'L'Estetica dell'Espressionismo' in *Marcatrè* 1964, nn. 8–10, where he sees Expres-

sionism's *antilinguistic* and action-like nature as its main characteristic form. This, besides confirming our thesis, provides a criterion to define the limits within which one can speak of 'Expressionist architecture', completely ignored by the more recent studies on the subject. (cf. note 21.)

[7] P. Mondrian. 'The Realisation of Neoplasticism in the Distant Future and in Architecture Today', 1922, in *De Stijl* op. cit.

[8] It is important to note – although this may not be the right place for such an analysis – that Paul Klee's theoretical positions were not diametrically opposite to those of orthodox Constructivism, but compensated them through a fruitful criticism from within. However the architects only caught the marginal aspects of Klee's criticism. Cf. L. Benevolo *Storia dell'architettura* op. cit.; G. C. Argan *Marcel Breuer* op. cit. Id. *Salvezza e caduta dell'arte moderna* op. cit.

[9] Walter Benjamin 'Das Kunstwerk in Zeitalter seiner technischen Reproduzier-barkeit' in *Zeitschrift für Sozialforschung*, Paris 1936, now in *Schriften*, Suhrkamp, Frankfurt a M., 1955.

[10] 'What does disappear – Benjamin says (op. cit.) – can be summed up in the notion of "aura"; and we can therefore say: what disappears in the epoch of technical reproduction is the "aura" of the work of art.'

'. . . The reproduction technique . . . *steals what is being reproduced from tradition.* By multiplying the reproduction it substitutes a quantitative series of events to the unique event. And by allowing the reproduction to meet the user in his particular situation, it realises what is being reproduced. *Both processses lead to a violent upheaval of tradition.* And this is the other face of the present crisis and of the present renewal of humanity.' (Our italics.)

[11] Cf. G. C. Argan, *Walter Gropius e la Bauhaus*, Einaudi, Turin 1951.

[12] W. Benjamin op. cit.

[13] Ibid.

[14] Ibid.

[15] Cf. Preface *Opera d'arte* op. cit.

[16] Renato Solmi, Introduction to the anthology of W. Benjamin's writings, *Angelus Novus*, Einaudi, Turin 1962, p. xxvii ff.

[17] Although they should cause a fair amount of reflection, the meeting points between *Verlust der Mitte* by Sedlmayr and the writings of a 'leftist apocalyptic' like Adorno are paradoxical.

[18] B. Brecht 'Die neuen Zeitalter' in *Gedichte* VI, Frankfurt a. M. 1964, p. 69.

[19] Cf. G. Lukács *Aesthetik, I. Die Eigenart des Aesthetischen*, Neuwied 1963, II, p. 489 ff., op. cit. in the Preface to *Opera d'arte* op. cit. p. 9.

[20] Cf. H. Lauterbach and Jürgen Joedicke, *Hugo Häring, Dokumente der modernen Architektur*, Stuttgart 1965; the chapter 'Hugo Häring e L'Espressionismo organico' in: Franco Borsi e G. Klaus König *Architettura dell'Espressionismo*, Vitali e Ghianda et Fréal, Genoa-Paris 1967, p. 195 ff.; and Jürgen Joedicke, 'L'idea di architettura organica in H.H.', in *Edilizia Moderna* 1965, n. 86.

[21] Cf. Bruno Taut, *Alpine Architektur*, Folkwang, Hagen 1919; *Die Auflösung der*

Städte, ibid. 1920; *Der Weltbaumeister, Architektur Schauspiel für symphonische Musik*, ibid. 1920 (architectural spectacle for symphonic music, dedicated to the spirit of Paul Scheerbart). Taut's drawings as well as those still full of traditional representational qualities contained in *Die Stadtkrone* (Jena 1919), have been re-published recently in the op. cit. by F. Borsi and G. K. König, who have painstakingly transcribed and translated Taut's captions, placing them beside drawings with a particular graphic function.

We do not agree, however, with Borsi and König's over-valuation of this work. One should distinguish, in fact, between experiences that are at the base of a new code of values and those that are nothing more than clever eversions or tightrope walks. The same criticism applies to the volume by Conrads and Sperlich, *Fantastische Architektur*, that includes many letters of the *Gläserne Kette* (the 'Glass Chain') lumping a-critically together avant-garde utopism and new utopism. Cf. also: Dennis Sharp, *Modern Architecture and Expressionism*, Longmans Green 1966 and Pevsner's review: N. Pevsner, 'The 'twenties Kick', in *Architectural Review 1967*, vol. CXL, no 48, p. 407.

[22] On this theme are of interest, even to those like us that don't share his approach, Cesare Brandi's observations in 'Le due vie' op. cit. (*Lo spettatore integrato*, p. 101 ff.)

[23] Ernst Gombrich, *Art and Illusion. A Study in the Psychology of Pictorial Representation*, Phaidon Press, London, 1960 p. 244.

[24] Selden Rodman, while interviewing Pollock in 1956 two months before his death, observed that his paintings, like those of Tobey, Hedda Sterne and O'Keefe who admitted it, expressed the turmoil of the modern capitalistic city or the reaction to it. 'What a ridiculous idea – answered Pollock – to express a city: it never occurred to me in my life!' In a certain sense Pollock was right: the experience of the city may have conditioned his painting activity but certainly not in an 'expressive' sense. Rodman's interview is published in Jürgen Claus *Teorie della pittura contemporanea*, Il Saggiatore, Milan 1967, pp. 149–51.

Among the more recent literary texts that propose again the experience of the city as a condition of artistic activity may be of interest: Alfredo Giuliani, *Immagini e maniere*, Feltrinelli, Milan 1965. Cf. also: Manfredo Tafuri 'Architettura, "town-design", città,' in *D'Ars Agency* 1967, nn. 36–7 (Summary of the lecture given at the 'XIX Congresso dell'AICA' at Rimini, Sept. 1967), in which we dealt with the theme of the correlations between urban images and visual communications.

[25] Cf. Marcel Duchamp 'Discussion' at the American Federation of Arts, Houston (Texas) 1957, in *Arts News* 1957, vol. 56, n. 4; Willi Baumeister *Das Ubenkannte in der Kunst*, M. DuMont Schauberg, Köln 1960; André Masson *Eine Kunst des Wesentlichen*, Wiesbaden 1961.

[26] Cf. Umberto Eco, Opera aperta, Bompiani, Milan 1962, and the criticism of his application of information theory to aesthetic interpretation by: Emilio Garroni, *La crisi semantica delle arti* cit., and Eco's answer: *Appunti per una semiologia delle comunicazioni visive*, Bompiani, Milan 1967. See also R. De Fusco, *Architettura come mass-medium* op. cit.

[27] '. . . One of the aspects of the crisis of contemporary bourgeois society [Eco writes in *Opera aperta* op. cit., pp. 126-7] is its inability to produce new and autonomous assumptive worlds at the level of daily life. This would imply the definition, within the terms employed up to now, of the anonymous and *heterodirectional* condition of the contemporary mass-man, anchored to a stable and static assumptive world, on which act with great ease the 'occult persuasions' from outside. So that one asks oneself with legitimate hope and anxiety . . . whether the proposal of contemporary art of a continuous free choice and conscious splitting up of the stabilised assumptive worlds . . . may be an instrument of freedom that acts not only at the level of aesthetic structures . . . but also at the level of the education of contemporary man towards self-direction.'

We must mention though that Eco's expectations from contemporary art are the same as the expectations of the avant-gardes. The relations between theory of language, technological aesthetics and capitalist development have been perceptively studied by Giangiorgio Pasqualotto in *Avanguardia e tecnologia. Walter Benjamin, Max Bense e i problemi dell'estetica tecnologica*, Officina, Rome 1971, in which he deals with the many mythologies dear to the successors of the Frankfurt School.

[28] Very much to the point is Eco's observation – made about television language but that fits our theme equally well – on the function of the 'Aristotelically conceived woven structures' in dealing with the poetics of the *opera aperta*. Cf. U. Eco, op. cit., pp. 186-7.

[29] Up to now we have been referring to residential buildings, but, in spite of the change of size, the problem itself does not change substantially whether one considers highly specialised textures and nodes of the city, mixed structures or the entire territory. Cf. some interesting notes on the theme in: J. Marston Fitch, *Architecture and the Aesthetics of Plenty* op. cit., and id. 'Prototipie copie. Crisi (per eccesso) della struttura della comunicazione' in *L'Architettura cronache e storia*, 1963, IX, n. 92. pp. 112-13, in spite of the generic aspects of the prospects contained in it.

[30] Cf. G. C. Argan, 'Il banchetto della nausea', in *La Botte e il Violino*, I, n. 2, pp. 3-8.

[31] We can in fact say that a good part of that utopism is simply the rhetorical amplification of contemporary mythologies and *disorder*. It has been noted already that Italian Futurism (and one could add the early Russian Constructivism) *mimed* rhetorically a world that existed already, and projected it into the future only because of the impossibility of realising it in a technologically backward country. The young Vanderbilt and Ford, with the Grand Central Terminal Station in New York (1902) and with the revolution of the traffic systems, realised what Sant'Elia, Marchi, Chiattone and Depero simply dreamt of, without an effective re-organisation of the meanings of the technological world. Cf. Douglas Haskell, *75 Years of Change – Mostly Unpredicted* op. cit. p. 75 ff. See also as an instance of experimentalism adhering to the things: B. Arvatov, 'Materialised Utopia' in *LEF*, 1923.

Contemporary utopianism, for example the utopianism of ARCHIGRAM, is not experimental. It treats science-fiction, the comic strip, chaos, technology, heterodirection, as myths to take to the extreme and not to be revolutionised. Being, in this sense, mere ironies, *Archigram's* projects are more positive than those of the *Metabolism* group and of GIAP. Cf. numbers of the magazine *Archigram*; the retrospective: 'Archigram Group. A Chronological Survey' in *Architectural Design*, Nov. 1965, p. 559 ff.; and Mike Jerome, 'Whatever happened to the Metabolists?' in *Architectural Design*, May 1967, vol. xxxvii, p. 203.

[32] Cf. George Kallmann, 'La Action Architecture di una generazione nuova', (*Casabella continuità*, 1964, no. 269) in *Architectural Forum*, Oct. 1962. Some observations by Boyd on these architectural groups dealt in depth with the historical aspect of the theme; cf. R. Boyd, *The Puzzle of Architecture*, op. cit. p. 133 ff.

3

Architecture as Metalanguage: the Critical Value of the Image

So far we have analysed the situation of architectural culture, and not the concrete ways in which the public receives such a culture. We have considered architecture and the town as transmitters of information, focusing on the sources rather than on the receptors. But we know that the way a message is received, the relative decoding processes, the 'errors' made in decoding, are the decisive factors in creating a productive relationship between communication and social behaviour.

Therefore, the present impossibility of carrying out an adequate analysis of the reception of the communications transmitted by architectural or urban images – except for a few limited studies, like those of Lynch and Meier – says something about the situation of architectural culture: did not the architectural avant-gardes in fact start with the aim of conditioning the relationship between artistic communications and public reactions?

Since the thirties architectural culture has preferred to deduce from its own centre what could have only been found by a complete and unprejudiced analysis of the ways in which the mythical *society* being addressed decodes, distorts, transforms, makes factual use of the messages launched by the *builders of images*. And this is a sign of the insecurity of architectural culture itself.

It is an insecurity that stems from two main causes:

A. The wish to contain all the problems within the architectural discipline, to avoid well-founded outside examination. The interdisciplinary myth itself emphasises issues marginal to the problem of visual communication. Sociology, ecology and the empirical sciences are invoked in the planning of territorial operations, but psychology or (in extreme cases) psycho-analysis, are not used in the studies of the behaviour of social groups or social classes in their daily reading of the architectural and urbanistic messages.

B. The unwillingness of the younger generations to abandon the myth of the perpetual avant-garde. For the avant-gardes, in fact, the problem of checking the effects on the public has little importance. By its own nature, a break-away work cannot continually stop to pick up and catalogue the fragments of its own explosions. This, if anyone's, is the task of those who want to carry on the constructive side of the avant-gardes, modifying, of necessity, the angle of fire. When one sees that the request for a new architecture goes arm in arm with *exploits* that raise the avant-garde flag on wobbly life-rafts, one begins to understand (though not to justify) the lack of rigorous analysis mentioned earlier.[1]

We will have to probe a little deeper, though, in the context of the present situation. It may seem, in fact, incomprehensible or even contradictory to denounce a lack of criticism in a situation that seems, on the other hand, caught in inextricable intellectual knots.

But what type of criticism dominates the present architectural situation? What is its extent and its real range? And how, if this criticism exists, does it enter the debate between the avant-garde and experimentalism from which we started?

The existence of a deep contradiction between the *avant-garde* and *experimentalism* has already been accepted.[2] Avant-gardes are always affirmative, absolutist, totalitarian. They claim peremptorily to build a brand new context, taking for granted that their linguistic revolution not only implies but actually 'realises' a social and moral upheaval. When Picasso states 'I don't look for, I find', he expresses perfectly the assertive character of the avant-gardes. Those who *look for* must, more or less, work on existing material, choosing, assembling and disassembling. But avant-gardes ignore *existing materials*. For them nothing is taken for granted or *a priori*. Their constructive act is radical, with Malevitch's 'pure desert' as its symbol.

Experimentalism is, on the contrary, constantly taking apart, putting together, contradicting, provoking languages and syntaxes that are nevertheless accepted as such. Its innovations can be bravely launched towards the unknown, but the launching pad is solidly anchored to the ground. Architectural experimental research has all the characteristics of tight-rope walking – the wire might break at any moment; or to leave the metaphor behind, one can always discover how absurd or worn out is the theme taken as a research hypothesis – with the protection of a strong net below.

The avant-gardes, by definition, perform without a net: they look in the face of disaster and accept it from the start, not only as a danger but also as an inevitable, although freely chosen, destiny. One could add that the avant-gardes seldom stop to argue with what they are destroying; even where they seem to indulge in contests, they prove themselves *beyond contestation*, by their quality and ability *to plan* future history.

Experimental movements can hide behind revolutionary statements as much as they like, but their real task is not subversion but the widening, the decomposition and recomposition in new modulations, of the linguistic material, of the figurative codes, of the conventions that, by definition, they have assumed as reality.

The epic clash of some figures that, in the course of history have been (not by chance) romantically mythicised, with the stability of the codes can be deeply dramatic: what the anti-Classicist heresies of Peruzzi, Sanmicheli and even of Michelangelo manage to show is the stability, the solidity, the actuality of the Classicist language. It can be distorted, enriched, pulled to the breaking-point of some of its internal cracks, but through all this bending and shattering it will show its ability to absorb all the eversion, which is not yet capable of overthrowing it completely.

This shows that, when speaking of *revolutions* in the history of architecture, one should, to avoid unverifiable and useless statements, refer to the real upheavals caused by the phenomena in question in the existing institutional codes.[3]

We will take up again this theme, later on: now we will try to understand how architectural experimentalism operates and its consequences. First of all let us try to link directly experimentalism and the infringement of the codes: this is a datum we can draw, empirically, from historical analysis. Late Antique and late Gothic, Mannerist, eighteenth-century and contemporary experimentalism find their own *raisons d'être* in the battle against the existing languages. And just as, in the end, it becomes almost too clear that the true objective of this battle is not a radical upheaval, so it also becomes evident that the most positive results of the experimental attitude – old or modern – consist, on one side, in the fractures and valencies introduced in the codes of the time (like time bombs, they will often only explode in the future) and, on the other side, in testing and probing. It is a testing that, in some cases, has the rather important result of uncovering and making conscious the ultimate meaning of the code introduced, in a mythical way, by the avant-gardes.

Experimentalism as de-mythicisation, then; but also as criticism in action, as a search for a criticism completely absorbed in its own planning.

Is the hypothesis of an independently *critical* architecture (or, more generally, art) theoretically justifiable? Ragghianti has shown that the entire work of the Carraccis can be interpreted as a critical operation; Argan, too, has spoken of Carracci's criticism as opposed to Caravaggio's rigorism, of the critical value of the French Illuminist paintings and of reproduction etchings; Zevi has carried out a study on the theme of a criticism developed with images, thus redeeming *visual design* from its historical conditioning and from its subjection to a tired alliance with *Gestalt* psychology:[4]

> The flow history-design [he writes] is not unidirectional. If history finds an outlet as a methodological component of planning, in its turn planning extends its criteria and its instruments into history; that is, it proposes a new type of historico-critical operation, a history of architecture carried out with the expressive instruments of the architect and not only with those of the art historian.[5]

Let us leave, for the moment, the final purposes of this tight joining of history and planning proposed and tried by Zevi,[6] and remain with the specific problem of criticism carried out through architectural means. With the theme, that is, of *creative* criticism, able to develop into a service for teamwork, as a voice in the interdisciplinary choir, able, also, to 'inject into mass production the qualities that the great architects have found in élite production, making sure of a coherent flow from the poetical language to the language of use'.[7]

It is the theme that Zevi dealt with more extensively in 1964 in his lecture at Cranbrook's AIA-ACSA Teacher Seminar:

> In point of fact, a great many works of art, even very famous works of art, are of a critical nature. You can use words to write a poem, or just to tell a story or to criticise an event. It is the same with painting. You can sing and you can speak. Modern art criticism has been able to show that many painters were really not artists but critics, great critics who used the medium of words to express not their feelings but their ideas. And it is the same with architecture. . . .[8]

> The challenge for us, in the next few years, will be to find a method by which historical research can be done with the architect's instruments. . . . Why not express architectural criticism in architectural forms instead of in the words?[9]

And it is important to note that Zevi quotes Ragghianti's opinion on the Carracci to enforce his thesis. Indeed, later in his analysis, he leans also on Gramsci (or rather on the passage in which he recognises in the structure of Dante's poem a proper semantic value) and on Della Volpe so far as the organicity of the work of art is concerned: once the fact that the aesthetical product belongs to a sphere of rational and controllable values is acertained, the way is clearly open to the possibility of an architectural production as consciously elaborated criticism.[10]

Zevi manages a logical leap in his argument by deducing from all this the possibility of an organisation of images equivalent to a critical discourse. The insistence that architectural and linguistic structures are within the same area of logical values does not mean, in fact, that they should share the approach to these values or that these values should be perceived identically in a literary essay or in an architectural work. The distinction made by the semantic schools and, in Italy, by Della Volpe, between 'omnitextuality' of the scientific processes and 'contextuality' of the artistic processes, is too well known to need any further examination here.

From this distinction we can derive the point that a criticism realised through images is not equivalent to a critical analysis that employs the instruments of language. In the first case the artistic language can, in fact, explore all the limits it can reach – even though the initial arbitrary choice of a code is taken for granted through a cruel and systematic opposition, but it cannot point out the reasons that have historically determined that initial choice. In the second case we are already beyond that linguistic choice; what we explore are the reasons within the structure of the reference code. This criticism operates in a situation of more radical contestation, for, by ignoring the linguistic organisation to be analysed, it is not in the position to point out, on one hand, the historicity of that code, and, on the other, the underlying and inexplicit ideologies, active at a not always conscious level.

The alliance between *visual design* and the history of architecture is not, then, as obvious as it seemed at first.[11] When in 1964 at the exhibition of Michelangelo's works in Rome, the visual interpretations by the students of the Venice Istituto Universitario were shown, many were, näively, scandalised. The models, the tormented iron trelliswork, the superimposed and dynamic photographs were harshly criticised as totally unrelated to Michelangelo's architectural work.[12]

Why have we called this scandalised attitude näive when we ourselves have criticised similar attempts?

With great perception Roland Barthes has theorised the right or, better, the duty of criticism to start from the work, not in order to make its meaning clearer – nothing is *clearer* than the work itself – but to generate new meanings from it, to multiply its metaphors, to satisfy, somehow, the inquiry that the work of art incessantly proposes on the sense of its construction. If the work, in fact, contains more than one meaning at the same time, if it is *symbolic* just because of the plurality of its meanings, if it is nothing but a proposal or a challenge to linguistic conventions, then the critic is, of course, compelled to develop, to multiply further, to freely (or almost freely) re-assemble the metaphors and the signs that are woven, available and *open*, in the work itself.

Consequently:

Le critique dédouble les sens, il fait flotter au-dessus du premier language de l'oeuvre un second language, c'est-à-dire une cohérence de signes. Il s'agit en somme d'une sorte d'anamorphose, étant bien entendu, d'une part que l'oeuvre ne se prête jamais à un pur reflet... et d'autre part que l'anamorphose elle-même est une transformation *surveillée*, soumise à des contraintes optiques: de ce qu'elle réfléchit, elle doit *tout* transformer; ne transformer que suivant certaines lois; transformer toujours dans le même sens.[13]

The critic's right to this constant transformation of the work is due to the fact that both work and criticism use the same means of communication: language. For literary criticism, the use of language in finding different ways of using language represents an essential condition: language speaks of itself, and because its intrinsic symbolism (as presence and planes of meanings) does not allow an a-symbolical description from the outside, criticism will have to accept reality, multiply the stated or potential meanings of the work, and renounce the impossible narrative from the outside.

When Barthes, in answer to Picard, retorts that all criticism is autonomously symbolical – a descriptive criticism symbolises the *interested* renunciation of finding out the ultimate meanings of language – he clears an intrinsic ambiguity of literary criticism: analyst of the 'writing' and of itself as literature at one time.[14] Barthes's statements could attract all sorts of comments, but for the moment we prefer to compare them with the different reality offered by the *binomium* architecture-criticism. Architecture and criticism, in fact, do not act on the same linguistic area. The doubling of meanings, Barthes's 'anamorphosis', is possible in architecture only within the limits of the critical use of the linguistic instruments of the work to be analysed: and it is obvious that in our case these instruments can only be found within the architectural language itself.

It is in architecture, then, that the multiplication of the metaphors left *open* by pre-existing architectures can be fully realised. We can say, in fact, that every new architectural work is born in relation – no matter whether of continuity or antithesis – to a symbolic context created by preceding works, freely chosen by the architect as terms of reference for his themes; nor has the distance or proximity of these terms from the present any importance. This gives further confirmation to the fact that every architecture has its own critical nucleus. What interests us is the possible emphasis one can give to this nucleus, to the point of making it the absolute protagonist of the work. At this point we can go back to the problem of the 'critical models' shown at the Michelangelo exhibition.

We think it is clear, by now, that those elaborations were, in fact, *anamorphoses*, in Barthes's sense, of Michelangelo's work. That so very scandalising independence was only the consequence of an intentional '*doubling of the meanings*', of an intentional '*fair flotter*' a 'second language' above the language being analysed. The incoherence of those products was, on the other hand, two-fold: their transformations were not '*surveillées*', and they did not present themselves with all the characteristics of a *second* architectural *language*; and they attempted an amateurish translation of the architectural language into abstract and a-historical sculptural games.

From all this we can derive three considerations:

A. The alliance between *visual design* and history of architecture can only happen at a level of considerable abstraction: the graphical themes that go with Zevi's 'Biagio Rossetti' are particularly effective because they are nothing more than abstract visual examples of an independently structured critical analysis; outside the reference to the literary text these schemes are – justly – silent;

B. The possibility of a critical study conducted through images and through architecture is still there: but it will have to climb back into real architectural structures;

C. There cannot be a true complementarity between architectural and historical critical discourses: they can converse with each other, but they cannot complete each other, because the two find themselves, inevitably, in competition.

Point C needs further clarification.

We have already said that the difference between a criticism from *within* the architectural language and the criticism that makes use of a specific metalanguage consists, mainly, in the different possibility that the latter has to throw light on the ideological systems underlying the various codes and the various works.

As we will be dealing with the methods, the instruments and the tasks of architectural criticism in the following chapters, we will now analyse in isolation the ways and the limits of *critical architecture*.

We have seen that to operate critically with the instrument of architecture implies a deformation of architecture itself: it has to change from language into *metalanguage*, it must speak of itself, it must explore its own code without leaving it, except for very carefully measured experiments. These are in fact the cautious eversions that characterise this type of operation; and we must add that the study in question can cover both the entire extent of the architectural code (in the global complexity of its typologico-functional, symbolical, syntactical, etc. layers) and its single sections. Consequently we will not consider critical architecture as a metahistorical category, but, more simply, as a phenomenon recurring in different forms, but with sufficiently similar structures.

We will deal with some instruments typical of architectural experimentalism, identifying five different types of experiments.

A. The emphasis of a given theme, exasperated to the point of the most radical contestation of the fundamental laws governing it, or disjointed in a sort of disassembly of its single parts: this is the case of many *late-Antique* architectures, from Villa Adriana to Piazza Armerina, of many late-Gothic experiences, of the whole vast debate on the central plan from the fifteenth to the late eighteenth century, with the heresies of Peruzzi, Serlio, of Palladio's Venetian churches and of the projects preserved at the RIBA, of French and Bohemian Rococo, of Piranesi's utopias, and, within the Modern Movement, of De Stijl's and Rudolph Schindler's studies, of the late production of Behrens and Van de Velde, of the New Brutalism and of Japanese Mannerism.

B. The insertion of a theme deeply rooted in a particular, totally different context: this is the case of the commixture of sacral emblems and civil functions in works like Sangallo's Villa di Poggio a Caiano, of Palladio's Villas, of the use of elements with a definite symbolic charge in a-symbolic contexts (like the nineteenth-century domed stations, libraries and stock exchanges), of the systematic introduction of *quotations*, in many eclectic works, first of all those of Gaudí (but, more to the point, those of Frank Furness and Victorian architecture).

C. The *assemblage* of elements from ideally and historically different and distant codes: like Notre-Dame at Le Puy or St-Front at Périgueux (where the Byzantine succession of the domes is inserted into Romanesque contexts), S. Giustina in Padua, much architecture of the late English seventeenth and eighteenth centuries (from Wren to Vanbrugh), Illuminist and Romantic periods, and part of the neo-eclectic production.

D. The compromising of architectural themes with figurative structures of a different nature (we are thinking of the Mannerist and Baroque *contaminations* of architecture, painting and sculpture, or of many recent attempts at dissolving the semantic autonomy of the various visual arts), or through their sudden insertion into a *series*; and here we are thinking of the typological use made of the themes drawn from archaeology by architects like Quarenghi and Schinkel.

E. The exasperated articulation of a theme originally taken as absolute: it is still the case of the late-Gothic and Mannerist typological *inventions*, of Piranesi's *Iconographia* Campi Martii, of many 'critical restorations' by Albini and Scarpa, of Kahn's last work.

Of course all these instruments (and many others that we have not mentioned) do not constitute, by themselves, an architectural criticism. We have quoted Gaudí's example; but it is clear that neither the Güell park, nor the Milà or Battlò houses play a real *critical* role. The first essential condition of this role is, in fact, the isolation of the various themes, so that they can emerge as protagonists in an architectural narrative that is complete in itself; the second essential condition is the rigorous and conscious check of this narrative.[15]

A further condition of seeing the work as a critical sounding is the meeting, in it, of *aesthetic and semantic information*. A cycle such as that of Chandigarh can be read as a critical cycle, but only by isolating, in its complex stratifications, those features containing communicative valencies that, in the totality of the work, belong to secondary informative structures. (It is equally so for the cycle of Michelangelo's drawings for S. Giovanni dei Fiorentini, and for the criticism of the concept of typology carried out by Borromini and by the masters of the Austrian and Bohemian eighteenth-century Baroque.) But in the cycles of Peruzzi's drawings, in Serlio's *models*, in Wren's work, the structure of the form is independently informative, and if there is any secondary information it is the very quality of the image.

Let us try to analyse some works or cycle of works that intentionally play a critical role. (It should be clear that in referring to pre-Illuminist architecture the term 'critical' takes on a relative meaning: this does not however seem to us an illegitimate transvaluation, as this criticism can always be related to the cultures it has entered with analytical and experimental intentions.)

We must distinguish, within this analysis, between criticism and irony. Irony, we know well, is also an aesthetic dimension rich in critical valencies: Klee's example leaves little doubt. But in it opposites merge in a continuous exchange between affirmation and negation, and one is not able to recognise a clear unequivocal alternative in the play to and fro. In other words the critical content of an intentionally ironical work is more in its allusions than in its demonstrations, more in what seeps through than in what is clearly said, more in what is stated paradoxically than in what is denied.

Let us take, for example, a work like the St Urbain in Troyes. It represents, as is well known, an extreme case of Gothic structuralism; the reduction to pure skeleton of the static lines is so emphasised as to appear prophetic, like a sort of anticipation of the language that will appear in the nineteenth century, in some open-structure iron and cast-iron examples.[16]

Johannes Anglicus began the construction of the choir of St Urbain in 1262; between 1248 and 1258 Master Gerhard started working on the choir of Cologne cathedral, while in 1258 Thomas de Cormont started on the upper part of Amiens choir, carrying on Robert de Luzarches' work. The foundations for a criticism within Gothic structuralism had then been laid, freeing the narrative elements that dissolve the walls from the laws of space organisation by means of decorative artifices connected to scholastic symbolism. Regarding the Amiens nave, the two de Cormonts act critically;[17] as regards the problems then on the table, Johannes Anglicus indulges in taking the dissolving of the wall, the play of transparencies, the fusion of the decorative elements, the reduction of the supports to pure and abstract force-lines to the extreme. The outside choir, transept and west façade of St Urbain are linguistic paradoxes. But on the other hand, all the instruments of architectural experimentalism mentioned above lend themselves to paradox.

Giulio Romano exercises his caustic irony by fusing together architecture, painting and natural elements that claim to have a decorative role; and, conversely, he introduces in his complex pastiches decorative elements masked by organic forms: from the saloons and grotto of the Palazzo del Te, to the façade of the Rustica in the Mantua Ducal Palace. For him – as, later, for some work of Bernini's and a few of his followers (we are thinking of Antonio Gherardi and the brothers Asam) – the ideal of the *synthesis of the arts* is a theme for irony, to be made absurd and paradoxical.

It is sufficient to compare Giulio Romano's work with the intersections of architecture and sculpture of firstly Giuliano da Sangallo, and later, of Michelangelo, to measure the distance between an ironical attitude and a fully felt critical probe.[18]

We could continue to simplify by examining the work of Jean Androuet du Cerceau, Alessandro Antonelli, or, today, of architects like Philip Johnson (and also some of Paul Rudolph's work such as his Jacksonville house). In Antonelli the paradoxical multiplication of the architectural orders by splitting the functions between real and figurative structures – we are thinking of the Casa delle Colonne or of the S Gaudenzio dome in Novara – are evidence of criticism directed towards the new techniques, dug in to defend a floundering architectural language that can be used only as a slightly *blasé* lexicon, declined with self-ironical detachment.

The abstract stylemes of Philip Johnson also makes use of irony. But their meaning is rather that of a disenchanted game: it is not by chance that the New York World Fair Pavilion of 1964 (in collaboration with Richard Foster) is perhaps his best work, in as much as the *fun-fair* use of the image finds a functional correspondence.[19]

In other words, with irony we have an 'interrupted criticism', folded on itself. It does not concede anything beyond ambiguous evidence about the limitations of the language: its use is intentionally made very difficult, because this is not a problem that interests those who use it.

The realisation and the logical control of a strictly critical formal process must reject these limits: not objective limits, we must add, but relative to the specific task of any form of criticism.

The disarticulation of the spatial successions, in the Villa Adriana or in the Piazza Armerina, are so coherent with the premises that justify them – the test of the autonomy range of the single spatial fragment, modulated, contracted or made elastic, to emphasise its absoluteness and to increase its ambiguity within the entire context[20] – as to make these works a sort of *anthology*, not only for successive studies, but also as sources to draw from: not by chance was a whole number of *Perspecta* taken up by the Villa Adriana, and Kahn often showed his interest for this singular group of architectural *objects*.[21]

What is of value in those exceptional late-antique monuments is the *series* of differentiated spaces that join and clash with one another: Piranesi's Campo Marzio, that owes so much to the study of the Villa Adriana, takes to the limit its formal *bricolage*, moving its search for a semantic polyvalency to another scale and to another historical context.

Disarticulations, semantic deformations, grouping of the various studies into one casuistry: it is not difficult to see it all in the *variations* modulated by Serlio in his seven books on architecture. Serlio sets up a real typological criticism. Given a theme – the portal, the country villa, the bourgeois or aristocratic palace, the ecclesiastical building – he fixes its components and then proceeds to give a series of deformations that could, theoretically, carry on *ad infinitum*. In the sixth book the *rustic* doors are bent to take the most heretical arrangements, to arrive, from commixture to commixture, to the *bestial order*;[22] in the second book, the central plan types are assembled and disassembled according to modulations recalling Peruzzi – the most *critical* and experimental Italian architect of the first half of the sixteenth century;[23] in the unpublished sixth book the typology of civil architecture is shaped by the use of the geometrical themes typical, up to then, of ecclesiastic architecture (an obvious example of symbolical-functional *contamination*): courtyards and saloons with elliptical ground-plans become the pivot of composite spatial sequences, based on the contraposition of pure geometrical figures.[24]

Intersection of spaces, policentrism, contaminations: Serlio's casuistry is ready to compromise the absolutism of the classicist code with functional empiricism and with the suggestions offered by an unprejudiced reading of domestic French architecture.

In Leonardo empiricism, open-mindedness and naturalism merge with the vernacular and with residues of archaeological culture: Serlio's criticism, along the entire arch of his composite images, results in the systematic exploration of the limits that could be reached by the aulic language in its fusion with popular *idiolects* and with an accentuated pragmatism. Serlio organises systematically what Peruzzi had simply outlined in the series of drawings for unrealised architectural organisms: Peruzzi's anxiety is resolved in an ordered casuistry, ready to be exploited, enlarged and reshaped.

Serlio's influence on the whole of Europe is due to the meaning of his criticism of the classicist code. He shows rationally how much of that code was still an available instrument, and how much of it was complete and self-sufficient. Working on *ideal models* and on series of variations represents the essential condition of Serlio's criticism; allowing him to isolate and study the various elements.

The *series* had been realised in the Villa Adriana. But in Leonardo's and Peruzzi's sketches, in Serlio, in the urbanistic models of Francesco di Giorgio and De Marchi, in Montano's *inventions*, the series takes shape in the studied succession of types and variations.

When, from about 1580 onwards, Montano designed his famous small temples, hiding under a false antiquarian skin a free and surprising typological casuistry, he clearly shows his intention of reaching a critical value in respect of the inheritance of the fifteenth and sixteenth centuries on the theme of central plan organisms, to the extent of allowing himself an ironical and detached tone.[25]

Central spaces opposed by a swarm of minor spaces that make one lose any sense of formal hierarchy, use of *heretical* geometric matrixes, such as the triangle and the hexagon, spatial aggregates that hint at centric organisms (but if one looks more carefully, one sees a solid in the centre of the composition), paradoxically deformed and planimetric figures with false perspective: a whole repertoire of calculated 'errors', of surreal ideas, of linguistic absurdities, characterises this singular figure of engraver and amateur architect, who exploits the accumulated inheritance of Francesco di Giorgio, Leonardo, Peruzzi, Serlio and Michelangelo.

But perhaps it is this very amateurishness that allows Montano – as had happened, at a different level, with Serlio – to take such a detached attitude towards his surroundings. His heresies have the icy quality of laboratory experiments where anything goes, because one is already, by definition, protected from the reality that carries on independently outside. All the same the criticism of the concept of centrality had not been expressed, up to then, with such severity and objectivity. Nor, we would say, with such immediate consequences. Montano's is a partial criticism, carried out through images: perhaps none of his ideal projects would stand, if built, and the analysis of the detail or of the linguistic repertoire, in a scale other than that of the organism, is doubtless disappointing. But it is just because Baroque culture was ready to receive any message sent through images that the collections of the Milanese engraver, printed in quick succession from 1620 to 1691, influenced the *inventions* of Bernini (from the Assunta di Ariccia to St Peter's canopy), of Pietro da Cortona (il Pigneto), of Borromini (from the Spada Colonnade to the canopy of S. Paolo in Bologna) and of Carlo Rinaldi (the canopy of S. Maria della Scala in Rome). Montano's *naïve* criticism of perspective naturalism, of the un-elasticity of the wall, of the balance of the organisms, shows, then, its ability to provide new planning materials to those able to go beyond the contingent polemicism on to new syntheses.

The 'Montano case' is no doubt symptomatic. Outside Italy we could place him next to Du Cerceau: but the lack of systemacity in the French architect-engraver, as opposed to the Milanese engraver's stubborn codification of the heresy, shows a lesser critical potential typical of the few and well-mediated influences of his work on Europe in general.

In connection with Montano's work we spoke of *systematicity in heresy*: this is, in fact, a feature common to any criticism developed through images. And this explains the scarce and ambiguous influences of the few similar attempts in the Baroque age.

When Borromini or Pietro da Cortona articulate their spaces polemically and spread syntactical and grammatical heresies within their organisms, the results, in the environments that try to learn something from them, are anything but coherent. The non-explicitness of their *criticism* in the architectural context does not make ideal material for the purpose of our study. Borromini's criticism itself cannot be understood, in its didactical values (and they are there), by those who, in trying to follow through its assumptions, understand only its marginal aspects, or, at the other extreme, its partial meanings.

However, the Baroque age does not lack isolated attempts to reach a strict experimentalism. Pietro da Cortona, in some drawings for fantastic projects – Portoghesi published one of them[26] – is within the span of experimental research: or, rather, tries to distort experimentally the results of an already codified formal synthesis. In the drawing in the Martinelli collection in which Berrettini piles up paradoxical domed cylinders to form an absurd *Chigian* emblem translated into ecclesiastic organism, or in the other drawing, where he elaborates a criticism of the traditional compositive hierarchy, the result he aims at – but does not achieve – is the discovery of independent critical values in the organic synthesis.

It is important to understand the contradictory quality of this attempt to compromise a structure endowed with its own synthesis, through a criticism that cannot enter it – because of the hostility of the structure itself which is too dense and too little articulated. There is a precedent for the present situation in the failure of Baroque criticism.[27]

Although the research of Guarini and European Guarinism – from Dientzenhöfer to Santini, with eclectic additions such as those of Martinelli in Poland, Johann Michael Fischer in Bavaria and Vittone in Piedmont almost on the threshold of neo-Classicism – is structured in an experimental sense, the equivocation in which it is caught lies entirely in the contradiction between the basic criticism and the impossibility of following this criticism to its logical conclusion, because of the inability to depart from a system too solidly anchored to symbolico-rhetorical values to allow a coherent experimental approach. The poetic of the image and its criticism will not lie down together: this seems to be the lesson that

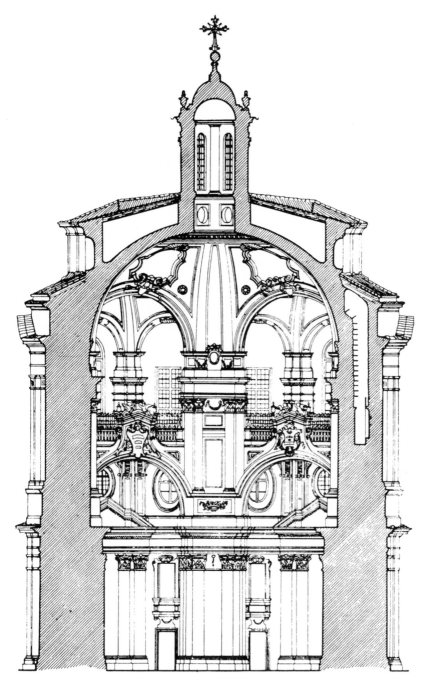

11.   Bernardo Vittone, Santa Chiara a Bra (c. 1742). Diagonal section. (Survey by Giovanni Joppolo)

European Guarinism offers to the consideration of a contemporary culture more and more involved in an analogous flowering of attempts to force the involutive situation with inadequate instruments that are as useless as they are generous.

Let us now consider the parallel and opposite style that has Wren as its main exponent. Wren, like Guarini, places architecture in the context of a wide range of scientific interests; like Guarini he treats every new project as an occasion for experimenting with a combination of mechanical forms tried out against a lucid appreciation of the structure; for him too the aggregation, on ground plan or in the vertical, of the most heterogeneous spatial and structural objects is a pitiless and critical scrutiny of the linguistic and syntactic inheritance of tradition; for him too the commixture of the main accepted code (that of Palladian Classicism filtered through the work of Inigo Jones) joins together the most varied linguistic sources in a clash meant to test the validity of the universalistic claims of Classicism. In works like St Vedast, St Mary-le-Bow and St Stephen's Walbrook, we can see how he adds the models of Flemish Jesuit and Dutch Reformed architecture to some Gothic suggestions and to an emotional use of light. But the sum total is now outside any 'rhetoric' or symbolism. Wren's detachment from his sources is total. He too behaves like a scientist, handling his test-tubes, lining up the retorts one after the other, ready for a new comparative test.

By linking Wren's experimentalism with its historical sources and by projecting it towards the anti-Baroque tendencies of *Whig* England (expressed by Campbell, Burlington, Kent, etc.), we throw light on the long tradition of criticism particular to English art. On the other hand, England's cultural position in the European debate, from the mature Gothic period onwards, is explicitly critical. In the Elizabethan era the *conceptism* of Raleigh's and Puttenham's poetry is found in many of the projects of Robert Smythson and Thorpe, where the ingenious combinations of geometrical figures seem to lead, on the one hand, to Wren's scientism, on the other, to the combinatory play of Illuminist eighteenth century.[28]

Girouard has recently concluded Summerson's work, analysing with acumen and a wealth of information the Elizabethan architectural *conceptism*.[29] But it seems to us that one element has escaped both these authors: the secular and anti-Classical value of the symbolism of Robert Smythson and of Thynne, in respect of the, at first, gnostic and cabbalistic movements of the Italian fifteenth and sixteenth centuries and, later, of the dogmatic and didactic movements of the Baroque age.

This is a decisive point in our analysis. It explains, in fact, the cultural antecedents of the first Palladian wave in England and of Wren's critical experimentalism. The geometric play of the Jacobean houses, the overlaying of quotations derived from the most varied lexicons, their contrivances, take conceptisms, symbolisms and heraldic scherzos into a geometry still hermetic but already trying to free itself from any superimposed content. It is for this reason that the linguistic commixture of the Elizabethan mansions, of the early Inigo Jones, of Wren, of Hawksmoor and of Vanbrugh assumes a strong experimental character.

No linguistic matrix is accepted *a priori*. The only real code used in the English sixteenth and seventeenth centuries, at least up to the second Palladian revolution, is the experimental clash of different codes, in tension with each other.

Let us examine a well characterised group of Wren's buildings, such as the parish churches of St Benet Fink and St Antholin (and one could add the project for the chapel of Whitehall Palace).

The main theme undergoing criticism is the typology of an elliptical space derived from Italian Mannerism. And it is clear that a *typological criticism* can only be achieved through an experiment expressed in typologies: the cycle of the three churches is compact and must be read in a unitary way.[30] In testing the functionality of a form, Wren has two conditions: its compromise with opposite and alternative geometrical forms and the isolation of the structural elements. The whole thing is, then, flooded with even light, to underline the *vivisection* carried out in this sort of *operating theatre* of architecture. (And here the functional motive of the Reformed Church, which requires maximum visibility in every point of the internal space and absolute unity of the space itself, merges with the expressive need).[31]

In St Benet Fink, therefore, the oval of the dome is carried by interrupted columns arranged according to a very elongated planimetric hexagon, so that the discontinuity of the supports contests the unity of the cover. But, at the same time, the geometric form also loses its absoluteness, melts into distorted figures: the perimeter of the church is a decagon joined to the internal hexagon by breaking the continuity. In the planimetric drawing we have a composition consisting of one oval, one hexagon, one decagon, two rectangles, four trapezia and four triangles: a whole repertoire of simple geometric shapes put together according to a merciless logic (Summerson described it as 'tyranny of the intellect').

St Antholin (1678–82) repeats the same experimental research. The Corinthian columns are isolated on terribly high and paradoxical pedestals that rob them of any intellectual value, reducing them to mere tectonic objects. The geometrical perimeter enclosing the vault is an octagon, and the flat surfaces cut by jutting out lintels underline the careful opposition between pure geometrical shapes and the building's luminosity. (Let us point out, again, the intentional contrast between the simple and naked shape of the perimeter windows and the Baroquism of the circular eyes of the dome that alter the geometrical purism of the ellipse.)

But that is not all. Wren's entire production can be read by following a precise typological reasoning.

In other words, what happened with him was similar to what had happened with Palladio: typological cycles, easily recognisable and with autonomous symbological attributes, solidly structured and coherently elaborated, emerge from the sequence of different architectures. Both Palladio and Wren present cycles of architectures that could be defined: *themes with variations*. Like Palladio's villas in the Venetian countryside, Wren's parish churches in the urban landscape of London were an autonomous 'landscape'. For Wren the city and for Palladio the country are nothing else but homogeneous backgrounds: the architectures inserted in them become 'focused landscapes' and recognisable outgrowths that qualify, restructure and give a face and a meaning to nature and to architectural pre-existences.

The horizontal nature and the volumetric solidity of Palladio's villas and, on the other hand, the spires of Wren's London churches, are like elements of a triangulation of the landscape. In this sense, the fact that Palladio and Wren foster a particular architectural quality that is realised in the sequence of buildings causes a jump in the concept of architecture itself.

Every villa and every church, besides its intrinsic value, takes a particular meaning from the fact that they are moments of unitary typological cycles. Wittkower and Ackerman have sensed exactly this feature of Palladio's architecture: from the Villa Godi to the Villa Piovene at Lonedo, from the Villa Poiana to the Villa Saraceno at Finale, Palladio carried out a tight typological criticism with highly experimental intentions.

In Palladio's architecture one can observe that the logic of the experimentation is in perfect balance with the expressive potential of the images: and it would obviously be very short-sighted to reduce the range of Palladio's art to simple criticism. Palladio – like Wright in the Prairie houses, Le Corbusier, or, in the cinema, Eisenstein – is at the same time poet, critic and a good theoretician; this is not the case with Wren. Wren's criticism is more absolute, the primary semantic value of his work is in the

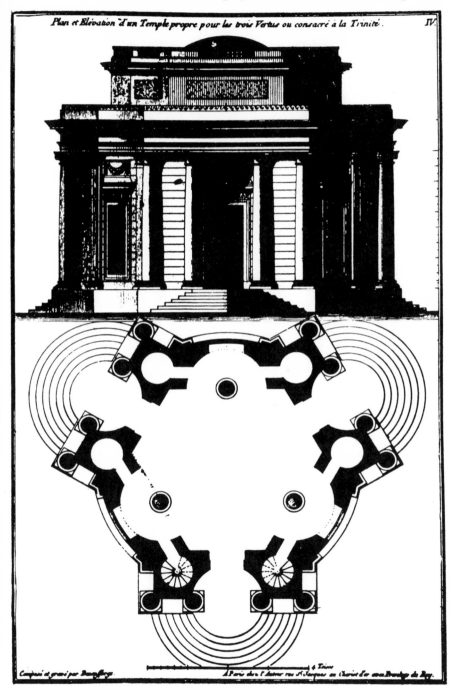

12.   J. F. Neufforge, Temple 'dedicated to the three Virtues or to the Trinity'. From *Supplément au Recueil Elémentaire d'architecture*, etc., Paris 1772, Plate IV

logic structure of his architecture. But it is his insistence on the rigorous construction of the form and the coherence with which his typologies become pivots of the urban scape that open a new chapter for modern architecture, later studied in depth by Quarenghi and Schinkel. Individual architecture sees its importance diminished in favour of a 'series', of an architectural cycle, of a new consideration of the value of typologies: the 'destruction of the aura' has its distant beginnings, and not by chance, in an architect whose activity makes full use of his experience as a modern scientist.

Palladio and Wren, consequently, translate into concrete architectural cycles the critical evidence of Peruzzi's drawings and of Serlio's and Montano's treatises. Their criticisms can be valued in different ways (they are, in fact, rather different, in purposes and cultural origins); but the problems set by them have, no doubt, enough common characteristics for our study.

The use of different and superimposed codes for experimental purposes does not necessarily imply that a particular historical moment is in crisis. Let us take the case of the seventeenth- and eighteenth-century late Classicism, in France and in England. We have already mentioned Wren, but the analysis could continue to include architects like Hawksmoor, Thomas Archer, James Gibbs, and – in spite of its polemic against this last group – all the neo-Palladianism of the eighteenth century, from Campbell to George Dance, Junior.

But the problem is not very different with, first, Hardouin Mansart and, later, Soufflot, at least in respect of some of their most advanced experiences. When Mansart (in works like the stables at Versailles, or the ground-floor vaults of Arles Town Hall) and Soufflot (in the exposed structural and luministic organisation of Ste-Geneviève), show a technological mastery that reminds one of the late-Romanesque and Gothic assemblages, they are certainly not attempting historicism. Rather, they compromise the apodictical classicist syntax with the empirical instruments of planning and execution, as if to test the resilience of that syntax. Theirs is certainly not an experimental criticism comparable to Wren's. But in Soufflot, in particular, one can see a conscious freedom of experimentation that coincides with the complex indictment against the classicist language.[32] It is the same indictment that will continue into the Illuminist age and that will lead to the definitive end of Classicism.

Perhaps it is not by chance that criticism and architecture of the last few years continually refer back to Illuminist culture. All Illuminism is

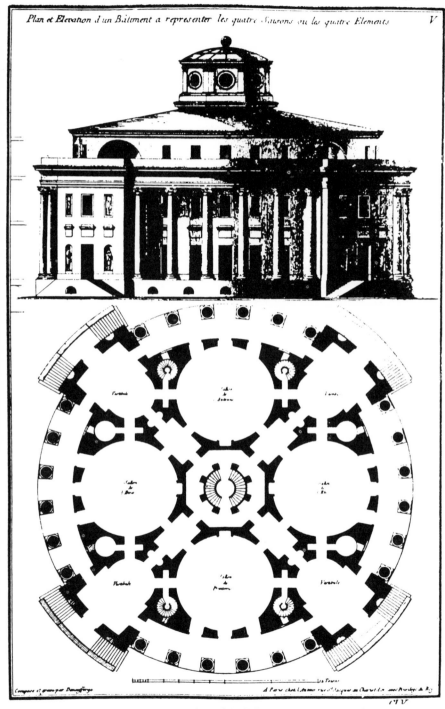

13.   J. F. Neufforge, Plan and elevation of 'building representing the four Seasons or the four Elements'. From *Supplément*, etc., Plate V

essentially critical: every problem is tackled with rational instruments, tending towards an identification of Nature with Reason that will conclude the search, already started in the sixteenth century, for a *mathesis univeralis*. But Illuminism is also the historical hinge between two incompatible universes of discourse: European Classicism and the Modern Movement. By referring to it, one can cautiously test the ground both up to the thresholds of the tradition we live in and towards a past that is unrecoverable as such, but with which one can still deal through its formal re-evocation.

In this way one is safe from accusations of neo-Classicism (for one is referring, in fact, to a tradition deeply critical of Classicism) and one is re-establishing, polemically, the link with a tradition too often seen as starting with William Morris.[33]

Here is a further explanation of why the *rigorist* American movements, with the related European movements, look for the recovery of Order and Form in the codes that are most eversive in respect of the old Order. The architecture of Kahn, Johansen, Franzen, Rudolph and of the 'Five' is, then, *critical* in a new sense. It does not deny the tradition of the Modern Movement but compromises it by comparing it directly with its origins: as if to find its certificate of historical legitimacy.

A few years ago this type of criticism caused quite a scandal. But it is not quite new. Peter Behrens, in one of his less well known works (and perhaps not by chance) – the 1930 block of flats on Bolivarellee in Berlin – assembled and disassembled the organism by using, in the nodal points, a casual sequence of protruding half-cylinders. The language that he is figuratively analysing is the language of the *Berlin school* (mistakenly identified with Expressionism).

It is very significant to find the same formal origin for this work of Behrens and for Rudolph's Endo Laboratories in Long Island (1960–4). Behrens puts in order and rationalises the criticism of Gropius's rigorism carried out, for example, by Scharoun in the same period but on a much less systematic basis. On this plane it should not surprise anyone that Behrens's criticism of the *wall as a limitation* of 'Rationalism' (and, at the same time, of the dissolution of the wall in Scharoun's work) should meet up with Rudolph's work and, even more, Ungers', who turned his attention towards an historical recovery of the valencies of the *Ring* and of its various tendencies.[34]

Because of what it suggests the independent volumetric articulation of Behrens's building may, therefore, still become productive after a lapse of time, as soon as its incidental motivations have been left behind. The case in question is certainly a precocious example of self-criticism on the part of modern architecture, outside the polemics of trends. (One, perhaps, could see a precedent in Olbrich's work, but with a quite different order of ideas and motives.)

The situation at the end of the sixties is, on the other hand, characterised by an architecture folding on itself, in search of its own 'why', of the 'why' of its structure and of its historical permissibility.

It is one of the inevitable contradictions of present day architecture. After having denied that it belongs to history, it has discovered, in itself, a new concept of history that, on one side, is projected on the pre-eighteenth century past, while, on the other, it enters insidiously into the development of the new tendencies. Having reduced antiquity to a simple *event*, lacking causal links, modern architecture cannot help trying to rebuild, and in a positively classic fashion, its own history. This explains the rising of all the series of phenomena connected to the exploration of the problems left open by the 'Masters' and by the avant-gardes of the twenties.[35]

We have a clear example in the entire movement conventionally called New Brutalism. In its funeral service sermon, Reyner Banham, the critic who has supported and in part invented and followed on its way this bundle of architectural tendencies, pointed out one of the basic contradictions of the movement (investigated, for the most part, in its English form) in the swing between a *new ethic* and a *new aesthetic*. Neither the Smithsons, in their reply in *The Architects' Journal*, nor Boyd in his editorial review in *The Architectural Review*, have been able to see the end of the problem set, but not solved, by Banham.[36]

> For all its brave talk of 'an ethic, not an aesthetic' [Banham writes] Brutalism never quite broke out of the aesthetic frame of reference. For a short period, around 1953–5, it looked as if an 'other architecture' might indeed emerge, entirely free of the professional preconceptions and prejudices that have encrusted architecture since it became 'an art'. It looked for a moment as if we might be on the threshold of an utterly uninhibited functionalism, free, even, of the machine aesthetic that had trapped the white architecture of the thirties and made it impossible for Gropius to reach through to the native American machine ethic that might have broken the back of the Beaux-Arts tradition that still cripples architectural thinking in America.[37]

And it is very significant that Banham feels the need to add that:

> The Johnsons, Johansens, and Rudolphs of the American scene were quicker than I was to see that the Brutalists were really their allies, not

mine; committed in the last resort to the classical tradition, not the technological.[38]

But the historicistic character of the movement had been openly declared in the 1955 Manifesto, where it was stated that the term New Brutalism was new, but:

> the method, a revaluation of those advanced buildings of the twenties and thirties whose lesson (because of a few plaster-cracks) have been forgotten. As well as this, there are certain lessons of the formal use of proportion (from Professor Wittkower) and a respect for the sensuous use of each material (from the Japanese). Naturally, a theory which takes the props from the generally accepted and easily produced 'Contemporary' has generated a lot of opposition. . . .[39]

But the basic criticism was compromised by a vitalistic impulse, that will split into two streams: one moving towards the recovery of the 'picturesque',[40] the other towards anticipations of New Realism and New Dada, as the London exhibition *Parallel of Life and Art* organised in 1953 by Alison and Peter Smithson, Nigel Hendersen and Eduardo Paolozzi, had so very strikingly forecast.[41]

But criticism, historicism (*malgré soi*) and *reportage* are not easily reconcilable. The acceptance of a given language – Le Corbusier's *materic and objectual* – leads to the coherent mannerism of the Japanese *new school* and to the too often frustrated aspirations of the English circle that will see Theo Crosby, one of the first instigators of the New Brutalism, trying new outlets in the *pop* fantasies of 'Archigram' and the Smithsons arriving at a dignified and agnostic professional integrity.

With New Brutalism we have an example of non-rigorous criticism, compromised (but also vitalised) by partially developed ideological superimpositions. Besides, the failure of New Brutalism sees a corresponding spreading of a diffused criticism that has led to international work of high quality not unrelated to the new tendencies of American architecture: from the production of Atelier 5 in Switzerland, to Mayekawa and Tange in Japan, to Aymonimo in Italy.[42]

However, the results of this diffused criticism cannot be said to be illuminating: a superficial observer could say that never has such an acute need of criticism generated so much confusion. But, if we go back to the historical precedents analysed earlier, we find many analogies with our own situation. The criticism developed by architecture seems permanently condemned to see its own objectives flounder. But what is the reason, then, for its appearance whenever a figurative system (and, therefore, a system of values) is on the verge of dissolution or radical change?

And again, shouldn't an art that offers itself as a desperate attempt at self-consciousness, be already beyond any myth? This is the contradiction of the type of architecture that claims to exhaust its meaning in the structure of a reflected action. On one hand it aspires to reveal values, difficulties, contradictions. On the other, it takes those very values, difficulties, contradictions to the extreme (so covering up their ultimate meaning). As revealer of myths it accentuates the rational polarity of its own structure; as architecture *malgré tous* it involves its own de-mythisation in the convolutions of the metaphor and of the images, making the meaning of its own discoveries equivocal.

'The architecture that speaks of architecture' rejects, after all, an in-depth dialogue with criticism. And, just as the best way to neutralise a feared opponent is to fully absorb his aggressive techniques, we find that the shaping of architecture as a critical experiment is revealed in all its essence to be a true exorcism of an authentic rational introspection.

The luministic dissonance of Hans von Steinhausen and Ulrich von Ensingen, then, does not quite *explain* the contradictions of late-Gothic; similarly, the hallucinated fantasies of Dietterlin and Montano explode but do not clarify the linguistic ambiguities of Mannerism; and the sophisticated, empirical and experimental eclecticism of Sir Christopher Wren does not influence in any substantial way the course of Baroque Classicism in Europe. Finally, the hedonistic, restless and rigorist criticism of Rudolph, Franzen and Ungers does not seem able to answer the questions that it is constantly posing.

The architecture that is on the way to becoming metalanguage, that turns constantly to question itself, that gives up its role as 'subject' to take on the role of 'object', is, then, also an architecture that either does not know how, or is unable, to go to the very end, that does not know how or is not willing to expose itself – without a safety net – to the dangerous test of an unprejudiced critical exploration, that prefers to punish itself masochistically rather than to open its eyes on itself and its own destiny. This architecture, therefore, wavers dangerously between unreality and play.

One could answer that unreality is the dimension of artistic language and that play is a constant component of European art. But in our case unreality means giving up influencing the process of transformation of architectural language, and the escape into play is nothing but the counter-altar of this renunciation.

The criticism that has entered the structure of artistic language is putting obstacles in the way of a full comprehension of the crisis. It slightly draws back the curtains, leaving the scene behind in darkness and winking with complicity at the public that is watching this comedy of indecisions. Here you have the reason why in history one constantly witnesses the misappropriation of 'critical writing' by architecture. On one hand, by pushing this architectural metaphor towards a rational and cognitive emphasis, one undermines the genuine critical excavation, because the latter is confronted by a product that, somehow, mimes its processes. On the other hand this type of architecture exerts a strong *persuasive* action on the public, by involving it (including the absent-minded) in its specific expressive values, in its own play of reticent allusions, of ambiguous references, of hermetic quotations.

At the level of the daily city experience, Rudolph's Yale Architectural School, Giurgola's Pennsylvania University Garage and Johansen's R. Hutching's Goddard Library are far more than mere fragments of an *action architecture*, as it may well seem at first. Once past the stage of the immediate perception of the image, they lead the spectator into a symbolic maze representing a sort of emblematic summary of the ground covered by modern architecture.

Of course, the more obvious the *quotations*, the stronger will be the psychological conditioning to a deciphering rite. But, at the same time, the various quotations must contain some sort of mysterious contradiction, something that makes them clash with each other in reciprocal endless references, something that can put in crisis the meaning of the single signs as soon as one perceives their historical origin.

In the Yale School, Rudolph plays the game of contrasting the tight composition of the internal spaces with the structural blocks of the organism, and Moholy-Nagy has rightly linked it to Wright's Larkin Building. Besides, the Le Corbusian Brutalism, evoked by the material quality of the geometrical solids and by the *Modulor* figures stamped on them, is compromised by the sophisticated vibration of the walls, that reduces the quotation to a mere expedient for an ironical lulling of the senses. Sensual hedonism is at variance with the emaciation of the didactical core of the building and with the fusion of the various types of space.

Are we, then, dealing with pure irony? Only in part. It is the *incompletedness* that becomes a sort of symbolic message in Rudolph's disenchanted work: Yale, and the designs for Tuskegee Chapel in Alabama, for the Government Center in Boston, for Stafford Harbor.

Incompletedness can mean *work in progress, open* architecture, expressive restraint. But this is not the case with Rudolph. In themselves his images are always redundant because he ignores the restrained allusions reached by reducing the images to pure signs and to 'objects', typical of Louis Kahn. Rudolph's truncated and contradictory phrases carry, rather, a sense of ambiguous contestation. Taken together – and it is particularly so in the Boston project – they tend towards a polemic summary of the history of modern architecture, bringing out its tensions and dichotomies (Wright versus Corbu, the winks at a vaguely medieval historical source and the academic use of worn out compositional formulae, the figurative ransom of technology and its concealment in sculptural objects).

But from the inter-reactions of the signs employed by Rudolph comes a message of a very different nature, alarming in its sceptical disenchantment. Their complex composition shows a mood definitely not insensitive to the historicisation of architectural activity, but that starts its moves from a condition of impotence and saturation. The clash of images taken from the most distant sources of modern architecture and the coat of Surrealist paint on the resulting *pastiche* – see the astonishing house in Jacksonville – have a precise meaning. Rudolph wants to drive home the drama of the *Fourth Generation* (i.e. after the Masters) of architects; the drama of being tied to Mannerism and of the loss of the *red thread* in the over-rich repository of linguistic sources at their disposal; of the realisation of a different and wider frame-work reference and of the inability to cut loose from a too heavy historical heritage; of the loss of meaning with the consequent reaction of exalting to the limit, intelligence, culture and *bravura*: as if an intellectural *tour de force* would compensate for the opacity and the wreck of the aims.

We have spoken of Rudolph because he shows in a greater degree the tendency that we are trying to identify: but we must keep in mind that this is a sort of condition common to almost all the international architectural culture of the last ten years.

We are then in an extreme situation: between critical eclectism and pure play. Rudolph, Pei, Lasdun, Ungers all share the same direction of research and the contradictions met in the course of it. Within descriptive architecture, the experiences of the architects just mentioned have the fault of trying to hide their true purposes while, at the same time, revealing the existence of a dead end that should not be moralistically condemned if only because it is historically determined.

The observations made up to now are not judgments of value: we are, for the moment, far more concerned with clearing the meaning of more and more generalised attitudes than with absolving or condemning. If there is a judgment to give, it will have to find its parameters within the structure of each single work, after having verified its coherence in respect of the initial premises.

And, no doubt, between the critical rigour of the later Kahn, of Lundy, Stirling, Tange, Kallmann and the subtle balancing tricks of Rudolph and Pei there is a difference of objectives. For the former the critical probing is communicated directly, as a process to go through in the architectural experience itself; for the latter the probing is interrupted and diverted towards the most subtle evasions hiding the original intentions.

Architecture as game, then; a game played, however, to dissolve a too intense problematic charge. The alternative between *jeu* and *sérieux* recognised recently by Garroni in the tendencies of the 33rd Venice Biennale, can equally apply to architectural culture.[43]

But it is not at all certain that the game does not possess autonomous critical capacities, if nothing else as the revealer of a situation. Many of the pure geometrical objects projected by the cultured American architecture as obscure symbols of an existential condition torn between protest against the psychological squashing of *urban consumerism* and the fascination of the changeable, of the urban surreal, of *Kitsch*, are, in fact, architectural translations of the symbolism of the new *pop* realism.[44] (We are thinking here of the contorted spatial sequences of the Tuskegee Chapel or of the paradoxical *open boxes* of Rudolph's Jacksonville House, of Pei's geometricised dolmens and menhirs at the Colorado National Center for Atomic Research, and of the allusive objects winking at us from the compact mass of Johansen's Hutching's Goddard Library.)

Many European and, in particular, Italian experiences are, too, looking for a new symbolism. At the bottom of all this there is the wish to adhere with enthusiasm to the multiple pressures of urban reality and, at the same time, to introduce in it *architectural events* and fragments which might force the entire meaning of that reality. In this way architectural criticism merges with criticism of the city: Samonà's project for the new Parliament offices in Rome and, to remain within Italy, the silent architectural objects of Aldo Rossi, are effective evidence of it.

At this point, we think no one will be surprised if we say that architectural criticism puts in crisis the critics of architecture. On the contrary, since the traditional task of criticism is already realised within the architectural structures, one could say that an independently critical architecture has the objective of destroying any critical intervention from outside. In structuring itself by reflection, speaking of itself, analysing its own language, architecture takes the form of a continuous and taut discourse,

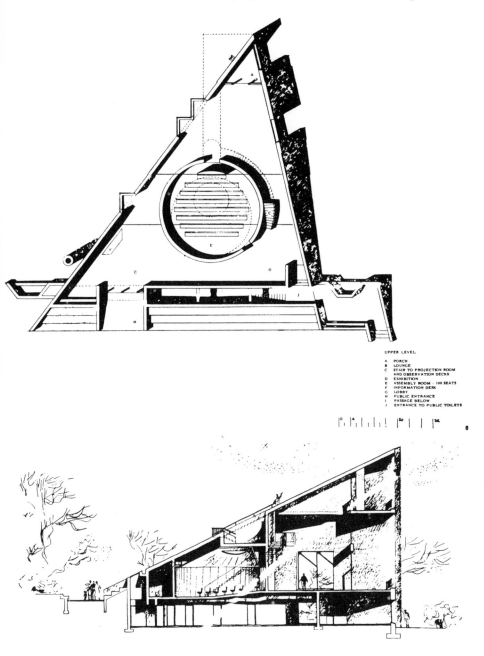

UPPER LEVEL

A   PORCH
B   LOUNGE
C   STAIR TO PROJECTION ROOM
     AND OBSERVATION DECKS
D   EXHIBITION
E   ASSEMBLY ROOM - 100 SEATS
F   INFORMATION DESK
G   LOBBY
H   PUBLIC ENTRANCE
I   PASSAGE BELOW
J   ENTRANCE TO PUBLIC TOILETS

14.   Romualdo Giurgola and Mitchell, Office building and study centre of the Acadia
National Park, Mount Desert Island (Maine) 1965

tries to demonstrate and, at the same time, to persuade one of its active role as configurator of space-environment at every dimensional level; and also tries to show, without false modesty, the genesis and the tricks of its organisation as a metalanguage.[45]

The second purpose of this activity is not as immediate as it might appear. Behind the anxious digging into its own *raison d'être* is the constant fear of an authentic critical process. Until the probing is conducted according to formal and organising principles inside the adopted languages, there is no danger of a radical eversion. Nor can one say that the linguistic contests of the most advanced experiences show a real and decisive revolutionary charge. (As is shown by Kahn's last works and by those young American architects in opposition.)

But we would not be fair to the present architectural tendencies if we did not consider the possible contributions of this way of working. To provide a *design* object, an architecture or an urban organisation containing a strong charge of criticism, means – on condition that the process is carried through – giving to the space thus formed a high degree of communication; it means, above all, showing the way to a *critical existence*, to a conscious fruition and to a correct use of the image.

Works like those of Kahn, of Samonà's last work, of Copcutt, of Stirling – as we have seen – are not satisfied with structuring forms and functions. They aim, first of all, at making their approach to form readable, they want, in short, to *historicise* themselves and to lead to a deeply reflected historicised fruition. It is by far the most important contribution made by this type of architectural research. But it is also where their dichotomy shows. On one side they direct their efforts towards a more and more conscious fruition of the city and the architectural object, by pulling the observer away from any automatic response: we have shown this by considering how, in many ways, they are trying to go beyond the condition of *absent-minded perception* without losing its acquisitions and within the complex stratification of the communication levels. On the other side, what somehow gets transmitted to the architectural culture is something more than a tranquillising tradition, but something less than the result of a constant and systematic examination of one's assumptions.

But we do not mean to repeat ourself by pointing out again the ambiguity of a criticism swinging between the fully demonstrated theorem and the *imagerie*: the most pressing question is the one about the attitude of the critics towards this constant, and often cited, attempt to overcome the obstacle.

The almost total silence of the critics on this point may seem at once normal and odd. Odd because one would expect a legitimate reaction; normal, because the close alliance of criticism and operation can only lead to a compromise even in such extreme case: it is almost impossible to be actor and spectator at the same time.

We have already seen that the phenomenon is not new. What is new is the process of global involvement started by contemporary art in order to absorb without residues of daily perception, critical analysis and history, within a single moment (of planning) and at all levels.

This general co-operation in forming and transforming architecture – the architect as direct configurator, the historian and critic as 'deeply compromised' analysts, the public as co-helper in the birth of the work and as determining interpreter of its meanings – seems to realise Gropius's dream of architecture as collective work achieved by teamwork and widened through concentric circles to include the whole of society, then reproposed in the new decisions of the planning group once its social productivity has been tested by the wider group represented by the public.

But it only seems so. There is no need to use too many words to show that this ideal process, if it does exist at all, is wholly mystifying. Of the specimen process idealised by the ideology of the Bauhaus, only the skeleton remains, while in the praxis of the artists, the memory remains, often brought back nostalgically.

'Critical architecture' has the architect as its authentic interlocutor, and, as object of its analysis, the highly intellectualised figurative processes. It is for this reason that the articulation of forms is translated into the Baroquism of the images, and that an effective analytical message in the global sense (committed to burrow into the totality of the structures, and, particularly, into the criticism they contain) is to be found only in few current experiences.

The slipping of the critical momentum into the slimy bog of a-critical images is perhaps one of the most serious symptoms of the uncertainty of both means and ends that dominates a good part of international culture. But this *crisis of criticism* has a further outlet, that represents a sort of counterpart to the phenomenon described up to now. The answer to critical architecture, to an art, that is, that tends to assimilate the instruments proper to analysis, is *operative criticism*: a criticism that carries out an opposite process and that tends to absorb in itself the moment of planning. *Architecture as criticism* is contraposed by *criticism as project*.

Notes to chapter 3

[1] Cf. chap. 5 on the possible links between analyses of experimental psychology and architectural analyses.

[2] 'The end of the avant-garde [Brandi writes] is connected to the loss of the future as the ontological dimension of human existence. An avant-garde of the present cannot be taken seriously because it is a contradictory concept. . . . It is essential for the avant-garde to be not only innovative but also eversive towards the past that reaches the present . . . in order to start a new tradition, set a new course away from retroactive values and the fossilisation of the very near past.' Experimentalism, on the contrary, lives only in the *hic et nunc* of the present and 'deliberately ignores the point of arrival and the projection into time'. C. Brandi, *Le due vie* op. cit. pp. 137–9. Cf. also Renato Poggioli, *Teoria dell'arte d'avanguardia*, Bologna 1962, and Edoardo Sanguineti, 'Intervento per Burri', in *Marcatrè* 1964, nos. 6–7. Brandi had already dealt with the theme of the end of the avant-gardes in 1949, cf. 'La fine dell'avanguardia', in *L'Immagine*, 1949, nos. 14–15.

[3] Cf. chap. 5.

[4] C. L. Ragghianti, 'I Carracci e la critica d'arte nell'età barocca', in *La Critica* 1933, p. 65 ff.; G. C. Argan, 'Cultura artistica alla fine del Cinquecento', in *L'Arte*, Feb.–March 1942; id. *La pittura dell'Illuminismo in Inghilterra*, Bulzoni, Rome 1965; id. 'Il valore critico dell'incisione di riproduzione', in Marcatrè, 1966, nos. 19–22, p. 293 ff. Among the most important studies on the critical function of contemporary art, see Zevi's on the critical value of the figurative splitting of neo-Plasticism, and Boatto's on the criticism of the painter Lichtenstein. Cf. B. Zevi, *Poetica dell'architettura neoplastica* op. cit. and Alberto Boatto, 'Il fumetto al microscopio' in 'Lichtenstein', *Fantazaria*, 1966, no. 2, p. 14 ff. (now in *La Pop Art negli USA*, op. cit.)

[5] B. Zevi, *La storia come metodologia*, op. cit. p. 13.

[6] 'The purpose [of the cultural re-integration of history and planning] is the reduction and the weeding out of the enormous waste of history. It is also the opposition to the squandering of the revolutionary heritage mortified and reduced by laziness, pride and insufferance and its defence and revitalisation by a criticism able to put it back on the drawing-tables.' Ibid. p. 17.

[7] Ibid. p. 22.

[8] B. Zevi, *History as a Method of Teaching Architecture*, op. cit. p. 15.

[9] Ibid. pp. 17–18.

[10] Besides the authors already quoted we could mention, as a further confirmation of our thesis, the work of the American semantic schools: Dewey's *Art as Experience*, and a considerable part of the structuralist and semiologic analyses, which we will deal with more specifically in chap. 5.

[11] We agree however with Zevi's criticism of the topicality of visual design in a discussion at the INARCH in Rome during the winter of 1963. Cf. also B. Zevi, 'Visualizzare la critica dell'architettura' in *L'Architettura cronache e storia*, 1964, X, no. 103, pp. 2–3, where he supports the possibility of a visual criticism of

architecture in respect of the items shown at the Michelangelo Exhibition.

[12] Cf. 'L'opera architettonica di Michelangiolo nel quarto centenario della morte' and B. Zevi, 'Michelangiolo in prosa' in *L'Architettura cronache e storia*, 1964, IX, no. 99; Paolo Portoghesi, 'Mostra critica delle opere michelangiolesche al Palazzo delle Esposizioni in Roma', ibid. 1964, X. no. 104, pp. 80–91; Renato Bonelli, 'La mostra delle opere michelangiolesche' in *Comunità*, 1964, XVIII, no. 122, p. 22 ff.

The Michelangelo Exhibition was set up by Portoghesi, Mario Boudet, Vittorio Gigliotti and Luciano Rubino, under the direction of G. C. Argan, G. de Angelis D'Ossat, N. Sapegno and B. Zevi (co-ordinator). Cf. also 'Michelangelo Pop' in *Marcatrè*, 1964, nos. 6–7, p. 125 ff. (contributions by Battisti, Bonelli, Maltese, Portoghesi and Zevi).

[13] Roland Barthes, *Critique et Vérité*, Du Seuil, Paris 1965, p. 64.

[14] We are referring to R. Picard's pamphlet. Barthes answered it with his *Nouvelle critique ou nouvelle imposture?*, defining his choices and his analytical methods.

[15] We have intentionally grouped together architectures that are formally very distant from each other, to emphasise the structural character of the phenomenon.

[16] On St Urbain in Troyes cf. Lefevre-Pontalis, review of: G. Minvielle, 'Histoire et condition juridique de la profession d'architecte' (Paris 1921) in *Bulletin Monumental*, 1922, LXXXI; Lisa Schürenberg, *Die kirchliche Baukunst in Frankreich*, Berlin 1934, p. 206 ff.; Paul Frankl, *Gothic Architecture*, Penguin Books 1962, p. 129 ff.

[17] On Amiens Cathedral, as ref. to our theme, cf. P. Frankl op. cit.; id. 'A French Gothic Cathedral: Amiens' in *Art in America*, 1947.

[18] We are referring to Sangallo's drawings for S. Lorenzo's façade, to the courtyard of the Palazzetto di Bartolomeo Scala in Florence and to the Michelangelesque studies up to about 1530.

[19] The opinions on Philip Johnson are varied and contrasting, from the accusations of betrayal by Zevi to Hitchcock's agnostic exegesis. It would perhaps be better to look at this architect as a phenomenon of a sceptical and impatient situation, as did, at least in part, Manieri-Elia. Cf. M. John Jacobus Jr., *Philip Johnson*, Braziller, New York 1962, and *Il Saggiatore*, Milan 1964 (with the recognition of the ironical character of Ph. J. wanderings); id. 'Miesless Johnson' in *Architectural Forum*, Sept. 1959, CXI, pp. 114–23; Henry-Russell Hitchcock, 'Current Work of Ph. J.,' in *Zodiac*, 1961, VII, pp. 64–81; id., *Philip Johnson's Architecture 1949–1965*, Thames and Hudson, London 1966; M. Manieri-Elia, *L'architettura del dopoguerra in USA* op. cit.; Massimo D'Alessandro, 'Note sull'opera di Ph. J.', in *Rassegna dell'Istituto di architettura e urbanistica*, Facoltà di Ingegneria dell'Università di Roma, 1967, n. 7, p. 11 ff.

[20] On Villa Adriana cf.: Heinz Kähler, *Hadrian und seine Villa bei Tivoli*, Gebr. Mann., Berlin 1950.

[21] 'It is probably no accident that both [Wright and Kahn] turned to Hadrian, since that haunted Emperor was perhaps one of the first, certainly one of the

most conspicuous, men in Western history for whom – all ways having opened, which more true than another? – conscious, selective memory was a major determinant of life. Is this a pervasive problem of the modern world – all possible, nothing wholly serving, no way the only way, memory all too free to choose?' Vincent Scully, *Louis Kahn*, Braziller, New York 1962, p. 38. The measure of Kahn's anti-pragmatism is given (as far as this is possible) by comparing Scully's interpretation with John Dewey's passage in *Art as Experience*, New York 1934, on the double meaning that can be assumed by the past as an oppressive weight invading the present with a sense of nostalgia and unfulfilled possibilities, and also as a 'store of resources' for those able 'to befriend even their own stupidities'.

[22] 'This door [Serlio writes about Plate XXIX in his book on doors] has in it the Doric, the Corinthian, the Rustic, and even (in truth) the bestial: the columns are Doric, and the capitals a mixture of Doric and Corinthian. The row of columns either side of the door are Corinthian, because of the indents; the same applies to the Architrave, the frieze and the cornice. The whole door is surrounded by Rustic.... And one cannot deny the presence of the bestial order, seeing there the several stones, shaped by nature into the resemblance of beasts.' Sebastiano Serlio, *Il libro delle porte di S. S. bolognese*, in Vicenza, p. 17. Serlio often underlines the experimental character of his *doors*, warning that by ignoring the formal heresies of his drawings one would revert to orthodox models.

[23] In Peruzzi's drawings at the Uffizi (and in the Siena copies) one can trace the rich casuistry that Serlio, as is well known, will move, polarising it, into the pages of his books. Rather symptomatic are Peruzzi's researches into the compentration of finite and contraposed in shape spatial cells, developed in his studies on central plan organisms, some for S. Giovanni dei Fiorentini, some for S. Pietro and some as ideal studies. With Peruzzi's studies we are already within an advanced criticism, that started with the most analytical of the architects of the early sixteenth century: Bramante. (Cf. Arnaldo Bruschi, *Bramante architetto*, Bari 1969.) From the compromise of the central space through peripheral crowns of independent and alternative spatial nuclei, typical of Leonardo's and Peruzzi's drawings, will spring a whole movement of sixteenth-century architecture that, from S. Giustina at Padova to the Duomo di Carpi, will arrive at Palladian experimentalism.

[24] Cf. Marco Rosci, *Il trattato di architettura di Sebastiono Serlio* (comment on the unpublished sixth book in Munich, now published in full), ITEC, Milan 1966: a very good study that brings out clearly Serlio's contribution to the sixteenth-century debate in Italy and in France.

[25] Cf. G.B. Montano, *Li cinque libri di architettura di G. B. M. milanese*, Rome 1691 (the last of the seventeenth-century editions). On Montano see: Giuseppe Zander, 'Le invenzioni architettoniche di G.B.M. milanese (1534–1621), in *Quaderni dell'Istituto di storia dell'architettura*, 1958, no. 30 and 1962, nos. 49–50; M. Tafuri, *L'architettura dell'Umanesimo*, Laterza, Bari 1972; P. Portoghesi, *Borromini: analisi di un linguaggio*, op. cit.

[26] Cf. P. Portoghesi, *Roma barocca*, op. cit.

[27] With the diffusion of Baroque Art in Europe, the theoretic literature loses the speculative vigour of the sixteenth century and is divided into: (a) conventional treatises (comments on Vitruvius, etc.); (b) geometry applied to architecture and projected geometry (Desargues, Guarini, Caramuel, etc.); (c) historical treatises (Fischer von Erlach, Wren, etc.); (d) pre-Illuminist literature (Perrault, Boffrand, Blondel, etc.); (e) iconographic collections (De Rossi, Specchi, Falda, Fürtennbach, etc.). One can demonstrate, therefore, in more than one way, the hypothesis of a close link between the crisis of theoretic literature and the crisis of Baroque criticism.

[28] The 'continuity' of English architecture, already mentioned by us, finds further confirmation in the continuity of its *critical* tradition.

[29] Cf. Mark Girouard, *Robert Smythson* op. cit. and John Summerson, *Art and Architecture in England 1530-1830*, Penguin Books, Harmondsworth 1953, 1963. Cf. also: N. Pevsner, 'L'Inghilterra e il Manierismo', in: *Bollettino del Centro intern. A. Palladio*, 1967, IX, pp. 293-303.

[30] Wren's church production is modelled, anyway, on well-defined typologies, as far as the space, the external solutions and the volumetric aggregations of the church towers are concerned. Sekler has set up graphically the formal cycles of Wren's parish churches, but, apart from Pevsner's acute and brief observations, no detailed critical reading yet exists. Cf. E. Sekler, *Sir Christopher Wren and his Place in European Architecture*, Faber and Faber, London 1956, figs. 3-16 and pp. 102-3, chap. IV; and N. Pevsner, *Chr. Wren*, Astra-Arengarium, Milan 1957.

[31] Kerry Downes relates the two (destroyed) churches of St Antholin and St Benet Fink with the polygonal theatre built by Robert Hooke for the College of Physicians (also destroyed). Cf. Kerry Downes, *English Baroque Architecture*, Zwemmer, London 1966, p. 24.

[32] Cf. Soufflot, *Mémoire sur l'architecture gothique*, Lyon, Académie des Sciences (12 April 1741) M. 194, cit. in: J. Monval, *Soufflot*, Paris 1918; and: Wolfgang Herrmann, *Laugier and the 18th Century French Theory*, Zwemmer, London 1962.

[33] We think Edoardo Persico represents the most rigorous and aware forerunner of this recovery of Illuminism, seen as an ideal relationship with a classical dimension more 'dreamt of' than archaeologically analysed. For Persico 'rationalism' was also an effort to reach a new classical dimension. Persico (like, in almost the same span of time, Le Corbusier) can, therefore, use the language of modern architecture as a docile metalanguage, capable of speaking about classicity metaphorically. There are two ways of looking at history in Italian architecture between the wars: Pagano will soon turn to *minor* and rustic architecture; Persico frees the monument from the layer of rhetoric of academic literature. Giolli understood perfectly the value of the Sala della Vittoria at the VI Milan Triennale. Cf. Raffaello Giolli, 'VI Triennale di Milano. La Sala della Vittoria', in: *Casabella*, 1936, nos. 102-3, pp. 14-21.

[34] Several works of the *Berlin school* show a geometrism either inhibited or only partially used as a linguistic element (we are referring to many residential

architectural works by Martin Wagner, Bruno Taut, Fred Forbat, etc.): the criticism carried out by Behrens, in the house on the Bolivarallee, is very much to the point.

[35] Apart from international Lecorbusianism in its various national and regional variations, the phenomena of 'rigorous Mannerism' are not very diffused. A few years ago, in Holland, a 'neo-De Stijl' movement enjoyed a certain success. (Cf. *Structure*, 1961, with the project for a single family house by Joost Baljeu and Dick van Woerkom, and: B. Zevi 'Attraverso, ma oltre "De Stijl"', in *L'Architettura cronache e storia*, 1962, VIII, no. 83.) We cannot ignore the studies in depth of Wright's poetic by Carlo Scarpa and Luigi Pellegrin, those of the French *constructivist classicism* (on the line Durand-Choisy-Garnier-Perret-Le Corbusier) by Samonà, nor those of the themes of Le Corbusier's last work by Mayekawa and Tange.

[36] Cf. Reyner Banham, *The New Brutalism*, op. cit., and Robin Boyd, 'The Sad End of New Brutalism', in *Architectural Review*, 1967, vol. CXLII, no. 845, pp. 9–11, where the author sees the cause of the failure of New Brutalism in its limited appeal: 'the failure of New Brutalism [Boyd writes (op. cit. p. 11)] along with other parallel ambitious efforts to this date, was that it preached almost exclusively to the converted. It was a would-be "sort of social language" (the Smithson phrase) that remained an architectural monologue.' And with this we have confirmation that a critical architecture can talk to other architecture, but finds it rather difficult to talk to the public: a feature that is, perhaps, already contained in its premises and may not be necessarily a fault or an inevitable fault. Cf. also the Smithsons' answer to Banham, in *The Architects' Journal*, and J. Rykwert's review 'Gregotti, Banham', in *Domus* 1967, no. 451.

[37] R. Banham, op. cit. pp. 134–5.

[38] Ibid. p. 135.

[39] New Brutalism's Manifesto, in: R. Banham, op. cit. p. 45.

[40] Cf. R. Banham, op. cit. pp. 74–5.

[41] The movement's Manifesto ended with the statement: 'The New Brutalism has nothing to do with craft. We see architecture as the direct result of a way of life. 1954 has been a key year. It has seen American advertising rival Dada in its impact of overlaid imagery; that automotive masterpiece the Cadillac convertible parallel-with-the-ground (four elevations) classic box on wheels; the start of a new way of thinking by CIAM; the revaluation of the work of Gropius; the repainting of the villa at Garches.' (op. cit. p. 46.)

About the exhibition in London cf. Banham, p. 61 ff. ('*Brute now and other art*'). He speaks of 'Pop Architecture' (p. 62) about the Smithsons' House of the Future (1956), and of 'Architecture autre' about Frederick Kiesler's Endless House (1957), Herb Greene's House at Norman (1961) and Fuller's Studies (pp. 68–9). Cf. also R. Banham, 'My Machine Aesthetic', in *Architectural Design*, 1955, no. 171.

[42] The term Eclecticism has often been used to describe many of these experiences: we can accept this term when related to the will to take over already experimented facts in order to develop their premises and compare them with

each other. 'Wogenscky [Banham writes, for example (op. cit. p. 90)] was not influenced solely by the work being done in the office while the house Rémy-les-Chévreuses was being designed: his view of Le Corbusier has greater historical depth to it, even a touch of book-learning'; he also recognises, later, similar motives in the work by Atelier 5 (E. Fritz, S. Gerber, R. Hesterberg, H. Hostettler, N. Morgenthaler, A. Pini and Fr. Thormann). Cf. Neave Brown, on 'Atelier 5', in *Architectural Design,* no. 2, 1963 ('The eclecticism of "Atelier 5" or any other group with a similar attitude is something of an act of faith. It affirms that if the future course is not clear, to progress at all it is necessary to adopt the successful forms and idioms of the immediate past'). Cf. also: R. Boyd, *The Puzzle of Architecture,* op. cit. pp. 131–3.

[43] After having admitted that 'the use of a programmed object is never really factual or even critical', because the 'manipulator . . . will inevitably behave in front of it as a *consumer of possibilities*' (pp. 29–30), Garroni analyses the positive aspects of the artistic play particularly as presented at the XXXIII Venice Biennale: 'The playful [he writes (pp. 44–5)] . . . has two faces: one turned to the present, where it is consumed without, practically, any appreciable cultural residues; and one turned to the future (*today* turned to the future), where it is charged with seriousness and new meanings, offering itself as an object of intellectual and contemplative understanding, as a place of "positive exchange", to be not only used but also continued further. We would leave the first face to the saddened jugglers (not to be confused with the "sublime" jugglers of the first avant-gardes), while the second belongs inevitably to our cultural inheritance.' Emilio Garroni, 'XXXIII Venice Biennale: "Jeu et serieux"', in op. cit., 1966, no. 7, pp. 25–48. Also important, for their extension of the criticism of architectural utopia, Garroni's passages on the utopianism contained in the playful experiences. (Cf. op. cit. p. 37 ff and id. 'Arte, mito, utopia', in *Quaderni di Arte-oggi,* Rome 1965.)

[44] Calvesi has recently suggested a similar critical reading for some American experiences (Lundy, Fuller) and for those of *Strutture primarie,* in his contribution at the Convegno della giovane critica. Cf. M. Calvesi, 'Da Giorgione alla pittura al neon', in Quindici, 1967, no. 4. Enrico Crispolti has criticised the 'realism' of Pop Art in his booklet on this movement (Fabbri, Milan 1966, p. 144 ff.)

[45] Although completely extraneous to our line of thought, in its premises and conclusions, the *critical* character of contemporary art has been emphasised – as regards the consequent 'difficulties' of criticism – in Giovanni Urbani's essay, 'Il silenzio della critica' in *I problemi di Ulisse: le vie della critica,* Sansoni, Florence 1962, vol. VII, p. 111 ff., in which the author takes up again the themes of a previous radio talk, published under the title: 'Difficoltà di linguaggio nella critica d'arte contemporanea', in *Terzo Programma,* 1961, no. 4, pp. 246–50. These writings are typical of a reading of contemporary art filtered through the Hegelian concept of the *death of art* caused by the arrival of a self-destructive intellectualism, on which cf. Sabatini, Morpurgo-Tagliabue and Formigari, op. cit. in chap. 1.

4

Operative Criticism

What is normally meant by *operative criticism* is an analysis of architecture (or of the arts in general) that, instead of an abstract survey, has as its objective the planning of a precise poetical tendency, anticipated in its structures and derived from historical analyses programmatically distorted and finalised.[1]

By this definition operative criticism represents the meeting point of history and planning. We could say, in fact, that operative criticism *plans* past history by projecting it towards the future. Its verifiability does not require abstractions of principle, it measures itself, each time, against the results obtained, while its theoretical horizon is the pragmatist and instrumentalist tradition.

One could add that this type of criticism, by anticipating the ways of action, forces history: forces past history because, by investing it with a strong ideological charge, it rejects the failures and dispersions throughout history; and forces the future because it is not satisfied with the simple registering of what is happening, but hankers after solutions and problems not yet shown (at least, not explicitly so). Its attitude is contesting towards past history, and prophetic towards the future.

We cannot pass abstract judgment on operative criticism. We can only judge it after we have examined its historical origins and measured its effects on contemporary architecture: no other yardstick will do.

In order to find one of the first sources of an *operative* attitude in modern criticism, we will have to go back to Bellori, rather than to pseudo-Manetti or Vasari. Before Bellori's *Vite* there certainly had been a *commitment* by theorists within a group or a movement, in the texts of *Anonimo brunelleschiano* and Vasari, for example (as well as in those of Lomazzo and Serlio); but it had always been a partial commitment, often faded and elusive. Vasari himself, although an enemy of the Sangallian circle, felt the need to show some objectivity in the biography of Antonio il Giovane; in the same way Lomazzo's insults against Serlio are of a very particular nature, and would disappoint anyone trying to find in them a critical choice in the anti-Mannerist sense.

In Bellori's *Vite*, on the other hand, there is an apodictical historical choice. All objectivity is banned and the artistic world is divided into two sides: on one side the *goodies*, Poussin's Classicism and Carraccio's historicism; on the other the *baddies*, all the Masters of the Roman Baroque, without exception.[2] But the title of Bellori's volume is *Le vite de'pittori, scultori et architetti moderni*. Clearly the author does not take history for granted; he does not accept reality as it is and he thinks that critical judgment cannot simply influence the course of history, but must also, and mainly, change it, because its approval or rejection have as much real value as the work of the artists.

What is the difference between Bellori's rejection of Baroque – we should perhaps say rejection of the existence of Baroque – and the strict rejection of the Middle Ages and of Gothic by the theorists of Humanism and Classicism, as expressed, for example, in the famous letter from Raphael to Leo X?[3] The stand of Raphael and the entire culture of Humanist extraction against Gothic serves only to justify rationally the validity and the absoluteness of the classicist code. The partiality and engagement of the artist cannot be called *operative*, because nothing in them speaks of choices for the future: the letter to Leo X sanctions and theorises a revolution carried out in the previous century, and its value, if any, is as evidence of the continuity of the new tradition founded by Humanism.

For Bellori such a generic statement has lost its value. The classicist language, in the mid-1600s no longer needs justification: what has to be recognised is its breaking up into antithetic lexicons. The critic's commitment can only be within the cultural choices founded on two centuries of research: one cannot even think of a programmatic eversion, a new revolution or a backward leap. But the classicist code no longer offers stable values and prospects. The antithesis hidden under the inhibited sixteenth-century debate must explode, become obvious, place the artist at a cross-road, place the critic in the situation of one that, having pointed out the reasons for that antithesis, makes a choice: a choice that is, substantially, a gamble on the future.

On one side are Bellori, Poussin, Félibien, Dubos, and, later, Boileau with his *Art poétique*; on the other Pellegrini with his *Delle acutezze*, Gracian, Tesauro.

Let us put aside, for the moment, any observation on the specific character of the two tendencies, and suspend our judgment as regards their historicity and the general analogies that, in spite of the antithesis, could very well be there.[4] What, besides the theses put forward by Bellori and Tesauro, links these authors, is the coincidence, in their theorising, of *what is* and *what should be*, of historical survey and projection of values into the future, of judgment of value and analysis of the phenomena. Their criticism is *operative* in so far as the system of choices made by them does not present itself as a well founded cognitive process, but rather as a suggested value, or, better, as an *a priori* discriminant between values and non-values. Somehow operative criticism already contained the seed of anti-historicity in the Baroque Age. At least in this sense: if, like Bellori, in order to make history we start from a well founded and personal order of values, so apodictical as to make superfluous, in the end, any objective survey, we will no doubt, get to an obvious operativity of the critical product, but, at the same time, we will not be able to demonstrate the validity of the proposed choices.

Removing Bernini, Borromini and Pietro da Cortona from the historical scene is in fact a self-explanatory gesture of *critique passionnée*. But, having cut any connection with the historicisation of the critical choices, Bellori throws his own choice back into the most absolute relativity; he seems, in fact, to realise unconsciously that any judgment of value has irrationality at its foundation, and, as such, can only shrink from fully showing its hand.

We have stayed with Bellori not only because his *Vite* are objectively a formidable historical precedent for modern operative criticism, but also because it is often easier to read objectively the phenomena of the past than to recognise the structures of the phenomena in which we are deeply involved. Nowadays what appears paradoxical in Bellori is, in fact, daily and punctually repeated by the most orthodox operative criticism: if no one goes so far as to eliminate from his historical treatise figures and happenings of the past, this is certainly not the case with figures and phenomena nearer to us. The result is not all that different from that obtained by Bellori: we know all about the personal choices of contemporary historians, but at the price of introducing serious mythicisations in the corpus of history. And with the gradual demolition of myths, however strongly built – carried out, now, within a few years if not months – one loses the main objective of those histories: operativity, and one generates, at the same time, a symptomatic distrust of history's capacity to assume a productive role in the contemporary debate.

In other words, we see already a typical feature of operative criticism: its almost constant presentation of itself as a prescriptive code. This code may be dogmatically systematic or methodologically wide open, but the difficulty in placing this kind of operativity in history comes, doubtless, from its wavering between the deduction of its values from history itself and the attempt to force the future by introducing – on a critical level only – brand new values and *a priori* choices.

It should not surprise us, then, that the ambiguity between deductive and inductive method is typical of one of the most *operative* tendencies of modern criticism: that of the Illuminist age, at least from Cordemoy onwards. It can be shown more clearly by underlining the gap existing between a text like Jacques-François Blondel's *Architecture Françoise* (that, although published in 1752 is still prescriptive in the Classical sense and very far from the modern criticism of Diderot's *Salons*), and Campbell's *Vitruvius Britannicus* that, with its precocious dates (from 1717 onwards), announce the principles of the *critique passionnée* that found its expression in the theories of Baudelaire.[5]

Blondel's cautious historicism soon clashed with the new theories of Laugier:

Le livres d'Architecture [Laugier writes in 1765, in controversy with Blondel] exposent et détaillent les proportions usitées. Ils n'en rendent aucune raison capable de satisfaire un esprit sensé. L'usage est la seule loi que leurs Auteurs ont suivie, et qu'ils nous ont trasmise. L'usage a un empire certain dans les choses de convention et de fantaisie; il n'a aucune force dans les choses de goût et de raisonnement. . . . C'est aux Philosophes à porter le flambeau de la raison dans l'obscurité des principes et des règles. L'exécution est le propre de l'Artiste, et c'est au Philosophe qu'appartient la législation. . . . J'entreprends de rendre aux Architectes un service que personne ne leur a rendu. Je vais lever un coin du rideau qui leur cache la science des proportions. Si j'ai bien vû les choses, ils en profiteront. Si j'ai mal vû, ils me relèveront, la matière sera discutée et la verité se fera jour.[6]

Not far from Laugier's position, Memmo, reports Lodoli's thought:

It is the philosopher that brings the light of reason to the darkness of principles and rules: to him the legislation, to the artist the execution.

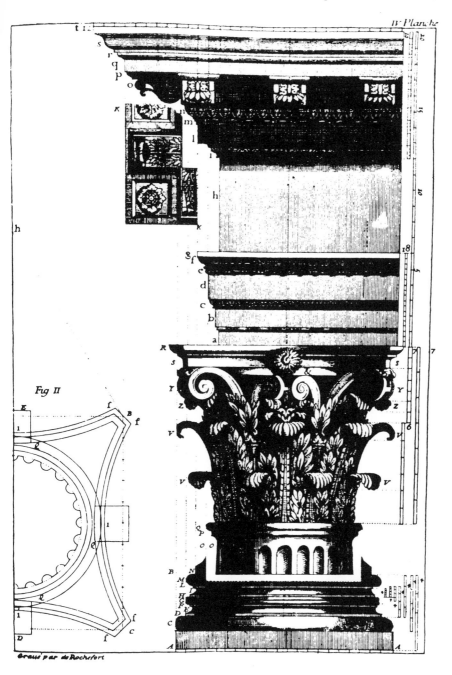

15. Rochefort, Corinthian order engraved for the *Nouveau Traité de toute l'Architecture* by Cordemoy (1706)

> Poor the artist that is not a philosopher, and even poorer if, not being one himself, from the philosopher he does not take guidance.[7]

The technician of rational analysis and the technician of the form are, then, split into two different figures: even if 'artist' and 'philosopher' co-exist in the same person, the two processes - critical-analytical and configurative - can be isolated and re-joined only *a posteriori*. The critic is the depository of the rationality and of the internal coherence of language while the architect confirms, by his activity, the range of applicability of that language.

What is behind this division of competence and this apparent dogmatism?[8] A theorist such as Milizia, with his eclectic experience of the first wave of Illuminist criticism, expresses it fairly clearly:

> The philosophical spirit, attacked by some as the destroyer of good taste, extends itself to everything. A half-way Philosophy takes one farther from the truth, but a well-meant Philosophy leads to it.... How could, then, the true philosophical spirit be opposed to good taste? On the contrary it is its stronger support, because it goes back to the true principles, it recognises that every Art has its own nature, every object its particular colour and character; in one word it does not confuse the limits of each different kind.[9]

The *Philosopher's* research, then, is into the structure and meaning of language. While criticism is at once a yardstick of the norms drawn from the rational analysis of history used according to present needs, the deduction of new norms from the operative experience (see, for example, the principle of *variety*, the concessions to Gothic and eastern suggestions, the interest towards an architectural *picturesque*) and a constant check of the quality, in the process already in action to quantify architectural production.[10]

History has, therefore, an instrumental value. For Laugier and Milizia - but not for Lodoli, perhaps the first to carry out a pitiless and determined *reduction* of architecture *to pure present* - and for Voltaire in his *Siècle de Louis XIV*, Illuminism is the landing stage of the history of man.[11] The future becomes the object of many expectations but, as Reason is taking the place of authority,

> ... to answer with examples and with authority, is not answering at all. Consequently Art is left in perpetual motion, and exposed to continuous upheavals: in executing it under the guidance of authority and examples, one is like the blind who are led by the blind and the helpless, not to the right path, but to be lost in errors. What one needs is

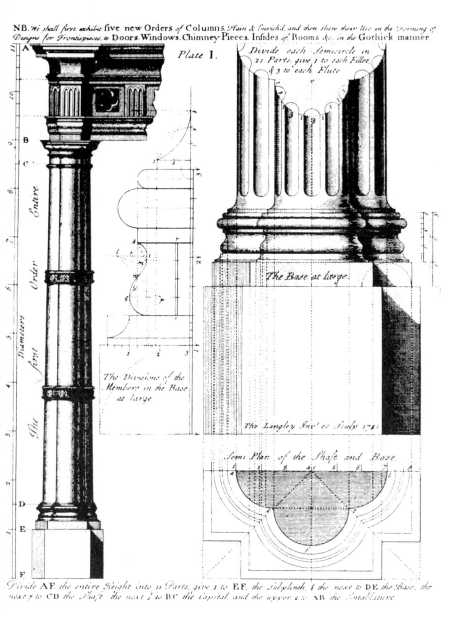

NB. *We shall first exhibit* five new Orders *of* Columns. *Plain & Enrich'd, and then shew their Use in the forming of Designs for Frontispieces, to* Doors, Windows, Chimney-Pieces, Insides *of* Rooms &c. *in the* Gothick *manner.*

16.   T. Langley, Contamination of classic order and Gothic structure. From B. and
T. Langley, *Gothic Architecture improved by Rules and Proportions*, London 1747, Plate I

true and constant principles deduced from the nature of the thing itself. From these principles Reason may draw the right consequences about what should be done or not be done in Architecture. Only then will we have a trusty and sure guide to lead us safely to our goal.[12]

Historicism and anti-historicism, inductive and deductive methods, rational examination and arbitrary choice, all merge in Illuminist criticism. Ambiguity is the condition that gives criticism the absolute leading role in the artistic revolution of the second half of the eighteenth century, preceding, with its pitiless analysis, the work of the architects that will put an end to the great chapter of Classicism.

Illuminist criticism, which is able to project into the future only the results of a colossal work of rationalisation, desecretion and systematic control, tends to overlap reflection and operation but it avoids turning on itself the weapons of criticism. The ambiguity of Illuminist criticism is the ambiguity of operative criticism: it touches Laugier as well as Milizia, Boito as well as Selvatico, Dvorák, Giedion and Kaufmann. It is an ambiguity, besides, that operative criticism accepts willingly and consciously. With fine insight, Zevi recognised, in a famous passage by De Sanctis, the manifesto of the identification of civil and critical courage that characterises historians like Compagni, Dvorák and Wickhoff (and, we would certainly add, Zevi himself):

> Dino's Compagni Chronicle and the three Chronicles of the Villanis cover the thirteenth century. The first tells us of the fall of the Whites, the other three of the rule of the Blacks. Among the losers were Dino and Dante, among the victors the Villanis. The latter tell with quiet indifference, as if drawing up an inventory; the former write history with a dagger. Those happy with the surface, let them read the Villanis; but those who want to know the passions, the customs, the characters, the interior life where facts come from, let them read Dino.[13]

History written with a dagger: it is not by chance that Dino Compagni is among the *losers*, and, rather more importantly, that he is involved in a revolutionary historical moment. He may not be objective, because, unable to use the dagger in the civil struggle, he discharges his anger into his writings: not able to change, in politics, the course of the events, he forces instead written history. It is not by chance, on the other hand, that history and *operative* criticism both flourish in two typical situations: when an uneasy stasis renders necessary a new courage, stimulated by criticism; and when an artistic revolution is establishing itself and needs the clarifying and divulging support of a deeply involved and committed historiography.

These are opposite situations: Camillo Boito, Viollet-le-Duc, James Fergusson are the historians that precipitate the impatient request for a new architecture, in the second half of the nineteenth century. Diderot, Apollinaire, Behne and Pevsner are the allies of the fundamental revolutions in modern art while, around 1945, Sartre, Vittorini and Zevi are among the champions, in Europe, of an ideological wave trying to fill the gap between civil commitment and cultural action. [14]

Action is always, anyway, the specific dimension of operative criticism. It starts – even in its eighteenth-century forms – from the discovery of the *active* qualities inherent in any form of contemplation, and from the introduction of a high degree of identification of thought and action.

In order to find the precedents for this extension of the operativity of criticism to historiography, we must go back to the ideological historicism of Pugin, Ruskin and, mainly, of Fergusson.

Fergusson's work is in many ways ahead of its time. His historical study is all directed towards finding, in the evolution of past forms, the link that will help create a theory of architecture valid for his contemporaries. It seems, therefore, that the dichotomy between *history* and *theory*, introduced by Leroy in 1758, has been left behind. But Fergusson's historical relativism, by simply showing how Renaissance, Chinese or Indian architecture adhered to functions and social customs in order to bring the nineteenth-century architects to an anti-eclectic study of the conditions and needs of their time, becomes a sterile moralism. [15]

The fact that Fergusson (like Viollet-le-Duc) contested the dualism between the history of art and the 'theory of art', sanctioned in 1818 by the statutes of the *Ecole des Beaux-Arts*, revised by the French Government (after Leroy's *Ruins of the Most Beautiful Monuments in Greece*), has not been without consequences in the historiographical field. [16] To re-join history and theory meant, in fact, making history itself into an instrument of theoretical reasoning elevated to a planning guide; and it is – at least at first – of secondary importance that Ruskin on one side and Viollet-le-Duc on the other (with Boito in an independent position) gave this lesson almost opposite interpretations.

The attempt to *actualise* history, to turn it into a supple instrument for action, has deep roots in nineteenth-century historicism. And it should not surprise us if we see in the contribution of some members of the Viennese School the decisive step towards a modern 'operative' historiography.

In his 1895 *Wiener Genesis*, Wickhoff bravely introduces, on the basis of a tried philosophical certainty, an exceptionally wide diachronic analysis, bringing out the value of the reliefs of the Titus Arch by referring to the breath of Velazquez's paintings, and the quality of the Pompeian third style, going back, on one hand, to ancient Egyptian iconography, and, on the other, projecting its meaning onto eighteenth- and nineteenth-century *chinoiseries*. But it is Dvorák, even before Lukács, who legitimises historiographical transvaluation as a specific critical method.

> What Michelangelo painted and sculpted in his last years [Dvorák wrote] seems to belong to another world . . . having reached the extreme limits of art, he faces, then, the most profound questions of existence: why does man live and what is the relationship between the passing, terrestrial and material values of humanity, and the eternal, the spiritual, the supernatural?
>
> Materialistic culture is nearing its end. And I am not thinking of the external ruin, which is only a consequence, but of the interior crisis that, for a whole generation, can be observed in all the fields of spirtual life, of philosophical and scientific thought, where the sciences of the spirit have taken the lead . . . of literature and art that have turned, as during the Middle Ages and Mannerism, to the absolute value of the spirit, abandoning objective criteria; and above all of the reconciliation of all the events that seem to point the mysterious course of human destiny towards a new spiritual and anti-materialistic age.[17]

. . . Max Dvorák's words in his famous lecture on Greco and Mannerism, in 1920. The revaluation of everything in the past that might be taken as a precedent for the *way beyond materialism* of which Dvorák dreamt and for a positive interpretation of Expressionism – which last motive places his interpretation of Mannerism within a whole tendency of German historiography[18] – sets the tone of his transvaluations.

But at this point we must ask two questions: why shouldn't Expressionism and the situation of modern art and thought be examined in themselves, rather than be seen only fleetingly through distorting the past? And does the projection (on history and on the present) of the historian's personal ideology really help the knowledge of things and the action on them, once this ideology has taken the place of the objective survey of the situation?

One can give a satisfactory answer to all this. The need of artistic avant-gardes to legitimise themselves has always led to a paradox: the new is justified by deforming the past. What happened to Expressionism (through the action of German historiography) will happen, a little later, to Cubism and Abstractionism – their ideal 'history of abstraction' will be outlined by going back to pre-history and to Minoan or Egyptian art – as has already happened to Impressionism, in another form, with regard to Japanese art.[19]

On the other hand we know today how deceptive was Dvořák's vision of the situation in the twenties. The indiscriminate superimposition of the historian's hopes and of his personal values on a reality left untouched in its true dimensions, makes Dvořák's *actualisation* quite inoperable. Instead of making history one makes *ideology*: which, besides betraying the task of history, hides the real possibilities of transforming reality.

We have not given here a complete view of Dvořák. We have insisted on the negative sides of his position because his misunderstandings are still active: it is enough to think of the success of one of the last books of his best pupil – Hauser and on the very theme of Mannerism – in spite of its naïve and mythical deformation of historical reality.[20]

A primary characteristic of both *operative* historiography and criticism has, however, come through: their didactic quality. One could add, too, that they make explicit, by forcing it, an inevitable condition typical of every history: that the philological recovery of the codes of interpretation of the past can only be achieved by starting from the present codes. History, then, is by its own nature, a balancing act, that operative criticism forces and precipitates into the dimension of the present.

Books like Giedion's *Space, Time and Architecture*, or Zevi's *Storia dell'architettura moderna* are, at the same time both, historiographical contributions and true architectural *projects*.

Let us try to analyse some of Giedion's historiographical deformations. Undoubtedly one of the most important chapters of *Space, Time and Architecture* is the one on the Sistine structures of late sixteenth-century Rome, realised under the direction of Domenico Fontana. Let us keep in mind the meaning of this historical episode within the economy of the book: in Sixtus V's street network Giedion sees one of the sources of that new dimension, perceptive and physical at the same time, that characterises the entire cycle of contemporary art. Furthermore, as the *space-time* category finds its specific setting within the urban structure, the empiricism and anti-schematism of the Sistine plan become, for Giedion, an exciting anticipation of that free and open experience of the form that the modern city has introduced into our vision of the world as the capacity for critical reception.

The 'actualisation' of historical data seems perfect, with a minimum amount of deformation, so that the thematic reading of the phenomenon seems to acquire a greater historical understanding. But if we analyse those data more deeply we find that Giedion's constant attention to the present has created a prejudice that is regularly paid for in this criticism:

paid for in those intentionally ignored aspects that could have thrown far more light on the present. Modern architects and the historians sensitive to contemporary art have willingly accepted Giedion's historicisation, and it is easy to see why. Through the reading of the Sistine structures in a modern urbanistic key, Giedion has on one side eased the minds of those architects who had started the examination in depth of the Modern Movement the hard way, by showing them how well based their studies were; on the other side he has demolished polemically an academic historiographical tradition by demonstrating its poverty and the narrowness of its instruments and arguments.[21]

This is the historical sense of Giedion's work: but we still have to judge its actuality. What has he ignored or been unable to examine with his choice of instruments? First of all the not at all innovative, indeed positively reactionary character of the Sistine plan, if it is seen within the parameters of an historiography that takes into account the earlier attempts at compromising the concept of unity of space with empirical principles (theorists and military architects from Sanmicheli to Michelangelo), the tragic failure of the secular humanist town, the thinning out into game, theatre and mere stage designs of Alberti's concept of *varietas*, the far more fundamental and earlier building regulations of Gregory XIII,[22] the universalistic and not at all libertarian meaning of the Sistine operation itself, within the stream of a long anti-humanist tradition typical of the Roman climate from the second half of the fifteenth century onwards, and, finally, the unproductiviness, in an urbanistic sense, of a street plan that, even in the late eighteenth century (as is shown by Nolli's plan), had not in the least revolutionised the urban structure of Rome and that, once filled in, has shown itself very far from constituting a significant autonomous *system*.

All the observations made so far would indicate that the modern urbanist should give up this 'safe' precedent and tradition: but we are not accusing Giedion of a mistake. When he brought out the final version of his book, his position became legitimate as is shown by its cultural productivity. If, today, his historical forcing does not satisfy us any more, and if we have made use of a more careful philology to contest it, this is because the discovery of an unstable dialectic in history, of a continual mutual presence of positive and negative, of an unresolvable multiplicity of meanings and directions matches the need to make its meanings operative.

This kind of observation can be applied to other themes that Giedion tackled, first of all the evolutive continuity of visual modes and the concept of art: what is deformed, here, is the revolutionary value of the historical avant-gardes and the fractures introduced by them at all levels.[23]

The exceptional importance of Giedion's history is in its being one of the first attempts at re-linking modern architecture to the past, as a pointer for future developments. In this sense the past is continually used as a confirmation of the present: history legitimises what is already there, has a tranquillising function and may stimulate slow or lazy experiences. This objective limitation, clear in Giedion's work, is typical of the greater part of present historiography and criticism. It is, however, a historical limitation, tied to the incidental situation, and not a limitation in the absolute sense.[24]

Operative criticism is, then, an ideological criticism (we always use the term ideological in its Marxian sense): it substitutes ready-made judgments of value (prepared for immediate use) for analytical rigour.

Now, criticism as one of the dimensions of architectural activity, has to satisfy two basic conditions:

A. It has to renounce systematic expression in favour of a compromise with daily contingencies. Its model should be journalistic extravaganza rather than the definitive essay which is complete in itself. The continuity and promptness of the polemic is, in this sense, more valuable than the single article. Criticism as intervention in depth is dropped in favour of an uninterrupted *critical process*, valid globally and outside the contradictions met in its evolution. The varying objectives of the polemic will justify the arbitrariness of the critical cuts, their alteration and the casual errors committed on the way.

B. The critical *field* will have to adjust its scale: from the analysis of the architectural *object* to the criticism of the global contexts that condition its configuration. The structure of this context – laws, regulations, social and professional customs, means of production, economic systems – will confront individual works only in a secondary way: these will appear as particular phenomena of a more general structure representing the true context on which criticism will act.

Let us consider, now, the pre-war work of Behne, Persico, Pagano, Morton Shand, the self-publicity of Le Corbusier, May, Bruno Taut, magazines like *Frühlicht*, *l'Esprit Nouveau*, *Casabella*, *Das neue Frankfurt*, and, in part, *Wasmuth's Monatshefte für Baukunst* (up to 1933, at least).[25]

This is a kind of literature that gives up an historiographical arrangement in order to bite into the present, accepting the risk of contradiction – Persico's writings, put together, give exactly the measure of this lack of concern, unusual in the traditional scholar, for the coherence of opinions in the course of time;[26] and its historical impact, compared with that of the more systematic attempts of Platz or Behrendt, is fully in its favour. We could say, in fact, that this new critical habit has found its way into the most important volumes of the historians of the Modern Movement: from Pevsner to Giedion.

Both criticism as an incessant polemical operation and the historiography of the 'Masters' of contemporary criticism are happy to produce a *short-lived*, consumable (even rapidly consumable) literature. As the judgments of value are measured by the pregnancy of events, and as planning behaviour – explicitly conditioned by consumption – is the model of operative criticism, both historiographical orientation and critical prospects can only adjust to the continuously changing criteria. It is not only the question of self-surpassing common to every scholar not riveted to a preconceived position but also, and in greater part, of an effort dictated by external conditions, by the variable pulse of events. Every scholar knows, of course, how to anchor himself to stable choices, derived from his multiform activity. Argan's constructivism guides his slashing of the later Le Corbusier, his appreciation of programmed art, and his cautious and recent acceptance of Pop Art; in the same way faith in anti-Classicism and in the *organic* myth leads Zevi to certify Le Corbusier's premature death in 1950 and his recovery after Ronchamp and La Tourette.

At this point a doubt arises of an *operative nature*. Is not confronting a cultural situation of the *consumerist* type with a *consumer criticism* an operation too much *on the inside* to be really productive? Is not *operative criticism*, in this respect, too much compromised by the attitudes of the planners to be able to bring out the non-obvious structures and the meanings implied in that very same planning?

It is a fact that the critical proposals of the last thirty years have acted as stimulants, but they have also failed to reach their objectives. Giedion's orthodoxy, in its simplification of the historical arc traced by the Modern Movement, has not been able to understand its heterodox developments (the introduction of Utzon as a representative figure of the Fourth Generation, in the last edition of *Space, Time and Architecture*, is a very significant point); the myth of *organic architecture* actively raises again, at least in Italy, a rather stagnant situation: but its use in populist and stylistic recoveries betray all its mystifying radical ideology; Hauser's sociologism appears completely unproductive; while Benevolo's, more rigorous and coherent, appears outside a dialectical conception of history, and has to exclude – in grappling with the new *myth of orthodoxy* – many of the most important experiences of contemporary architecture.[27]

The hazard of a 'planning criticism' is, then, punctually paid for: and we do not think that those who, today, have faith in it, complain excessively of it.

The problem is of a different nature, and it can be summed up in one question: if we take for granted the possibility of the presence, at the same time, of the various types of criticism, each with its well-defined role, what are the margins of validity for operative criticism? Is its insistence on taking a traditional literary form really useful, or is there already some new field of application? And, again, what is the reason for its persistence, after its obvious failures?

The simple fact that about 90% of architectural writing is produced by architects who are active in the profession, is the very important factor that answers the last question. Particularly because, if one compares the literary production of architects with that of other categories of manipulators or creators of forms – from painters to film directors – one quickly notices a singular difference. While the latter are conscious, in their writings, of giving discursive form to a personal poetic or of expressing problems relative to a highly distorted perspective, the former mostly tend to give objective form and scientific dignity to their speculations.

We do not think that the presence of a strongly distorted or instrumentalised critical and historiographical production is necessarily harmful or incorrect. If it were possible to use this kind of literature in assisting the comprehension of the methods and poetics in their evolution, or as evidence of the links between the various architectural tendencies and the problems faced by them, we could accept its accentuated tendentiousness, at least as a symptom.

Unfortunately, at least for the present, this is not possible. This is not only because of the lack of a rigorous scientific tradition in the subjects relative to architectural disciplines, but also because the way in which studies, examinations, historico-critical valuations are presented prevents the separation of a nucleus of coherent elaborations from their superimposed deformations, through the continuous confusion of cleverly disguised value judgments with the analysis of data.[28]

The historiographical salvage of the *abandoned mines* of the Modern Movement is precisely to the point here. Once these distortions have been registered it will be easier to answer the question of why there is so much interest in the actualisation of history: those committed in this sense are aware of the gap between history and architectural activity, and try to bridge it by using the historical example as a didactic and moral instrument (reduced in the worst cases to exhibitionism or moralism).

But there is not much evidence that these deformations of history have had much impact, especially on the younger generations. In the last resort, *operative* historicism fails completely, precisely in the field of concrete action: if we take for granted the inability of architects and of the public in general to state the complexity and specificity of historical events, then the actualisation of history consciously ratifies the proliferation of myth. And myth is always against history.

When Zevi, however, forces the intentions of Biagio Rossetti, or intentionally ignores the ambiguity of Borromini, if we keep in mind that we are not facing a *planning of history* we will not be so naïve as to take his propositions in a mere historiographical sense. The tension and interests behind those readings of the past filtered through hopes for the future are autonomous facts, and go beyond their productivity: they must, in fact, be valued as *projects*. [29]

Why not, then, use the instrument of the image directly, explicitly overlaying research and planning in a unitary plexus that would free historical analysis from the tasks that are not specific to it? The analysis of two critical instruments only recently introduced as such may give us some new answers.

We could charge criticism – as another of its failures – with the prevalence of pure and simple graphic and photographic images in the diffusion of architectural problems and fashions. We could try to work out a scientific and statistical study of the influence of images on the planning praxis of even the most prepared architects. Critical praise or rejection counts, in fact, less and less, when the sophisticated photographic images on the smart glossy pages of architectural magazines ooze with often cunning visual seduction. But it would be childish to be scandalised by this phenomenon, typical of the present cultural situation.

The problem consists, in fact, in controlling the images rather than showing them casually, in a sort of self-service for architect-consumers: it consists, too, in being able to *speak critically* through the images.

The first way is the most difficult and, so far as we know, has not been attempted yet: Italian and foreign magazines are not all that concerned about the selection and the significant arrangement of their material. And we must add that since a real committed magazine does not exist today – apart from marginal, confused and insignificant attempts like *Carré Bleu*, *Archigram* and the architectural section of *Marcatrè* – we cannot see by what principles an operation of this kind could be conducted.

The second way – the critical use of the camera – has, on the other hand, been attempted, and is becoming more and more widespread. Among the most significant examples are those by Zevi, Benevolo and Portoghesi. But already we are beginning to see the dangers of this way. Like any other critical research based on the instrumentation of images, 'critical photography' risks being caught by the very devil that it is trying to exorcise: it often ends by becoming an end in itself, an autonomous image only very slightly related to the linguistic structures that it is trying to explore.

How can photography lend itself to a critical interpretation? As it offers us fixed and isolated images of a whole that it is defined as a *process* (architecture or town), it becomes obvious that its main characteristic is the elimination of the temporal succession of images. The photographic sequence that reproduces the physical movement of the observer *in* an architecture, will assume a naturalistic and descriptive value, certainly very useful but not very suitable to a critical narrative.

One of the specific instruments for the critical use of photography is, then, the accentuation of representational discontinuity. The suspension of the moment and of the single image from the spatial-temporal continuity of the organism, can be used to focus aspects such as articulation, organicity, disaggregation, proper to isolated spaces and linguistic elements: in such case the pausing of the camera on the single element takes the character of a *reductio ad absurdum*.

The critical use of the camera is, then, by its own nature, strongly anti-naturalistic. The deformation of the architectural object tears the building from its context and from the perception and interpretative laws specific to the time in which it was built and places it in a new context, ruled by an already familiar a-perspective, fragmentary and discontinuous reading code.

Critical photography fixes, therefore, the ambiguous meeting of the structure of the work and the arbitrariness of its interpretation. Consequently, the camera makes explicit and evident the vast range of interpretations that the architectural text can make available and the problem of setting limits to this arbitrariness becomes a rather difficult one.

The rigorous use of the camera can, then, make concrete the systematic and intentional misunderstanding of the philological reality of architecture and the urban environment. (The same observations apply to the use of the cine-camera – according to Ragghianti's theory; while the possibilities of the television screen would require an altogether different study.)

We must also emphasise here, the fact that a careful photographic *montage* of, for example, naturalistic and critically deformed pictures, arranged in a contrasting order, can make more objective the photo-graphic irrealism that finds its compensation and clarification in the photographs' relationship with the literary text.

We are left, however, with the problem of critical communication through images. And architectural magazines should feel particularly committed to make full use of this information channel that, with time, could change from a mere visual hedonism into a formidable operative instrument.

In the last ten years we have seen the appearance of a new type of operative criticism, that takes up an aspect of the architectural culture of the twenties, widening it and developing it from new bases. Faced with the studies of Smithson, Copcutt, De Carlo, Aymonimo and Aldo Rossi on the architectural aspects of urban morphology, of Canella and Gregotti on the town structures in respect of the infra-structural systems, of Copcutt and Tange on the ability of the architectural fragment to give new meaning to a preconstituted environment, of a great part of English culture on the problem of housing, of the LCC on Hook 'New Town' and of the Buchanan Report Commission on traffic systems and their implications in the city-plan, we can certainly speak of a new boom in *typological criticism*.[30]

'Criticism' because it carries out its research from the vast mass of existing material: it departs from the analytical studies of the Masters of European 'rationalism' and their followers – Taut, Klein, Hilberseimer – because of its historicistic character. 'Typological' because it insists on formally invariant phenomena: here the meaning of the term 'typology' changes radically, because it has to be redefined each time according to the concrete problems facing it. (Its size can be reduced to the study of a single *object*, and immediately afterwards can stretch out to consider that very same object in its urban thematic; or it can touch on brand new themes, formulated on a pure experimental basis; the themes, for example, of the directional and tertiary structures of the town and of service systems not necessarily realisable into buildings.) The *operative* character of this typological criticism is due to the contemporary nature of its planning choices, even if only on the level of the structure of the image.

When the Smithsons and the *Buchanan Report* hypothesise a stratified and complex urban structure, intersected by through routes, or when Canella and Aymonimo examine the problem of directional systems with instruments that are already within the configurative process, they go beyond the simple checking of available data and studies, although remaining on this side of true and genuine planning.

There are, in fact, two types of critical values in these analytical perspectives. On one side the object of criticism is the architectural situation. The style of the studies confirms it: the very kind of appraisal of the renewing qualities of the formally and functionally complex and multi-valent (or, on the contrary, simple and mono-valent) systems, spread in regional areas and without a proper physical structure (or precisely located and perfectly structured in an architectural dimension), *open* to time and space (or *closed* in their definition of monumental objects) gives a typically operative angle to the reading of the architectural phenomena.[31]

On the other hand we have a criticism of the urban system as such. Rather than follow an ideological criticism, according to the tradition that goes from Pugin to Mumford, the critical stream we are dealing with takes reality as its starting point and models on it a reading immediately translated into systems that modifying its single components, or, in extreme cases, its fundamental laws.

It is obvious, anyway, that typological criticism is an essentially urban criticism. Furthermore, this type of research strongly contests apocalyptic ideologism, resulting from the many readings of the town carried out by the criticism of visual arts.

In place of a sterile utopianism, with its empty intentions to change, in one single sweep of re-planning, the entire urban environment (in its form and institutions), in place of the aristocratic detachment with which the critics of the contemporary city see its secondary phenomena as fundamental, the typological studies we are speaking of share the common feature of a temporary suspension of judgment as regards the city in its global character, in favour of concentrating the analysis on limited sector-environments, that are seen, however, as among the most vital aspects of urban structure.

Realism, then, in the choice of the samples, and unprejudiced experimentalism in the formulation of the new *models*. Even if differently orientated, Aldo Rossi's studies on the role of the *primary places* of the town, Canella's on the urban morphology and on the educational and theatrical systems of Milan, Aymonimo's analysis and projects for the directional system of Bologna, all converge on this very point.[32]

In their function as critical analyses they upset, examine, reassemble in new forms, the structural elements that the contemporary city tends to see as immutable and undisputable values. In their function as operative criticism, they commit themselves, immediately afterwards, to the formulation of planning hypotheses that will make clear to everyone: first, the possibility of different solutions from those passed off as real and natural by the *consumption conditioned town*; second, the connection between formal ideas and new typologies, within the compass of the new relationships between urban morphology and architectural *figures*. In this type of experience, historical analysis, critical examination, critical function of the image and demonstrative value of planning, are all indissolubly connected.

Historically style, they carry on the typically Illuminist tradition: Pierre Patte's *Essai sur l'architecture théatrale* (1782), Tiercelet's *Architecture moderne* (1727), J. F. Blondel's *Distribution des maisons de plaisance* (1737), Loudon's *Encyclopaedia of the Cottage* (1833), Baltard's volume on prison architecture (1829), and Louis Bruyère's treatise on building typology – beside the better known writings and drawings by Ledoux, Boullée, Durand and Dubut –[33] distinguish themselves from the pure functionalist treatises because of the determining value they give to the images and to the figurative formulations of the new functional programmes. Through the particular, typological criticism carries on, whatever its ideal bases may be, an operation of proposals in respect of the present dimension of planning.

By not taking for granted an *a priori* existence of well-defined forms to which the idea of organism relates – in extreme situations, as in some studies on city services, one can deny the necessity of a precise configuration for structures such as educational and tertiary systems in favour of their diffusion in the city – typological criticism continuously takes its problem back to the origin of the architectural phenomenon. These studies are compelled to continuously redefine architecture and then, each successive time, to reject it, to salvage it, to upset its meaning: not on the bases of abstract generalisations, but by founding the research for a new quality on the solid ground of the partial questions asked by architecture of architecture. It is in this sense that these studies are far more linked to Illuminist criticism than to orthodox functionalism. Not taking for granted even the physicality of the organisms or the possibility of defining some functions (we are thinking, for example, of the debate on the *containers*), typological criticism puts again in question all the problems that functionalist literature had taken as already solved. *Form* becomes, now, an object of study as a typological theme in itself – from opposite quarters, both Louis Kahn and Aldo Rossi have insisted on this theme – and the models formulated in the laboratory begin to create new instruments to check their hypotheses. Here we find the entire inheritance of the Modern Movement undergoing a operative critical

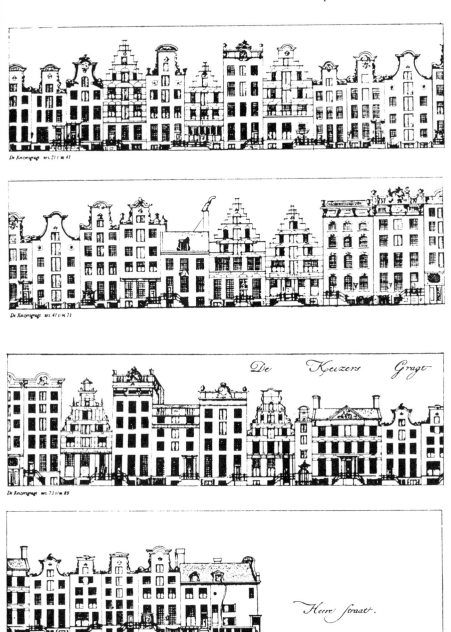

17.   Profile of the Keizersgracht in Amsterdam, from *Grachtenboeck von Caspar Philips*. In the Dutch experiences of the seventeenth- and eighteenth-centuries building typology and urban morphology are smoothly integrated

valuation. The point of view of typological criticism is not exactly historical: but it manages *to become* historical by using instrumentally the results of historical criticism as a support for its current analysis.

When Kahn, Copcutt, Samonà and Aymonimo, in their experimental projects for directional systems (we are referring to the project for *Market East* in Philadelphia, for the Glasgow regional system, for the Turin Directional centre), set up a dialectic between symbolic value of the organism in its complex but *finite* articulations, and open and flexible functional systems, they put in crisis the entire tradition of the *città di tendenza* typical of the Modern Movement.[34] It is for this reason that those projects lean on complex analyses, being nothing more than possible exemplifications of their results.

Typological criticism, in this sense, is beginning to create independently a new critical history of the Modern Movement: the interaction between literary instruments and graphical instruments ensures an easy operative diffusion, charged with new responsibilities in respect of the traditional typological studies. And we must add that its deformations, typical of every operative criticism, are perfectly justifiable: its historiographical instrumentalism, with its perspective on experimental planning choices, is taken for granted.

Having started from critical experiences that are trying to overcome the traditional barriers between criticism and the concrete intervention, we have come to an in-between land where, we think, history, criticism and planning can all meet with mutual advantage.

The problem facing us now is the following: does this new type of operative criticism absorb all the qualities proper until now to the various disciplines converging on it, or are there still some specific spaces left for them? And if these spaces do exist, how can history and planning realign themselves as regards planning?

In other words, it does seem that the historian is, at this point, faced with two choices:

A. Either to regain a specific role, concentrating his attention on his own autonomous instruments, renouncing the role that can be carried out much better by the new architectural disciplines placed somehow between criticism, the empirical science of planning methods and planning itself.

B. Or to shape his own studies as a specialist destined to have a role within an inter-disciplinary group formulating new architectural and urbanistic programmes.[35]

But note that in both cases the result will be an operative criticism raised to a higher level, with all the attendant ambiguities. Typological criticism and purely contestive criticism, unable to recognise the ideological roots of architecture *as discipline*, show themselves to be instruments of the integration of criticism and the proposals. (And here the role that Illuminist culture gave to the *Philosopher* is definitely ended: today, the historian, rather than working out comprehensive visions of architecture, finds partial causal connections, always on the point of being contested.)

But before specifying any further the possible present tasks of the criticism of ideologies, we should move our analysis to the structure of its working tools.

Notes to chapter 4

[1] Calvesi has spoken recently of 'planning criticism', not so much as a 'guide' to artistic activity, but as an influence on artistic processes due to stimuli that do not require to be exactly realised. Cf. M. Calvesi, Introduction to *Le due avanguardie*, op. cit. Cf. also: V. Gregotti, *Il territorio dell' architettura* op. cit. and E. Garroni, *La crisi semantica delle arti* op. cit. (chap.: Conclusioni e prospettive storico-critiche, p. 305 ff. in particular).

[2] On these aspects of the *Vita de' pittori, scultori et architetti moderni* by Gio. Pietro Bellori (Rome 1672), cf. C. L. Ragghianti, *I Carracci e la critica d'arte nell'età barocca*, op. cit.; D. Mahon, *Studies in Seicento Art and Theory*, London 1947; Erwin Panofsky, *Idea. Ein Beitrag zug Begriffgeschichte der alteren Kunsttheorie*, Leipzig-Berlin 1924; Ferruccio Ulivi, 'Il classicismo' in *Galleria di scrittori d'arte*, Sansoni, Florence 1953, p. 165 ff.; Paolo Marconi, *Giuseppe Valadier*, Officina, Rome 1964 (Introduction).

[3] The famous letter to Leo X, attributed to Raphael, is, for more than one reason, the 'manifesto' of classicist historicism: its condemnation of the Gothic has a decisiveness and clarity of ideas, unknown to, for example, Ghiberti's *Commentari*, and fixes the 'field' within which sixteenth-century Classicism admits the positive nature of history. In this sense this text clarifies what is already present in the more advanced culture and it does not put forward new possibilities of action.

[4] Bellori's intellectualism cannot be too decisively contrasted with Tesauro's 'conceptism': from our standpoint both are exponents of a renewed conscience of the operative value of reflection on art – not the least consequence of the new post-Tridentine climate. On Tesauro's *Cannocchiale aristotelico o sia Idea dell'arguta e ingegnosa elocuzione che serve a tutta l'arte oratoria lapidaria e simbolica*, etc. (1655), cf. G. R. Hocke, *Die Welt als Labyrinth* op. cit.; id., *Manierismus in der Literatur*, Rowohlt Taschenbuch, Hamburg 1959; Andreina Griseri, *Le metamorfosi del Barocco*, Einaudi, Turin 1967 (chap. VI in particular, pp. 147–68, and notes 1–6, pp. 168–71, with an extensively annotated bibliography.)

[5] Cf. Jacques-François Blondel, *Architecture Françoise*, Paris 1752; id. *Cours d'architecture*, Paris 1781, and, on Blondel's theories: Louis Hautecoer, *Histoire de l'architecture classique en France*, Paris 1943; Anthony Blunt, *Art and Architecture in France, 1500–1700*, Penguin Books, Harmondsworth 1953; E. Kaufmann, *Architecture in the Age of Reason*, op. cit.; R. Middleton 'J. F. Blondel and the Cours d'Architecture', in: *Journal of the Society of Architectural Historians*, 1959, p. 140 ff. On Campbell's *Vitruvius Britannicus* (London 1715) and on the English neo-Palladian movement see, besides Kaufmann op. cit., John Summerson, *Architecture in Britain, 1630–1830* op. cit.; N. Pevsner, 'Palladio and Europe' in *Atti del XVIII Congresso Internazionale di storia dell'arte*, Venice 1956, p. 81 ff; R. Wittkower, 'Lezioni sul palladianesimo inglese', in: *Bollettino del Centro Internaz. di studi di architettura A. Palladio*,

1959, I, p. 65 ff., 1960, II, p. 77 ff., and id. 'La letteratura palladiana in Inghilterra' ibid. 1965, VII/II, p. 126 ff.

[6] M. Antoine Laugier, *Observations sur l'Architecture*, The Hague 1765, le partie, p. 4.

[7] A. Memmo, *Elementi dell'architettura lodoliana*, etc. Rome 1786, vol. I, p. 177. Milizia will take up this proposition again and insert it (as usual, without quoting the source – a habit that provoked Temanza's protests) in the first part of his *Principij*: 'An ancient Sage said that it belongs to the Poet to make poetry, to the Musician to make music, but that it does not belong to the Philosopher to speak well of either. It is the philosopher (always an odious name) that brings the light of reason to the darkness of principles and rules; to him the legislation: to the artist the execution. Pity the Artist that is not a philosopher, and even more pitiful if, not being one himself, from the Philosopher he does not take guidance.' F. Milizia, *Principij di Architettura civile*, Finale 1781, part 1, p. 277.

[8] In fact most of the theorists of the second half of the Settecento compensate the manualistic analysis by identifying the sectors in which the architectural experiment can enjoy an independent articulation. For both Laugier and Milizia, the *variety* of the Picturesque is linked to its *naturality*: the *ingenious* intersection of unusual geometrical figures compensates for the rigorism of the reference models, leaving the combinatory play of the figures quite recognisable. The problem for them, as for Peyre, Neufforge, Camus de Mézières, Soane and then for Valadier, Poccianti, Quarenghi, consisted in the analytical check of all the assembly stages of the architectural product. Nature's authority (schematised and reduced to *code* by Morelly) filled the gap between rigorism and articulation. See some interesting observations on the topic in: Giorgio Grassi, *La costruzione logica dell'architettura*, Polis (Marsilio), Padua 1967.

[9] F. Milizia, op. cit. part I, p. 24.

[10] Eighteenth-century criticism expresses perfectly its 'functionality' by placing itself at the forefront of an architectural production more and more spread out and left to the *professionals* rather than to a few exceptional intellectuals. 'Not even England [Milizia writes (op. cit. part I, p. 25)] has now a Newton, a Locke, a Pope, a Jones, but it too is more than ever flourishing in every kind of Science and Art ... the fact that in a nation there does not appear a man greatly above the rest may sometimes be due to a universally spread culture; as in a well-formed wood where no tree towers above the others, because all the trees have grown well and they are all of more or less the same size.'

[11] Dilthey's work on Illuminist historicism is very illuminating on the subject: Wilhelm Dilthey, *Il secolo XVIII e il mondo storico*, Comunità, Milan 1967. See also, on the relations between architectural renewal and eighteenth-century historicism: Peter Collins, *Changing Ideals in Modern Architecture. 1750–1950*, Faber & Faber, London 1965, chapter: The Influence of Historiography, p. 29 ff.

[12] F. Milizia, op. cit. part I, p. 29.

[13] Cf. B. Zevi, 'Uno storico ancora vitale: Franz Wickhoff', in: *Annuario*

dell'Istituto Universitario di Architettura di Venezia, and in *Pretesti di critica* op. cit. p. 20 ff.

[14] All the theoretical works by the 'romantics' (such as Boito and Selvatico) should be re-read on those lines. Totally unsatisfactory, as regards this subject is, Carroll L. V. Meeks, *Italian Architecture 1750-1914*, Yale University Press, New Haven and London 1966. On Viollet-le-Duc, besides the few perceptive pages by Renato De Fusco in *L'idea di architettura*, Comunità, Milan 1965, cf. *Viollet-le-Duc, 1814-1879*, a commemorative volume by the Classe Nationale des Monuments Historique, Paris 1965, with a complete bibliography and an exceptional amount of reference material. In the text we are mainly referring, apart from Vittorini's contributions on 'Politecnico' from 1945 onwards, to the famous presentation by Sartre of the magazine: *Temps Modernes*, later in *Situations I, II, III*, Gallimard, Paris 1947, '48, '49, and to the programmatic manifesto of the APAO (Associazione per l'architettura organica) in *Metron* 1945, no. 2, pp. 75-6.

[15] Cf. J. D. Leroy, *Ruins of the Most Beautiful Monuments in Greece*, London 1758; James Fergusson, *History of Architecture*, London 1855. Note that Fergusson represented the rationalist wing of nineteenth-century British culture – anti-eclectic and antithetic to Ruskin's romanticism.

[16] P. Collins has insisted on these aspects of eighteenth-century theories and on the move from the split caused by Leroy to a new synthesis, in *Changing Ideals in Modern Architecture* op. cit., and in the article: 'Oecodemics', in *The Architectural Review*, 1967, no. 841, in which, by criticising some of Banham's propositions in a review of R. De Fusco's *L'idea di architettura* op. cit., he re-states the importance of a modern 'theory' as an approach to architecture. In Collins's book the analysis of the nineteenth-century architectural magazines, from *The Builder* to the *Revue Générale de l'Architecture*, is significant to the birth of the modern operative criticism.

[17] Max Dvorák, 'Ueber Greco und den Manierismus' in *Repertorium für Kunstwissenschaft*, 1925, no. 46, pp. 243-62. But Dvorák's lecture was given on October 28, 1920. On Lukács' position as regards the theory of criticism as a transvaluation see: G. Lukács, *Beiträge zur Geschichte der Aesthetik*, Berlin 1954.

[18] The German historians' studies on Mannerism are deeply linked, whether intentionally or not, to a reading of an anti-classical, expressionist or surreal key of sixteenth-century art: from the analyses of Friedländer to those of Loni Ernst, Michalski, Hoffman, Gombrich and Wittkower, this transvaluation has dominated the main contributions on the Cinquecento. Cf. for a synthetic and to the point panorama on this theme: Maria Luisa Becherucci, item: 'Maniera' in the VIII vol. of the *Enciclopedia Universale dell'Arte*, coll. 803-14.

[19] On the value of oriental art, seen as historicisation of the European avant-garde artistic movements in 1800 and the early 1900s, cf. C. L. Ragghianti, *Mondrian e l'arte del XX secolo*, Comunità, Milan 1962, chapter: 'Il contenuto storico della sintesi matura: l'architettura dell'Estremo Oriente' and the works quoted in the notes.

[20] The distance between an abstract historicism, bent on an indiscriminate 'actualisation' of the past as brilliant as it is rapidly consumable, and a more careful reflection on history's specific value, can be measured by comparing two texts on Mannerism: Arnold Hauser, *Der Manierismus. Die Krise der Renaissance und der Urprung der modernen Kunst*, C. H. Bek'sche, Verlag, Munich 1964; and John Shearman, *Mannerism*, Penguin Books, Harmondsworth (cf. in partic. chap. IV, p. 135 ff. in which the author expresses his historiographic criteria).

[21] Giedion ignored, because it would have opposed his historical reading, the introduction in the street plan of the figure '*in sideris formam*', justified by a typical rhetorical 'concept'. It is still the celestial Jerusalem that is mirrored, like a cosmogonic projection, in the network of the seven Roman Basilicas. In this sense the easy reading of the network has a double justification: firstly functional, and secondly propagandist and persuasive. (Cf. Franciscus Bondinus, *De rebus praeclare gestis a Sixto V*, Rome 1588; D. Fontana, *Della transportatione dell'Obelisco Vaticano et delle fabbriche di Nostro Signore Papa Sisto V, fatte dal Cav. D. F.* etc., Rome 1590. The chapter on Sisto V, like those on *Prospettiva e Urbanistica e Leonardo e gli inizi dei piani regionali* were added by Giedion to the Italian edition (Hoepli, Milan 1954) of *Space, Time and Architecture* (1st ed. Harvard Univ. Press, Cambridge 1941).

[22] The importance of Gregory XIII's urban statues has been recently recognised by P. Portoghesi in *Roma barocca* op. cit., pp. 26-7. Portoghesi, although justifying the novelty of the Sistine plan against the criticism of D'Onofrio's, who had called Sistus V 'the last medieval urbanist', recognises in the building policy of the Pope 'not a sudden turning away from the building tradition of his predecessors, but rather a widening and a generalisation of that tradition'. (Ibid. p. 27. Cf. also: Cesare D'Onofrio, *Gli obelischi di Roma*, Rome 1965.)

[23] Dorner sharply criticised *Space, Time and Architecture* (in: *The Way beyond 'Art'*, op. cit.) as regards Giedion's indiscriminate use of concepts like 'space' and 'art'. The opposition between Dorner and Giedion is interesting because it illustrates the clash between two types of operative criticism; Dorner's position is more within the new dimensions dictated by contemporary movements, while Giedion's is half-way between Dorner's and a more traditional evaluation.

[24] Zevi wrote the 'manifesto' of his historiographic method in: 'Attualità di Michelangiolo architetto' (in *Michelangiolo architetto*, Einaudi, Turin 1964, Introduction). This is doubtless the work in which the meaning of a modern operative historiography comes out most clearly and incisively. The relations found by Zevi between 'the world of the Abstract, of siding with annihilation and death, of social protest, of the sterile vitalism' of the twentieth century, and 'the politico-religious reaction, the intellectualism and the virtuoso elegance of the second half of the sixteenth century' are, not by chance, very near to those proposed, forty years earlier, by Dvořák. (Cf. M. Dvořák, op. cit., passim.)

[25] The continuous and insistent activity of avant-garde magazines represented the most suitable means for a really operative criticism. Between the twenties and the thirties there are, however, two types of commitment in print. The breakaway type of the magazines *Das Andere, G, Frühlicht, l'Esprit*

Nouveau, and the less avant-garde, less interested in the diffusion of the civil objectives of the new architecture, typical of the magazines edited and founded by Ernst May: *Schlesiche Heim,* and *Das Neue Frankfurt.* (Cf. the collection of the magazine *Frühlicht* 1920-22 published in the Ullstein Bauwelt Fundamente Series, Berlin 1963; Ulrich Conrads, 'Bruno Taut e la rivista *'Frühlicht'* in *Edilizia Moderna,* 1965, no. 86; Justus Buekschmitt, *Ernst May,* Koch Verlag, Stuttgart 1963.) A different type of criticism, performed almost exclusively through the selection and comparison of architectural examples, is represented by the very successful book by Alfred Roth, *The New Architecture* (1940), where he demonstrated the possibility of a *common language* for modern architecture.
[26] An analysis of Edoardo Persico's writings (published by Comunità, Milan 1964, edited by Giulia Veronesi) shows the price paid by an intellectual completely coherent with the basic principles of operative criticism: as the action's circumstances continuously change, Persico does not try to preserve a coherence of judgment in the course of time. (See his change of opinion about Loos and Le Corbusier, for example.)
[27] Until now only two ways have been tried to make 'operative' the past in the historical field. On one side are the analyses of Zevi, who, since he finds the features of architects like Alberti, Biagio Rossetti, Palladio, Sanmicheli, Michelangelo and Borromini relevant to the present, show that he is a follower of Wickhoff and Dvorák's methods. By choosing a historiographic method totally directed towards action, Zevi has to give up many objective examinations. However, given his aims, this cannot be considered the main limitation of his work. The true parameter for checking his historical criticism is the effect on the culture of active architects: and it is here that we see the failure of the operation Zevi tried. History, however deformed and made 'operative', does not become a vital stimulus for planning.

On the other side we find Benevolo's concept of history. Apparently more objective and without definitive judgments, Benevolo's 'history' inserts critical judgment into the exposition and 'montage' of the facts. Here the deformations are revealed by the 'forced' attitude with which the author chooses or ignores figures, movements and cycles of works. Also, compared to Zevi's work, Benevolo's *Storia dell'architettura moderna* is ideologically far more limited. In the end both bend history in order to demonstrate *a priori* choices for the future of architecture: what changes (and completely) is the quality of such choices.

We find an exceptional example of operative history in Ludovico Quaroni's essay: 'Una città eterna: quattro lezioni da diciassette secoli,' in *Urbanistica,* 1959, XXIX, no. 27, p. 6 ff. in which Rome's urban history is read through the filter of a strongly felt hope for a different future. Grassi's observations on modern historiography demonstrate a nucleus of problems similar to the one under analysis, though indirectly. Cf. G. Grassi, *La costruzione logica* op. cit.
[28] On the recent Italian literary production in the field of architecture cf. F. Tentori 'Le editrici di architettura e il rinnovamento delle università' in *L'Architetto,* 1967, no. 4; and V. Gregotti 'L'Architetto analfabeta' in *Quindici,* 1967, no. 6.

[29] One cannot sufficiently condemn the naïve or snobbish attempt to read historical phenomena by 'present' yardsticks of those, who, for the sake of feeling 'alive' and up-to-date, reduce critical transvaluation to exhibitionism and fashion. For example, finding a precedent for Wright in Genoa's Palazzo Rosso, for Tatlin in Borromini's S. Ivo, and a real happening (sic) in the work by the Asam brothers at Weltenburg.

[30] To define further the kind of research we are referring to we can quote the studies on housing produced by English-speaking culture, with recurring articles in *Architectural Review, Architectural Design*, etc.; the studies on university structures by Lasdun, J. L. Martin, De Carlo, etc.; research by Tange and Copcutt on the urban systems of Tokyo and Glasgow (cf. *Casabella continuità*, 1963, no. 280). Italian architectural culture has particularly developed, in the last ten years, this type of study; at first on *Casabella continuità*, from '60 to about '64, under the direction of E. N. Rogers, then with the publication of several volumes such as: *La città territorio*, Leonardo da Vinci, Bari 1964; *L'utopia della realtà. Un esperimento didattico sulla tipologia della scuola primaria*, ibid. 1965; N. Sansoni Tutino, *Scuola et territorio*, ibid. 1966; C. Aymonimo and P. L. Giordani, *I Centri direzionali*, ibid. 1967; G. Canella, *Il sistema teatrale a Milano*, Dedalo libri, Bari 1966; C. Aymonimo, 'Documenti dei corsi di caratteri degli edifici', Ist. Univ. di Arch. di Venezia, op. cit.; *Edilizia Moderna*, no. 86 (1966), special number on the form of the territory; A. Rossi, *Contributo al problema dei rapporti tra tipologia edilizia e morfologia urbana*, ILSES, Milan 1964. Argan gave an important theorical contribution in 'Sul concetto di tipologia architettonica' (in: *Boll. A. Palladio*, Lecture at the Facoltà di Architettura, Rome, and then in: *Progetto e destino* op. cit.). Also very important, among the many contributions from outside Italy, the Buchanan report on town traffic: *Traffic in Towns*, HMSO, London 1963; *The Planning of a New Town*, LCC, London 1961; G. Copcutt, *Planning and Designing the Central Areas of Cumbernauld New Town*, London 1965.

[31] The approach, for example, of Louis Kahn to the typological theme of the centre of Dacca starts from a system of figurative and functional values resolved through a closed, definitive and institutional configuration on all levels (from the symbolic to the formal): and we know very well that for Kahn every project is a pretext for a typological criticism. In the series of projects for Dacca, Kahn separates the parts to be considered fixed from those that his system of values allows freedom of formal aggregation in space and time. (Cf. Louis I. Kahn, 'Remarks' in *Perspecta, the Yale Architectural Journal*, 1966, nos. 9–10, p. 303 ff.: lecture at the Yale School of Art and Architecture, Oct. 1964; and the publication on the Dacca Capitol, Yale School, 1967.) Canella's system of values, used by him in his diagnoses on directional structures, on educational and theatrical systems, is based on the possible absorption by the urban continuity of a complex, differentiated and articulated system of functional 'loci' not necessarily architecturally defined. (Cf. G. Canella, op. cit.) This example can demonstrate the weight of initial choices in even the most objective analysis, and also their verifiability as regards formal choices with an independent *raison d'être*.

[32] Cf. A. Rossi, *L'architettura della città* op. cit.; G. Canella, 'Relazioni fra morfologia, tipologia dell'organismo architettonico e ambiente fisico' in *Utopia della realtà* op. cit., p. 66 ff.; id. *Il sistema teatrale di Milano* op. cit.; C. Aymonimo and P. L. Giordani, *I centri direzionali* op. cit.

[33] Collins made a brief historical analysis of eighteenth-century typological criticism, cf. P. Collins, *Changing Ideals* op. cit. chapters: 'Rationalism' and 'New Planning Problems' pp. 198–239. (See also: Giusta Nicco Fasola, *Ragionamenti sull'architettura*, Macrì, Città di Castello 1949, passim.) Of some interest is Aymonimo's proposed re-linking with Illuminist typological criticism, as a confirmation of the meaning given by us to the present recovery of a rigorous criticism. Cf. C. Aymonimo, *La formazione del concetto di tipologia edilizia*, IUAV, Cluva, Venice 1965; and G. Grassi, op. cit., chapters III and IV.

[34] The urban models of European Constructivism extended the typological object within the urban complex, forming a chain, perfectly described by Hilberseimer, with the town as the top link and at the end the design of the object or the residential unit. In this sense the town underwent an attempt at a figuratively verifiable global design: the administrative activity of Martin Wagner in Berlin, of Bruno Taut at Magdeburg, of Schumacher in Hamburg, of Van Eesteren in Amsterdam and of May in Frankfurt matches perfectly this failed attempt of modern urban planning. The return to an urban reading and operation *in sectors* can therefore be seen both as a 'renunciation' and as a realistic act with, perhaps, a wider understanding of the phenomena. The linking of this realism to that of American Pop Art has been implicitly identified by Donlyn Lyndon, in his acute comparison between the architects that save a few possibilities of action from the chaos of *refuse* of which the present town is composed, and the *assemblage* re-composed by Junk Sculpture. Cf. Donlyn Lyndon, 'Filologia dell'architettura americana' in *Casabella continuità*, 1963, no. 281. Cf. also G. Kallmann, *La 'Action' Architecture* etc. op. cit. which contains observations of great interest on the subject.

[35] Very interesting historiographic choices of this kind are to be found in: Reyner Banham, 'Convenient Benches and Handy Hooks. Functional Considerations in the Criticism of the Art of Architecture' in *The History, Theory*, etc. op. cit. p. 91 ff. (though we do not share his critical conclusions), and in: George A. Kubler, 'What can Historians do for Architects?' in *Perspecta*, nos. 9–10 op. cit., pp. 292–302. (We were not able to find Kubler's *The Shape of Time*, mentioned in the same magazine.)

5

Instruments of Criticism

A critical method can be established in many ways: one can start from the philosophy of art and deduce historiographic methods from it, go to already well established methodologies, to a more or less rigorous empiricism, or to fashionable analytical methods. These choices must, however, be judged on their degree of penetration into the reasons of history.

As far as we are concerned, the basis of our critical method is all contained in the previous chapters.

We have in any case already noted that we do not think it is possible to deduce a criticism from traditional aesthetics. The American semantic schools, as well as Plebe, Anceschi, Morpurgo-Tagliabue, Pagliaro and, most of all, Garroni, have, if nothing else, revealed a deep 'crisis of aesthetics'. It is a crisis that can only be solved, it seems, through a strongly historicistic attitude, able to determine, each successive time and with an eye to the future, a horizon for the study of aesthetic problems that is constantly variable and determined by the concrete experience of art's unforeseeable changes.[1] We are in complete agreement with Garroni when, taking up one of Anceschi's concepts, he writes that this horizon 'is not an a-historical methodological category, but rather a historical category (historically qualified), only valid within the limits of the *choices* of these manifestations'.[2]

This does not imply, of course, the disappearance of historiographical criticism into a historicistic aesthetics or vice versa. It implies, rather, that the two fields of studies – criticism and general reflections on art – become historically complementary. But only because they start from the same premise: the concrete experience of the dialectic inherent in the dynamic and changeable character of artistic studies.[3]

This is the most conspicuous consequence of the unavoidable crisis of any definitory aesthetics based on a static and metaphysical conception of 'art'.[4] In this sense the points made on the present conditions of architecture and criticism already belong to the study of critical methodology. The tasks and instruments of architectural criticism will be defined on those conditions. Furthermore they will have to be constantly checked, renewed and eventually revolutionised, as dictated by the changing historical contingencies.

It should be clear, therefore, that we have already stated a fundamental postulate: the identification of criticism with history. Any attempt to separate criticism and history is artificial and hides an unconfessed conservative ideology. To relegate criticism to a limbo, given to abstract analyses of the present – as if there really existed a 'present' time, quite apart from historical time – means accepting the ransom demanded by the most transient and mystifying mythologies.

Anyway, criticism always wrenches the present event from its daily context, simply by looking for its meaning and reasons: it is impossible to define those meanings and reasons without placing the artistic event back in the structure of history. Otherwise we shall not have criticism, but empty hagiography and abstract exegesis (in other words, failed criticism). The hypocrisy of these approaches to the basic themes of our time – including those of architecture – can be measured by the mountain of useless *exploits* that, day by day, threatens to crush the professional reader.[5]

For these reasons, all methods of architectural analysis based on a-historical criteria must be considered phenomena in need of historicisation: from the standpoint of criticism it does not make much sense to speak of *theory of architecture,* but it does from the standpoint of the definition of new planning instruments. It is symptomatic, in fact, that there is a demand from many quarters for the establishment of a rigorous theorisation of architectural problems. This need is felt by a considerable number of English-speaking critics – particularly by Collins[6] – by a historian like Christian Norberg-Schulz, by specialists of planning methods like Alexander and Asimow, by theorists involved in planning, like Aldo Rossi and Giorgio Grassi.[7] The reasons for the present new demand for the 'establishment' of an architectural discipline are many and differ considerably from scholar to scholar. It is, however, possible to find common features on which to base some criteria for the critical use of the vast *congerie* of studies accumulated on these themes.

We can therefore mention three basic motives for this type of research:

A. The confirmation of the loss of *public meaning*, on the part of architecture; a loss felt particularly at the level of linguistic communication.[8]

B. The need to check the meanings underlying the transformations – whether planned or not – of the physical and anthropo-geographical environment: which had produced the studies by Lynch, Kepes, Gregotti, Rossi, etc. on the form of the city, the territory and its sectors that one can use in the structurisation of architecture and the urban plan.

C. The need to substitute for the vanished linguistic unity, an objective, logical and analytical method of checking planning, to preside over planning itself.

At this point the research divides into: (1) studies such as Alexander's and those of many other American theorists, based on mathematical methods of examination, selection and assembly of data, with the intention of reaching a sort of *architectura ex machina;* (2) studies, on the contrary, like those of Rossi and Grassi, that work on rational criteria of description, classification and manipulation of the constant laws of architecture, in order to establish logical and unified methods of analysis and planning.

There is no doubt that the three motives mentioned above are only different expressions of the same concern. Even admitting that contemporary architecture grows from a revolutionary tradition, the semantic crisis that exploded in the late eighteenth and nineteenth century still weighs on its development, and it no longer seems sufficient to base the experience of architecture on *open* methodologies or on a too fragmented tradition. There is a more and more pressing request for a new institutionality of architectural language, with an equally pressing problem of direct communication with the public and of social behaviour towards images and structures. The departure from the criticism of a single section of theoretical research in the classical sense has, therefore, a precise reason. Taking architecture back to its prime elements and to its 'zero degree', introduces, in the survey of the phenomena, an objectivity that satisfies the more and more widespread wish to find not only a logical and verifiable process of form construction, but also constant and permanent principles – outside historical changes – of architecture.[9]

If criticism must place its analyses beyond such research – the research itself becoming phenomena to be historicised – it cannot ignore the needs from which it originates. The fact that we are witnessing today the decline of sociological criticism, that we have to admit the progressive depletion of operative criticism, and that many regard the need for a rigorous, verifiable and 'scientific' foundation of architectural criticism as central and unavoidable, does not mean that the new ferments have found real outlets.

The uncertainty of architectural culture following the great crises of the thirties, fifties and sixties, the new phase opened by the introduction of new and wider thematics in the last ten years, the more and more accentuated need for stricter controls of the products and of, mainly, processes and methods of planning, have for a long time put in crisis the traditional critical empiricism and the more sophisticated analysis techniques inspired by sociologism, such as those of Hauser and Antal.

The emergence, within architectural criticism, of the *language problem* is, then, a precise answer to the *language crisis* of modern architecture. The proliferation of studies on the semantics and semiology of architecture is due not only to a snobbish keeping up with the current linguistic *vogue:* every snobbism, anyway, derives its reasons from historical events, and the snobbisms of architectural culture do not escape this rule. The attempt to bring the 'sciences of man' under the unifying sign of linguistics is rooted also in the present historical situation. One looks for what has been lost, and the need for more and more complex reflex actions in order to discover the meaning of events and things, derives from the discovery that we are among *signs,* conventions, myths, that offer us artifical processes as *natural,* that manifest themselves as innocent images or rites just where they are least disinterested, and that carefully hide their meanings. From this comes semiology's frantic search for meanings; and it is up to us to make it a *new science* with a formidable capacity for demystification, or to let it become another transient fashion under the flag of evasion.

But it is clear that an architecture restless enough to turn into a self-critical study reveals the need for reading instruments able to show what is behind linguistic conventions and figurative poetics; it reveals also what has been unconsciously conditioning the architect's activity, and what, today, is the objective task of architecture and urbanism: the reduction, because of inadequate control, to dangerous persuasion techniques, or, in the best of cases, to the broadcasting of superfluous, rhetorical and exhortative messages.

For this reason those who warn against the new studies on architectural language, seeing that they hide the complex situation of the present crisis of modern architecture, its ambiguous relationship with clients, the hard struggle, still going on, for reforms of legislation, education, social and professional custom, are right so far as the explicitly evasive research goes, but not about the research that recognises all those difficulties as elements of the language itself. Nor does it seem wrong to us to project these new interests onto the past. We have known for quite a while now that historical reading is not conditioned by our commitment to the present. Even history needs to create a code of values to give sense to the past; and on this we are in substantial agreement with an heir of Crocian culture such as Sasso, an empirical historian such as Carr and an apparently anti-historical structuralist such as Lévi-Strauss.[10]

So the justification for the history of architecture is in the search for the meaning of present architecture: but it is useless to project outdated beliefs onto the past in order to solve the problems of the present. In this way architecture itself comes to be considered a problem. The apparent suspension of judgment of many recent analyses has, in its turn, a sense of unprejudiced research into the possible directions to be taken in the future.

To choose to examine architecture as a linguistic phenomenon corresponds, then, to a heart-felt search for what has evaded and still evades planning activity. But it means also avoiding running aground on the *consumption* of poetics and languages analysed by Gombrich, Dorfles and Bense.[11]

The present concern of the critic [De Fusco has written recently] is never to be surprised by the new artistic phenomenon, to have always ready a casuistry of values wide enough to contain and explain every new experience. Anyone can see in this critical activism a substantial renunciation. When anything goes, there obviously cannot be any value or any valuation; judgment is then exercised, in most cases, . . . in the hundred unsuitable ways we all know and, what is worse, among general indifference.[12]

A criticism that tries to be completely attuned to the events of architectural production can hardly avoid falling into the impasse denounced by De Fusco.

So the well-known formula of the French *nouvelle critique:* 'analyse the [architectural] language, rather than use it', can be a formidable aid in showing the mystifications contained in language itself. And the fusion of criticism and architecture in one operative methodology may still have many useful applications, but it cannot throw light on architecture's ultimate reasons. Even without making the revealing quality of criticism a determining factor, those who recognise the need for a radical clarification can only adopt a demystifying attitude by going beyond what architecture *shows,* in order to examine what it *hides.*

The price of this operation is certainly going to be a deep split between criticism and architecture. But it is as certain that this split is absolutely necessary, at least until the clash between those who use architectural language ambiguously (and we think this is undeniably the case with today's architects) and those who uncover the real meanings of architectural structures, has completely cleared the ideological and mystified character of the architectural discipline.

This premise seems to us adequate to place historically the choice of parameters and instruments for historical criticism.

The attribution to architecture of a specific range of meanings, the linguistic approach to visual communication techniques, the recognition of the structural laws shaping architectural products, the need for deep analyses to bring out the hidden mechanisms of the use and formation of language, all come directly from the themes that in the last fifteen years have become problems whose solution can no longer be deferred.

This approach to the thematics of history of architecture requires further clarification. A perfect identity of criticism and history may seem in opposition to the welcoming of structuralist themes. But we must keep in mind that: first – the possibility of a structuralist historicism remains and has been suggested by many;[13] second – the only non-metaphysical approach to structuralism is empirical, and structured, in its turn, on the concrete problems posed by the object under examination.

No doubt the reduction of the structuralist attitude to a simple analytical instrument alters the nature of the ideology underlying a rigorous structuralism. (But does *a* structuralism really exist, or are we not already into the problem of the distinction between opposing propositions?)

When dialectic historicism takes up structuralist thematics, it takes over, in fact, the weapons of the enemy.

But the alliance, already forming, between structuralism and some critical positions based on the most absolute rejection of the semantic value of architecture, is definitely not casual.[14] To deny architecture – and art in general – any sort of recognisable and explicit meaning in order to state the absolute, total and tautological character of the artistic product, has, in its turn, a meaning. When Furet (quoted in the introduction to this book), and many critics of the Marxist left analyse structuralism and bring out its ideological mystifications, they see not so much the objective contents of Lévi-Strauss's anthroplogy or Barthes's analyses, as the dangers implicit in their anti-historicist attitude.

The reduction of architecture to silence proves the *availability* of structuralism and its hidden sides behind the opening towards deeper aspects of human activity.

On the other hand, the structural reading of architecture (as has been already realised) is anything but new. The studies of Schmarsow, Frankl and Sedlmayr can be quoted as precedents, but it is interesting to note that, in Italy, Bettini's analyses not only anticipate by a couple of decades the themes in fashion today, but actually tackle the problem we have just mentioned.[15] In Bettini's fundamental introduction to the Italian translation (1953) of Riegl's *Spätrömische Kunstindustrie*, the structuralist tone turns into a beautifully measured critical method.[16] He has not only assimilated – almost alone in the Italian cultural scene of the time – the contributions of the English-based semantic schools, from Tarski to Carnap and to the *Meaning of Meaning* by Ogden and Richards, but has explicitly recognised the linguistic character of artistic production, linking the problem of criticism to, as he defines it, the paradox of metalanguage.[17] In re-examining Wickhoff's and Riegl's propositions on late Roman art and architecture, Bettini, from the standpoint of his personal interpretation of the links between antique works and the modern discovery of a space fused within a temporal dimension,[18] specifies 'that "space" and "time" are not in categorical opposition (this would take them back to nineteenth-century metaphysics, in which they represented the constant dimensions containing the phenomena: forms and events), but variable types of situations. It follows, in art criticism, that their function or prevalence can be explained by the "metalanguage" of criticism only on the basis of the *internal structure* of the works of art.'[19]

Bettini's problem is, after all, the problem of the functionality of the critical language and of the identification of the communicable aspects of the work. In his study on the instruments of criticism, he faces the great themes of modern linguistics: from the researches on the functional value of language to Moritz Schlick's study on the problem of knowledge.

Bettini's essay on semantic criticism, published in *Zodiac* in 1958, marks the meeting of the research on functional lingustics with a culture deeply immersed in phenomenological thought.[20] The themes already mentioned in the introduction to Riegl, have, here, a wider expression. Rejecting Panofsky's iconological method, Bettini starts off with an apodeictic statement: '. . . art is not representation, but formal structure of history. This is the case when we take art as language: we can then say that the language of art is the morphology of culture.'[21]

From this derives the inadequacy of any critical discourse on the meanings of the work of art: 'art as *Erlebnis* [writes Bettini][22] is not communicable through means other than the work of art itself. There should be no doubt, then, that what is communicable is the language: the *linguistic structure* of art.'

In spite of the fact that in too many ways Bettini's theses are completely antithetic to those of Brandi, as far as the problem of the semanticity of architecture goes, the two scholars seem to find many points of agreement. Brandi's most recent volume, on which he has been working for more than twenty years, takes these theses up again, and is symptomatic of the alliance between neo-idealism and structuralism. Besides, in his *Due vie*, Brandi had clearly stated the reasons that made him reject any communicative value in respect of art:

> We shall not have . . . to decode the message of the work of art as a message that structures the work of art, but, rather, as the series of messages that are channelled and pulled along by the work of art from the time of its birth, like a placenta. Therefore the work of art is not a message, it contains instead endless messages to be inferred by those who intend to make it explicit in the history where it was born and in the history where it is successively revealed.[23]

Here Brandi seems to be giving dangerous weapons to the theses opposed to his own. If the problem is to know what art *is,* we think that very few would care to follow Brandi's argument to its conclusion. The ideal isolation of Brandi's artistic phenomena does not come from an analysis of the historical phenomena, but from inductions of their essence and of their *noumenal* reality.

Brandi seems to state the supremacy of the work over any deformation caused by its being in history: in reality the statement of supremacy only expresses the critic's personal ideology, because the belief that one can define the reality of the work of art can only be taken as a statement of personal *faith.* (Mute, of course, towards its object, but eloquent towards the critic's subjective values.)

For those who do not share this kind of re-establishment of metaphysically flavoured *principia,* the artistic *object* cannot be considered a *thing,* but rather, a message *in fieri* or, if you prefer, the very (open) system of endless messages mentioned by Brandi.

In any case architecture shows continually that the very basis of its existence is in the unstable balance between a nucleus of permanent values and meanings, and their metamorphoses in historical time.

We have mentioned elsewhere the constant misunderstanding of the meanings piled up on architecture in the course of history. But we must specify that this 'misunderstanding' is not only constant but also the only way available to approach architectural reality.

Nor is this misunderstanding due only to the arbitrary use of the functions. The usual examples quoted on this topic are the possible use of the Pantheon as a commercial building, and of the Castello Sforzesco and many Dutch churches as museums or exhibition rooms. But the recently introduced perceptive distinction between *primary and secondary functions* can easily measure the historical scope of this kind of misunderstanding.[24]

There is, in fact, another way of absorbing the messages of a work of architecture: it is partial (because its complex stratification is not yet understood in its unity) but certainly more direct and authentic than the reduction to simple *use* of the contact with the work.

When Francesco di Giorgio, Giuliano da Sangallo and Baldassarre Peruzzi reproduced in their survey drawings,[25] the organism of the Oratorio della S. Croce (A.D. 461–68) near the Lateran Baptistery – so similar in plan to Hadrian's Sala della Piazza d'Oro – when Cronaca, Serlio and Palladio interpreted the organisms of the Roman Thermae in their attempts at restoration, and when Palladio and Pietro da Cortona tried to define the structures of the Prenestine Sanctuary of Fortuna Primigenia, they offered us the best possible demonstration of the (concrete because historical) dialectic that rules the deformation of an architectural message when confronted by different reading codes.

Faced with the mixtilineal, continuous and enclosed plan of the centric organism of the fifth-century Oratory, Francesco di Giorgio is lost for an adequate interpretative key. He cannot accept such a daring infraction of the classicist language, even as a curious exception. Although Francesco di Giorgio was already committed to a composition, according to an unprejudiced combinatory logic, of central matrix spaces in opposition, he cannot yet accept the principle of the elasticity of spatial filling. For this reason his 'survey' tends to reduce the scope of the contrapositions between concave and convex surfaces: the latter are represented as wall reliefs, almost as a mere bulging of the internal volume.

Francesco di Giorgio perceives perfectly, then, the *danger* charge transmitted by the Roman monument to fifteenth-century culture: in his own way, he transmits it back to us in an absolutely transparent fashion. Today, in his drawing, we can see:

A. The *heretic* value attributed to mixtilineal organisms by classicist culture.

B. The reactions to this provocation on the part of the late fifteenth-century culture and the uncertainty of the latter before the *antique* (Francesco di Giorgio deforms the building he is surveying, but agrees, at least at first, to a confrontation with it).

C. The humanist architects' identification of super-historical dialogue with architectural ideation: of the acknowledgement of the structural laws of their own formal codes with the exploration of the codes of antiquity.

All this information is referred, on one side, to the ancient archaeological finds, on the other, to Francesco di Giorgio's drawing. The first shows the presence of a specific *meaning* deformed and deformable in the course of history, the second (besides its own meanings) shows clearly its determining value in the philological acknowledgment of the humanist architectural codes.

Francesco di Giorgio carries out a real critical act, to be, in its turn, historicised and connected to the later acts of Giuliano da Sangallo and Peruzzi: the latter will not only absorb the spatial ambiguity of the Oratorio della S. Croce, but will multiply its values of tension and complexity in his Uffizi drawing,[26] allowing us to see, as in a diagram, the changes undergone by the perceptive laws and the spatial researches of Italian Classicism. And, furthermore, with his new availability towards the past he throws new light on the meaning given to history by the first experiences of Mannerism.

In this interpretation the Paleo-Christian room becomes a message with a form that admits a considerable *opening* towards the most varied decodings in the course of time. With the change of interpretative codes, the *meaning* of that particular work changes also: even if the various messages, successively read in it, pivot round a nucleus of permanent values.

Obviously, then, perceiving an architectural structure means the modification of a system of expectations, as we have learnt from modern psychology and as Gombrich has widely shown for other systems of visual communication.[27]

Let us go back to Brandi's propositions on the would-be a-semanticity of architecture, as they are presented in his most recent text:[28]

> ... the main stumbling-block [in considering architecture as language] is that any semiotic system works out a code in order to transmit a message, and this message is not transmitted by architecture: the information one can deduce or work out is not the message that should guarantee its semiotic structure. At this point we should put aside, once and for all, the semiotic analysis of architecture, because if those

works where it realises itself are works of art, it itself, like all works of art, realises a presence, and the conscious mind that receives it and recognises it in this presence does not receive it as a message to be decoded. If the work contains a cryptographic (allegorical or symbolical) message, the conscious, in order to get to it, will have, in a way, to neutralise, push back that presence and reduce it to an object. The question we were posed was of a different sort: is the essence of architecture semiotic?

Its secondary messages are not sufficient to make its essence semiotic. Therefore the meaning of the blue ceiling of the dome or the symbol of the Nile valley in the Egyptian temple pillars give neither the essence of the dome nor that of the Egyptian temple.[29]

We could cut Brandi's story short by stating frankly that we are not interested in his 'essences', because to propose these parameters again does not seem to us very useful for architectural research. But a part of his interpretation deserves careful consideration.

Brandi knows that his method reduces architecture to a pure tautological expression. Offering itself and nothing else, in a structure that leads only to its own internal laws of construction, architecture is void of meanings. But then one can well ask what is the use of criticism? Not being able to interpret – where there is no meaning there is no reading – or to historicise – the historical character of architecture is compromised by its reduction to a *presence* – criticism will have to limit itself to *description*.

Such criticism seems to be stating the supremacy of the work over every type of empty content, but falls, in its turn, into a sort of literal translation of the figurative structures. Brandi is open, therefore, to the very reservations expressed by the French literary *nouvelle critique* about critics like Picard.[30] Of course, we cannot say that Brandi is a 'naturalistic critic' because of the sophisticated intellectual construction of his analyses. Nevertheless, the following observation by Doubrovsky seems to make a suitable answer to his theses:

The profundity of a work must therefore be understood in a *perceptual* sense, as one speaks of the depth of a visual field, in which the multiplication of viewpoints can never exhaust the material to be perceived, or achieve the flat and total vision that would display its object in simultaneous entirety. So that there are indeed 'levels' of signification, defined by the level of perceptual acuity; there are indeed 'depths' of meaning, but not strata.[31]

And we think that this rejection of the 'layers' of meaning is of particular importance for architecture. The perceptive reading and the 'absent minded' reading, either of an architectural work or of an urban environment, do not receive different 'sectors' of the messages emitted by those works, they receive instead different 'zones' of meaning, still defined, however, by their unitariety and by their multi-valence.

In examining the different readings of a single monument in the course of time, from Francesco di Giorgio to Peruzzi (but we could have extended our examination to include Borromini, who had, perhaps, in mind the surveys of the Oratorio della S. Croce, as well as the heretical organisms of Hadrian's villa), we have put precisely into focus some of that monument's *zones* of meaning. When we spoke of ambiguity, heresy and conformism, we were in fact defining the historical meanings of buildings when confronted with the codes they were referring to. These meanings do not exhaust, of course, the sense of the buildings, but, at least, they get us nearer to the central nucleus of their values.

We could say, in this sense, that the reading of a work clashes not only with the historicity of its language, but also with the successive layers of meanings left on it by the history of criticism. It would be useless to try to sort out the *added meanings* from those internal to the work. The historian will have to accept, taking it into account, this interference of values and meanings, coming in part from the work itself, and in part from the history of its critical 'fortunes'.

History of criticism, therefore, has an important role in the philological reconstruction of historical codes. It can even become a fundamental yardstick in checking the validity of the reading, because the comparison between the reading and the interpretations gathered on the architectural text can be used to check the scientific character of the critical construction.

We will have to make a few distinctions in this philological recovery of the codes of the past. The *absent-minded perception* of Piazza Farnese in Rome, as a mere parking lot, does not automatically exclude the absorption of the specific values of that space. This particular use of the square focuses on one particular 'layer' – the functional layer – that, today, is specific to this urban environment: but the complexity of its meanings is also present in the character of its totality. The emphasis on the functional aspect pushes into the background of consciousness the primary functions of the square (at least from the point of view of an historical reading), but it does not nullify its complex symbolic values. They are simply perceived in an unconscious way: they are within a particularly narrow 'zone of meanings'.

When, in Baroque times, Tesauro writes that 'all the art of the Gospel speakers is in mixing the difficult with the easy in such a way that in the mixture of learned and stupid people, the learned are not sickened by too much understanding nor the stupid bored by too little', he foreshadowed a semantic complexity now on the agenda of the most recent architectural research. It is here, then, that the ideological meaning of Brandi's propositions takes shape. The *supremacy of the work*, re-stated by him, can easily be accepted; but if it becomes so absolute as to transform itself into critical silence, then it enters into a train of thoughts not by chance hostile to the entire problem of contemporary art.

Recently someone spoke of 'discordant criticism' in connection with Sedlmayr and Brandi.[32] We would add that their 'discordance' does not seem to raise healthy doubts for action, but rather apocalyptical doubts for paralysis.

> In stressing the primacy of the work it has been my intention [Doubrovsky writes again] for a single instant, to advocate the formalism in which English criticism frequently has its roots. For me, the meaning does indeed reside in the sensible material of the object; but the object is not closed in upon itself so that an investigation of its structures can never be related to anything other than the miracle of internal equilibrium. Any aesthetic object is also, in reality, the work of a *human project*.[33]

The reference to the *primacy of the work* can, then, – for those of us who accept this last proposition of Doubrovsky's unconditionally – merge with the analysis of architectural structures seen as 'human project'.

Having acknowledged our dissension from the a-semantic interpretations of architecture, we must now examine Lévi-Strauss's objections to extending structuralist methods to the reading of artistic phenomena.

> In anthropology as well as in linguistics [Lévi-Strauss writes] the structural method consists in the discovery of the invariant forms within different contents. Structural analysis, to which some critics and historians of literature mistakenly refer to, consists on the other hand in looking for recurrent contents behind variable forms. We see the rise, therefore, of a double misunderstanding: on the relation between substance and form, and on the relation between concepts as separate as those of recurrence and invariance, the former open to the contingent while the latter goes back to necessity.[34]

Lévi-Strauss's warning is very important and applies also, of course, to the history of architecture.

The typological problem, the object of so much equivocation from academic culture, is the characteristic example of a theme that has generated much confusion between formal recurrences and invariance of meanings. It is, on the other hand, even too obvious that anthropology and linguistics, on one side, and historical criticism of the arts, on the other, have completely different objectives. But there is still the possibility of a level of historical study in which the singling out of invariant forms from different contents has a meaning: perhaps the meaning of the comparison between forms that refer, even though indirectly, to common schemes. (The variations of the centric organisms from late-Antique to Illuminism, the aggregation of spaces with differentiated geometric matrixes, decorative repertoires seen repeated in the course of time and in distant geographical and semantic areas – Europe, Middle East, Asia, etc.)

Another warning from the French ethnologist seems to us equally important:

> Literary criticism and history of ideas can become really structural only on condition that they find, outside themselves, the instruments for a double objective check. And it is not difficult to see where they should be found. On one side, on the level of linguistic and even phonologic analysis, where the control can be exercised independent of the conscious elaborations of the author and of his analyst; on the other side on the level of ethnographic research, that is, for a society like ours, on the level of external history.[35]

This can apply also to architecture. The objective examination of the parameters of analysis consists, for architecture, in the comparison with the internal evolution of its historical conditionings. And this is certainly not new: what is significant, within the structuralist thought, is Lévi-Strauss's reference to history against the anti-historicism of so many of his followers. Equally significant, for us, is the passage that directly follows the previous one:

> Not only, therefore, can 'the structuralist methods be directed towards a mainly historicist critical tradition', but, in fact, only the existence of this historical tradition can supply a base for structural operations. To be convinced of it, it is sufficient to refer, within art criticism, to a fully and totally structuralist work such as the one by Erwin Panofsky. This author, in fact, is a great structuralist, first of all because he is a great historian, and also because history offers him, at the same time, an unrivalled source of information and a combinatory field in which the truth of the interpretations can be tested in a thousand ways. It is the

marriage of history with sociology and semiology that allows the analyst to break the circle of an atemporal confrontation, in which one never knows, while the pseudo-dialogue between critic and work carries on, whether the former is a faithful observer or the unconscious animator of a *piece* which he offers himself as a show, and whose listeners could always ask if the text is being performed by real characters or simply by a skilful ventriloquist to the puppets that he himself has invented.[36]

Lévi-Strauss is attacking not only the academic verbosity of exegetic criticism but also a 'structuralist' critic like Roland Barthes.

All the same it has been Barthes himself who has shaped structural analysis in the 'productive' sense (if we are allowed, here, this term):

The purpose of every structuralist activity [he wrote in 1963] whether reflexive or poetic, is the reconstruction of an 'object' in such a way as to show the working rules (the 'functions') of this object. The structure is then simply a *semblance* of the object, but an orientated and interested semblance, because the imitated object makes visible something that was not so before, or that was unintelligible in the natural object. The structural man takes reality, disassembles it and reassembles it; apparently not very much (and some think that structuralist work is 'insignificant, without interest, useless, etc.'). But from another point of view this is of little importance, because between the two objects or the two phases of the structuralist activity something *new* is produced, and this something is nothing less than the general intelligibility: the semblance is then the intellect added to the object, and this addition has an anthropological value, because it represents the whole man, his history, his situation, his freedom and nature's resistance to his mind.

This is why we can speak of structuralist activity: creation and reflection are not, in this case, original 'impression' of the world, but true fabrication of a world similar to the original, not in order to copy it but to make it intelligible.[37]

It is understandable that those who look fondly at the absorption of culture by nature, and reduce history to a system of data that confirms the character of *a priori* synthesis of the spirit, are not happy with Barthes's 'production *of the new*'.

Architecture, on the other hand, is always creation *against* nature: its history is the story of the subjection of nature to the constructive activity of the ruling classes. The historical criticism of architecture has, then, as its main object the discovery of this constructive activity. The alliance between history and semiology is only possible from this starting point. Semiology as a 'general science of signs' is an instrument in the hands of the historian – as an ideology it is an instrument of mystification.[38]

Beyond the identification of invariant forms, of linguistic and syntactical systems, of typologies, structural research in architecture cannot escape the great problem affecting all structural research: the network of unconscious and unknown links that underlies figurative choices, that is *behind* and informs the architectural codes, that ties these codes to social behaviour, to myths and to historical dialectic.

Cassirer and Lévi-Strauss seem to agree on this point. For both, the social and cultural institutions, the myths, the formative activity of *man*, are 'symbolic forms'; they follow conscious and unconscious 'models' and realise themselves on the basis of a deep and hidden structure that it is up to the analyst to bring to light.

The unconscious has, then, a primary role in structuralist research. The analysis of myths seems to prove that, beyond the images in which they manifest themselves, there is an *architecture of human spirit,* an underlying structure and a logic above historical changes.

To what extent is the prevalence of the unconscious and of the *system* a mere working hypothesis, and to what extent is it an ideology? Lévi-Strauss, in his analysis of Baudelaire's *Les chats,* recognises in the structure of the poem impressive analogies with those of the ethnologist in his analysis of myths.

Armanda Guiducci has pointed out correctly that the kind of perspective in which poetry and myth are complementary terms goes back to Cassirer and to his strong Freudian inspiration:

> What matters is that the influence once played by Cassirer on the aesthetic, critical and literary reflection between America and Europe, bounces back today from the structuralist anthropology of Lévi-Strauss. The latter represents a new, methodologically inspired, synthesis between the semantic interest for the linguistic symbol (so very pronounced in Cassirer), and the unconscious symbolism (that also inspired Cassirer) reconsidered through the achievements of structural linguistics – and all these new knotty considerations could not help touching on the literary reflection, already sensitised by Cassirer.[39]

The question remains substantially the same for architectural criticism. The reflection on architecture as a reading in depth, as a discovery, not of the clear   and   immediate   meanings,   but   of   the   architectural 'connotations', of the ambiguous, reticent, 'hidden' meanings, goes back to the tradition of Cassirer's *Philosophy of Symbolic Forms,* rendered into a coherent system of historical research by Saxl and Panofsky, and in a less coherent reading method by Susanne Langer that was nevertheless very influential on American culture.[40]

It is Cassirer, in fact, that introduces the possibility of seeing art as an independent 'universe of discourse', as a specific structure with its own meanings. As a *symbolic form,* that is as a product of a conscious-forming activity, art, like myth or ethics, is for Cassirer a *whole* with its own meaning that can only be understood by starting from the structural laws inherent to it. And as these laws are not only the product of the human activity that builds in this way its own reality but also, at the same time, the means to go beyond it, the study of the structure of symbolic forms becomes the study of the meaning of historical behaviour.

Cassirer has had an enormous impact on the history of contemporary criticism. From Warburg to Saxl, Panofsky, Langer, Battisti, the study of artistic structures has been deeply influenced by his salvage of the symbolic dimension not only (or not so much) as an instrument of human knowledge, but also as a constructive activity of the 'spirit'.

The objections raised by Cassirer do not seem to us to have touched the substance of his innovative contribution. Stripping his analyses of all the propositions linked to a contingent neo-Kantism, we can confidently state that Cassirer has adequately shown the existence of meanings proper to structures of behaviour, of the laws of vision and of the communication systems. After Cassirer one would find it difficult not to admit that the 'instruments' of communication define a 'field' of historically determinable meanings. Like the psychology of the Gestalt, the *Philosophy of Symbolic Forms* contests the thesis of association psychology, but, unlike *Gestaltpsychologie,* it does not reject history in its search for the laws of conscious-forming activity. Cassirer has taught us that any way of 'representing' the world is mainly a way of 'building' the world itself on the basis of a common network of underlying contents, an inter-subjective universe of meanings and a forming activity active *also* on the unconscious plane. In this sense the fundamental propositions of Fiedler, of the *Gestaltpsychologie* and of Cassirer are all directed towards a common problem. (The very one, in fact, voiced by Gropius, Kandinsky and Klee within the Bauhaus.) After them one takes for granted that there cannot be perception without an activity that organises consciousness within a *'field'*, and that there are not *ways of representing* but rather *ways of seeing* (that are at the same time ways of adapting psychological expectations to the reactions of the environment).

In addition Cassirer introduces a symbolic consideration of language, of myth, of rituals and of art that allows the interpretation of artistic phenomena not only as single structures dominated by a system of internal interdependence, but also as elements of wider structures of which they are expressive manifestations (*symbolic forms,* in fact). There is a clear affinity between Cassirer's themes and the results of the most modern structural analyses. Seeing myth, ritual and art linked together as distinct forms of unitarian systems, emphasises the question of unconscious and inter-subjective conditioning active in the formation of languages, of the architectural language in particular.

When Panofsky decided to establish a rigorous method of historical interpretation of artistic phenomena based on Cassirer's elaborations, he found himself faced by another kind of research, specific to art criticism. Brandi has very appropriately recognised in Wölfflin's *Kunstgeschicht-liche Grundbegriffe*[41] a system of five binary oppositions representing one of the first coherent attempts to reach the work's structure through the work itself.[42]

Cassirer's research is on the plane of meanings, those of Wölfflin's and Riegl's on the plane of formal structures, of the 'signifiers'. Panofsky's task was to link together these different streams of research.

So he elaborates the question of formal structures, introducing a series of correctives and enlargements to the Rieglian concept of *Kunstwollen,* and to Wölfflin's *Kunstgeschichtliche Grundbegriffe.*[43] So far as the 'artistic intention' is concerned Panofsky shows how it cannot possibly be considered an intention proper to the psychology of the time; he states further that 'the statements of the theory and criticism of art of an entire epoch will not be able to interpret immediately the works of art produced in that epoch; they too will have [in fact] to be interpreted by us, together with the latter'.[44]

The great importance Panofsky gives to treatises and literary documents contemporary to the works of art does not have for him – as it does for the greater part of his followers – a determining value in the identification of the structural characteristics of an age or a single work. 'Theories' do not 'explain' or 'designate' the values or the meanings of the works, but constitute parallel phenomena, with their own history – they are the *object* rather than the means of interpretation.[45]

Panofsky also specifies that 'we must make a clear distinction between the *artistic intentions* and the *intentions of the artist,* the intentions generated by his moods and the mirroring of the artistic phenomena in the conscience of the time or even the contents of the *Erlebnisse,* of the impression of the work of art on the contemporary onlooker: in short, artistic value, as the object of a possible scientific knowledge of art, is not a (psychological) reality'.[46]

In this way, Panofsky's *Kunstwollen* avoids both the limits of psychological definition and the character of instrumental abstraction. As the basis of the interpretation, in the immanent sense, of the work of art, it can only be perceived through 'categories valid *a priori*': the 'fundamental concepts of the science of art'.[47] Such 'fundamental concepts' are reduced to 'pairs of concepts whose antithetic structure expresses the "*a priori* fundamental problems" of artistic activity',[48] but:

> far from wanting to separate the world of artistic phenomena into two opposite fields, leaving no room for the countless artistic phenomena, the fundamental concepts designate only the polarity of two sets of values that are beyond the world of artistic phenomena, two zones that in works of art can be expressed in the most varied ways. The contents of the world of historical reality are not perceived through fundamental concepts, but rather by using them as a starting point. The fundamental concepts do not claim to classify the artistic phenomena, like a sort of *'grammaire générale et raisonnée'*, their task is ... to make the phenomena speak, like an *a priori* reagent. They in fact reduce to a formula the position, but not the solution, of the artistic problems, and therefore they determine the questions we have to put to the objects, but not the individual and always unforeseeable, answers that these objects might give.[49]

Therefore the surface values and the deep values, or the contiguity and compenetration values, lose the absolute meaning they had for Wölfflin. Being *a priori* conceptual models valid for an arbitrary (but historically founded) systematic reorganisation of the material offered by the artistic experience, they constitute the prime elements of a reference *grid,* of a 'super-code' for the interpretation of the artistic facts. This systematic construction has been recognised by Panofsky as a conceptual structure articulated and concluded in itself. Furthermore, the subordination of the particular historical problems to the 'fundamental concepts' is possible

> . . . because the particular artistic problems, in respect of the fundamental problems, can only be derived problems and, therefore, the corresponding 'special concepts' have, in respect of the 'fundamental concepts' the meaning of derived concepts: in fact the particular artistic problems are constituted according to an almost Hegelian scheme, so that the solutions of the generally valid

fundamental problems become, in their turn, in the course of historical development, poles of a particular problem and the solutions of this particular problem form, in their turn, the poles of a more specific particular problem of 'secondary importance', and so on *ad infinitum*. Therefore, if we take an example from architecture, both the solution that we call 'pillar' and the solution that we call 'wall' represent a clearly determined solution of fundamental artistic problems. If in particular historical conditions (Late Antiquity or Renaissance) we have the case of a building whose wall or pillar are connected harmoniously, then we have a 'new' artistic problem that, in respect of the fundamental problems, is particular and that can also generate several other particular problems, because its various solutions (Baroque or Classical) can, in their turn, generate a confrontation.[50]

This postulates the need for a close collaboration between historical and theoretical research. The constant reference, during the analysis of a single work or of a cycle of works, to a unitary *stylistic system,* poses the problem of the dialectic between the completed and singular artistic phenomenon inserted 'in the historical nexus of cause and effect', and the need to understand the very same phenomenon by withdrawing it from the nexus, in order to understand it 'beyond the historical relativity, like a solution, extraneous to the time and place, of a problem that is extraneous to the time and place'.[51]

Panofsky's essay on 'the relationship between history of art and theory of art' goes back to 1925, and anticipates in an impressive way the current polemics between the various factions within structuralism. The abstract but necessary character of what he calls – following Wölfflin – the 'fundamental concepts' of the 'theory of art' is underlined and defined in his polemic with Dorner, who had attacked him violently, rejecting any validity of the conceptualisation of artistic historiography.

Dorner's empiricism is typical of every 'impressionist' critic who is opposed to any verifiable criticism; Panofsky's answer still finds echoes today in the detailed analyses by not-dogmatic critics of the concepts of 'code' and 'structure',[52]

Dorner's accusation that the application of fundamental concepts were a 'usurpation of the legitimacy of history', was answered by Panofsky:

> ... if we start from the ... [given] definition of the artistic value, this usurpation will not happen because what must be perceived through those fundamental concepts finds itself in the same relationship that exists between 'case' and 'phenomenon'. For this very reason I

perfectly agree with Dorner when he denies to the 'conceptual construction' that I proposed the character of reality – a character that I have never meant to give it.[53]

That is like saying: the construction of interpretative codes is artificial, and only justified by the fact that comparison between them and the works *causes a reaction* in the artistic phenomena – it *makes them speak*. It is symptomatic that the most recent criticism has ignored the problems posed by Panofsky the heir of 'pure visibilism', and has concentrated on Panofsky the scholar and theorist of iconological interpretations.

But one cannot understand the value of Panofsky in the history of modern art criticism without keeping in mind that the whole of his activity as historian wavers between two kinds of analysis that he has not been able to integrate: the analysis of the systems of the signifiers (whose theorical bases are perfectly expressed in the 1925 essay mentioned above), and the analysis of the systems of the signified. With this in mind Panofsky can not only be re-read in the light of more recent problems posed by semiological analyses, but his work, rigorously faithful to the premises that originated it, can also constitute a true methodological test. His work seems to be saying that once the study of the formal structures is separated from the study of their meanings, they can't be rejoined *a posteriori*. He does in fact postulate the separation of iconology, iconography and criticism as the starting point of the study. But his own historiographical work shows that: first, this separation cannot be carried to its conclusion; and anyway the various parameters interfere with each other, continually changing the direction of the research.[54]

One cannot help suspecting, then, that the relationship between the symbolic element and its 'referent' (its specific meaning) may not be all that decisive in the reading of works or artistic cycles, even those deeply impregnated with symbolism. Or, rather, that the iconological analysis is better able to grasp the symbolic dimension specific to some historically well-defined communication systems than the meaning proper of the single works.

In recognising the existence of a specific 'symbolic form' in perspective representation, Panofsky has been able to confirm historically and objectively that there is no gap between ways of representing reality and ways of 'constructing' reality. The perspective of curved surfaces, multiple-point perspective and the Renaissance single-point perspective correspond to different systems of vision and the construction of the world: they define different artistic cycles and the laws inherent in them.

So the attitude towards perspective becomes an element of historical judgment:

> ... the concept of perspective [Panofsky writes] stops religious art from moving into the region of the magic . . . but opens up a brand new region, the region of the visionary, within which the miracle becomes an experience immediately felt by the spectator, because the supernatural events rush into the apparently natural visual space that belongs to it, thus allowing an adequate 'penetration' of their supernatural essence. Furthermore, for religious art, where the miracle happens in the soul of the man portrayed in the work of art it opens up the psychological region in its highest sense.[55]

There is, then, a meaning proper to perspective as a representational technique rich in symbolic values, and, at the same time, as an interpretative code of the world. In the Renaissance, Panofsky notes:

> . . . the subjective visual impression had been rationalised to such a degree that it could have at once constituted the foundation for a solidly built empirical world, and been at the same time 'infinite' in a fully modern sense (and we could almost compare the function of Renaissance perspective to the function of criticism, and the value of the Roman-Greek perspective to that of scepticism). The passage from psycho-physiological to mathematical space had been realised: in other words, we had an objectivation of subjectivity.[56]

The psycho-physiological space is the locus of pure facts, with no symbolic value, while the mathematical space is the result of the intellectual planning of human environment and has, therefore, a sense. Later Pierre Francastel, by grafting Panofsky's analyses on Piaget's and Wallon's studies on the origin of the notion of 'space', worked out a history of art on the lines of the three levels of spatial representation: typological, projective and perspective.[57] Though certainly debatable, Francastel's hypothesis confirms the thesis that space is not an *a priori* 'datum' of the conscious, but the product of a mental and inter-subjective construction, tied to the social and intellectual conditions of the various historical moments.

The notion of space is, therefore, a constitutive element of artistic codes and of common behaviour. If a code is, as commonly stated, a 'system of expectations', then Panofsky's analyses will allow us to build a bridge, extremely useful for the understanding of contemporary art and architecture, between the space of life and the space of the image.

Already then, in Panofsky's studies, the analysis of the problem of perspective takes on the character of a structural research. By linking ways of representation that are historically far apart and have different meanings he was able to see the different contents lying behind analogous forms.

Panofsky follows a similar method in tackling more strictly linguistic problems.

His analysis of the structure of Gothic architecture in relation to Scholastic thought goes beyond orthodox iconologism and also, if read carefully, the criticisms of those that found in it a naïve search for ephemeral ideal correspondences between architecture and philosophical speculation.[58] It would be a great mistake to read Panofsky's essay as a quest for characteristics common to philosophical thought and architectural praxis. It is fairly obvious and even, in part, made explicit[59] that the iconological research aims, in this case, at bringing to light an inter-subjective code of values underlying the entire ideal condition of the Gothic Middle Ages. At least, as a first instance, the fact that adherence to this code was conscious for the philosophers of the Sorbonne and the School of Chartres, semi-conscious for masters like Robert de Luzarches and Pierre-le-Loup, totally unconscious for the stone-masons and in the common use of the cathedral by the population, does not constitute a very important problem.

The true problem, in this case, is the identification of a structure specific to a period of history, and in order to define it the historian will have to hypothesise a unity (however relative it may be):

> . . . and if the historian wishes to verify this unity instead of merely presupposing it, he must try to discover intrinsic analogies between such overtly disparate phenomena as the arts, literature, philosophy, social and political currents, religious movements, etc. This effort, laudable and even indispensable in itself, has led to a pursuit of 'parallels' the hazards of which are only too obvious. No man can master more than one fairly limited field; every man has to rely on incomplete and often secondary information whenever he ventures *ultra crepidam*. Few men can resist the temptation of either ignoring or slightly deflecting such lines as refuse to run parallel, and even a genuine parallelism does not make us really happy if we cannot imagine how it came about. Small wonder, then, that another diffident attempt at correlating Gothic architecture and Scholasticism is bound to be looked upon with suspicion by both historians of art and historians of philosophy.[60]

Between the theses adopted by Antal in *Florentine Painting and its Social*

Background and those of Panofsky's *Gothic Architecture,* there exists, therefore, an irreconcilable opposition. Antal employs the criteria of sociological criticism. Panofsky, on the contrary, does not postulate a rigid cause-and-effect relation between social dialectic and history of art, but directs his research towards the discovery of the structures common to thought, custom, the myths acting on a deeper level, and architectural ideology.[61] In this way he can easily admit that Pierre de Monterau, Robert de Luzarches, Hughues Libergier or any other master of Gothic cathedrals may not have read the works of Gilbert de la Porrée, of St Thomas or of the philosophers of the School of Chartres[62].

What is important to him is to establish that Scholastic philosophy and the methods of the Gothic masters both start from common mechanisms of the intellect, from a common way of looking at reality, of interpreting it and of acting on it. So, when Panofsky finds, in the compositive method used by the Gothic masters, the same principles of articulation as those of the theological *Summae* – from the subdivision into *partes, membra, quaestiones, distinctiones* and *articuli,* to the schemes for *disputationes* such as the famous '*videtur quod – sed contra – respondeo dicendum*' – he not only sees into the intimate structure of twelfth- and thirteenth-century architecture, but also articulates his interpretation by recognising the historical and dialectical nature of that structure.[63]

In identifying the nuclei of his research Panofsky has well in mind that the historical unity of the period under study is not abstract and motionless in time, but rather a process, a chain of facts, a complex of events determined by the ideologies of the ruling classes. If the problem of the rose window in the western façades can be considered one of the primary *quaestiones* of Gothic architecture, the series of solutions in St Denis, Laon and Rheims cathedrals responds to a true *disputatio,* carried out in the course of time by their respective builders, according to the classic dialectical scheme of *videtur quod* (St Denis's rose window, isolated and unconnected to the organism), *sed contra* (Laon's organic solution), *respondeo dicendum* (the 'final' solution of the problem by Hugues Libergier in Rheims, where the two preceding and opposed experiences find peace in a brilliant synthesis).

Panofsky shows that the mental processes demonstrated in the structures of Scholastic thought are the same as those hidden in the structures of the great cathedrals.

However, even Panofsky's fundamental studies have objective limitations. Having defined the role of ancient, medieval and humanistic perspective, and having recognised the figurative dialectic of Gothic space, there still remains the problem of how to use these analyses. How can these comprehensive studies enter the history of architecture as a specific ideology? And how can the reading of the works in a symbolic key become a global reading?

Panofsky symbolism rests on verifiable data: at the basis of the readings of iconological criticism are the great symbolic systems of antiquity, and those codified by Ripa's *Iconologia*, Alciato's *Emblematum liber* and Tesauro's *Cannocchiale aristotelico*. But is post-Illuminist art really completely a-symbolical? Is not Mondrian's, Mies's and Le Corbusier's *angle droit*, in its turn, a symbol, like Wright's fluid space and Kahn's 'objectuality'?

But then are not the limits of iconological studies perhaps becoming methodological inadequacies? And how can one preserve the validity of Cassirer's premises in a context of considerations that would not artificially separate myths and classical symbols from the 'new symbols' and 'new myths' of the technological world?

Gombrich has recently denounced the deformations of iconologism: and the source of this denunciation should cause much reflection, especially among Italian epigones of this analytical method.

> All the field of allegory and emblematic representation which, a few years ago, was thought of as pedantic and abstruse, is now held in great honour; in fact the hunt for the symbolic meaning is in danger of becoming the latest fashion in scientific activity.[64]

Quite rightly, Gombrich tries to re-define and assess the meanings of the term 'symbol'. He places on one side the definitions of Hobbes and Peirce, with their coincidence between sign logic and symbolic logic;[65] on the other he puts the interpretations of the French and German schools that admit symbolic value only to signs able to act as vehicles to meanings that could not otherwise be rendered through other signs. Rejecting the interpretation of the first two theorists (because their excessive extension of the concept deprived it of any functionality) Gombrich states that 'every type of symbolic expression only functions within a complicated system of possible alternatives, that can be, perhaps, interpreted to a certain extent: but an adequate translation can only be given in the exceptional cases of the chance meeting of the two systems.'[66]

In the historical criticism of architecture the *hunt for the symbolic meaning* has already become a cultural fashion. And one would not complain of this phenomenon if it limited itself to a cautious and in-depth operation in preparation for historical interpretation, as was Panofsky's original intention when he defined the specific tasks of iconological studies. More deforming is the *reduced* meaning, given by more recent iconological studies, to the concept of symbol itself and to its value within the context of architectural structures.

The illusion of being able to reach the primary meanings of the planning act by referring to an exactly codified symbological lexicon, thus acquires a sense. To a critical method that is 'impressionistic' or, even worse, left to the uncontrollable discretion of the interpreter and to the pure-visibilist and formalist abstractions, neo-iconologism offers in contrast an undoubtedly verifiable criticism that redeems philology by giving it a new sense, that investigates extensively and in depth the mythical, ethical and institutional context of which art is part, without seeing – as does the historiography of sociological extraction – naïve cause-and-effect relations between architecture and social conventions. Furthermore, neo-iconologism does not stop at the immediately obvious relations between the components of a single work or of a cycle of works (it is, in fact, the analysis of 'cycles' that characterises iconologial criticism, because it is in those that the stratified structures of symbolic meanings are made evident), but goes from the immediate perception to the underlying layer, from what is given to what is presupposed, from the conscious act of planning to what is not conscious in planning, to what *speaks* through the planner and to what conditions and precedes the act of planning. A criticism of the most recent applications of this method would be their lack of courage in not going the whole way, and in not becoming 'criticism of the ideology' *tout court*.

It must be said, first of all, that in setting up a vocabulary of symbols suitable for translating univocally the system of signs evolved in the course of history, iconologism cuts itself off from the understanding of the specific value of a combination of the various signs, or of the *ambiguous* character acquired by the symbolic signs themselves, as soon as they are introduced in a complex structure like that of architecture. On one hand we see, then, the setting up of an excessively deterministic relation between symbolic signs and their meanings; on the other, we see the contradiction between the intention of throwing light on the underlying aspects of language and a research interrupted at a generic level.

Reading Bernini's S. Andrea al Quirinale through the *montage* of decorative allegories related to the apotheosis of the saint's martyrdom may well be a first element of critical probing but it certainly cannot be the purpose of historiographical analysis. It follows that to see in works even more tied to Mannerist or Baroque *conceptism* – Vitozzi's Parco di Viboccone, Della Porta's and Maderno's Villa Aldobrandini at Frascati

18.   Francesco Borromini, S. Ivo alla Sapienza (1642–60). Interior of the dome

and Guarini's S. Sindone[67] – a consciously orchestrated chain of symbols, can only constitute a 'moment' of the analysis, to be left behind and absorbed in syntheses verified through the comparison with all the new parameters offered by the complex stratification of the meanings of those architectures.

In reality every work of architecture can be referred to several symbolic systems. The fact that in Borromini's S. Ivo the myth of Babel's Tower, the ascent to Truth and Knowledge, the divine anti-Babel, the Pentecostal space, the superimposed allegories of Modesty and Knowledge (the emblematic bee and the *Domus Sapientiae* as the seven-pillared house) are fused with the passage from a space uncertain of its hierarchy (that of the lower level) to the unitary space of the dome, is not irrelevant to the formation of meanings specific to the spatial in-fill.[68]

Indeed, the fact that Borromini's symbology is ambiguous, that it lends itself to several interpretations, that it integrates itself indissolubly with a rigorous geometrical construction of the form, throws light on the general value that iconological interpretation can assume in critical evaluation. The symbol is, in fact, something that because of its nature rejects an univocal reading. Its meanings tend to escape and its characteristic is that of revealing and hiding at the same time. Otherwise, instead of a symbol we should speak of an 'emblem'.

It follows, therefore, that the qualities of the symbol are the same as those of the artistic 'sign': ambiguous, disposed to accept different meanings, transparent and fixed within a pre-established code, and, at the same time, able to transgress the laws of that code. So a reading of the more obvious meanings of architectural symbolism can, at most, place a work within the text of a certain culture; as when Baldwin Smith studies the propagandistic meaning given, in Imperial Rome, to the city gates and the entrances to the imperial palaces, or the religious meaning given by the Middle Ages to those same elements (the gates of Heaven, the analogy between earthly city and the *civitas Dei*, the walls of the celestial Jerusalem), or when De Fusco reads the messages of contemporary architecture as a *mass-medium*.[69]

Beyond these orientative readings, one must admit that the symbolism latent in architecture can be perceived by considering the relations linking the various symbolic signs, even without returning to their more apparent meanings.[70] Once the symbolic value of the dome, of the central plan, of the 'plans' based on 'magic' geometrical figures, of the anthropomorphism presiding over the use of classical orders, of the application of the harmonic-proportional modules, are defined, the study moves to a further level in which the analysis of the combination of the various signs, and of the eventual transgressions and enrichments of those symbolic systems, predominate. This more highly complex symbolic level is the same as that identified by Barthes in literature, in his polemic against what he calls *critical verisimilitude*: against the critical tradition that hides behind the screen of 'judgment' and the conformism of analyses and intends to leave the question of the meanings specific to writing wrapped in myth.

> L'ancien critique [says Barthes in answer to Picard's attacks (but his words will do perfectly well for the similar idiosyncrasies of the *ancienne* architectural *critique*)][71] est victime d'une disposition que les analystes du langage connaissent bien et qu'ils appellent l' *asymbolie*: il lui est impossible de percevoir ou de manier des symboles, c'est-à-dire des coexistences de sens; chez lui, la fonction symbolique très générale, qui permet aux hommes de construire des idées, des images et des oeuvres, dès lors que l'on dépasse les usages étroitement rationnels du langage, cette fonction est troublée, limitée, ou censurée.

Let us go back to the analysis of architectural facts. It is obvious that when we speak of co-existence of meanings in the symbolic construction of architectural organisms and images, we are already facing an interpretative dimension that goes beyond those already familiar to iconological criticism. We have also seen the consequences of a criticism committed to multiplying the metaphors of the work. The critical aversion to Barthes from unexpected sources is the same (or almost) as that to, for example, Vincent Scully, accused of emotive redundancy in his critical writings. (Collins has ironically compared Scully's prose to that of Ruskin, and his method to that enunciated by Oscar Wilde in *The Critic as an Artist*.)[72]

What, however, emerges from the *nouvelle* literary *critique* is the specific value of the polysemia of artistic language. Within Italian Marxist thought, Galvano della Volpe enjoyed some success a few years ago, by recognising in the figurative structures a specific logicity, a character of *system* that requires a self-examination and a stratified polysemia.[73] If in this way, Della Volpe freed Marxist thought on art from the low tide of 'vulgar' sociologism, by re-inserting it in the international debate on semantic problems, one cannot say for certain that his *Critica del gusto* has been at all productive in the field of architectural studies (not to mention his heavy ideologism). Or, rather, it has had only indirect effects, confirming the importance of the specific consideration of the architectural object as an organic system of linguistic-functional signs.[74] It is important to note, though, that, for Della Volpe also, artistic language is multisignifying. It contains the parameters necessary for its self-examination but, unlike scientific language, it is 'open', available and multivalent. The results of semantic criticisms have been, then, automatically transmitted to the criticism of architecture and of the visual arts: this is certainly one of the *merits* of Della Volpe, at least within the context of Italian culture.

But to what degree can semantic criticism penetrate objectively the ideological structure of architecture? And is not the 'organic' character of art, identified by Della Volpe perhaps inadequate for the reading of artistic phenomena that are not organic, but are disarticulated, 'open', like Dada, Abstract, Pop-Art or urban scale architecture?

Umberto Eco has tried to answer at least a few of these questions.

The work of art [he writes] is like a message whose decoding implies an adventure, just because it strikes us with its way of organising the signs not foreseen by the usual codes. From this point on, in trying to discover the new code (typical, for the first time, of that work – and yet tied to the usual code, which it partly violates and partly enriches), the receptor, one might say, enters the message, converging on it all the series of hypotheses allowed by his particular psychological and intellectual disposition. Lacking an external code on which to rely completely, he turns into a hypothetical code the system of assumptions on which his sensibility and intelligence are based. The understanding of the work springs from this interaction.[75]

It is clear, though, that this infraction, this offence to a known code, offers the possibility of measuring the new elements emerging in the work that is considered *eversive*, not so much in terms of the quantity of information as in terms of the degree of modification of the usual *system of expectations*.

Now, we must note that, particularly for architecture, the efficiency of a code is measured also by its ability to identify all the new information offered by a non-conformist work. Indeed, as the formation of a *system of expectations* is an historical operation, and can be judged as such, there follows the possibility of studying the evolution of artistic movements, each time adapting the instruments of reading to the variation of the phenomena.

We find, therefore, that the codification of the systems to be deciphered may change and involve the entire history of architecture because of the appearance of a single work that throws light on a previously unclear process – which has, in fact, partly happened with the appearance of Louis Kahn's work on the international stage between

1958 and 1961 – or with the discovery and critical evaluation of unknown or inadequately studied works such as Michelangelo's Florentine fortifications and Elizabethan architecture. From this it follows that one of the first and most important operations of historical criticism is the exact identification of the reference codes.

But let us note: criticism, in making explicit the structure of the codes, cannot help deforming – through the introduction of arbitrary and inevitable value principles – the systems of expectations acting on daily life. So there comes into being a complex exchange between codes, works and criticism. Linguistic conventions are shaken, enriched or put in crisis, by the mere fact that the demystifying activity of criticism makes explicit the character of their system and their most hidden implications.

In this sense we can easily say that every type of criticism that exactly identifies the relations between the work and the code underlying it is *operative*. It modifies, in fact, the very connections being investigated. By making rational what, normally, in aesthetic activity happens outside a strict logical check, and by discovering the ideological values of formal choices often made out of habit, criticism can face the architect with the responsibility of a continuous and pitiless check on the sources and symbolic systems to which he, consciously or unconsciously, trusts himself. By this constant demythologisation criticism can perform a 'political' rather than a 'productive' function. Compared with 'operative criticism' analysed in the previous pages, semiology's contribution reveals itself as symmetrically opposite. 'Operative criticism' accepts the current myths, enters into them, tries to create new ones, judges architectural production by the yardsticks of the objectives it itself has proposed and advanced. A criticism that pays attention to the relations between the single work and the system to which it belongs tends to throw light on and to unmask the current mythologies, even the most advanced, and, without proposing new myths, invites a pitiless coherence. Even the extreme coherence of those who decide to remain (but consciously and critically) in the most absolute silence.

One must also say that this kind of criticism has not been yet tried out with sufficient methodological rigour (and not only in respect of architecture). It meets, in fact, many difficulties, some political, others methodological. Zevi, analysing Eco's recent essay on the semiology of visual communications, reveals the difficulties met in trying to define a *code* for architecture.[76] Eco has examined the various hypotheses put forward on the subject, distinguishing between 'syntactical codes' (primary elements into which a building can be decomposed), and 'semantic codes' (denoting 'primary functions', like stairs, roofs, etc. and 'secondary functions', that is, all the symbolic elements of architecture, and all the building and spatial types that refer to an 'ideology of housing').[77]

We will criticise later the way in which Eco relates the concept of 'code' to architecture. What interests us, for the moment, is his recognition of the codifications to which the architect refers even without being clearly aware of it. But, Zevi asks, what is the meaning of 'code' in architecture?

> If it is about typological kinds and syntactic and semantic elements, the reasoning may sound almost reactionary, because the architect, condemned to deal with the 'base code', with traditional forms and schemes, would never be able to cause a movement in the events of history. . . . Architecture constitutes a challenge to semiology not so much because it is unable to 'speak about its own forms' (this, in spite of Eco's perceptive essay, has not yet been ascertained), but rather because its language has to continually refer to society and history, emphasising a close synthesis of signified and signifier. The crisis of architecture concerns not only forms, laws or syntactical relations within the architectural system (even if it would be wrong to ignore their problems) but, above all, the purposes of planning new towns and new buildings.[78]

Apart from the specific criticism of Eco's interpretation of the architectural codes, Zevi touches, accidentally, on the problem of the ideological attitude of structuralist analysis. By insisting so much on the permanent structures of human activity and, in particular, of architectural activity, is one not running the risk of falling into a new metaphysic of Being? If every action finds a place in pre-existing codifications acting on a subterranean level, how can one effect the introduction of the new, of what contests reality, of what causes – not, of course, in architecture but in politics – a revolutionary jump? It is not by chance that in the introduction we have mentioned the risks implied in the structuralist attitude. It is too easy to introduce through it, and under the counter, a new ideology of *tout se tient*.

But, as someone has mentioned recently, one must not confuse astrology and astronomy, condemning a science on the basis of its deformations and its secondary issues.

Underneath all this there remains the problem of the definition of the codes specific to architecture. We should mention that on this point the studies that try to 'translate' language research into architectural analyses too often show the functional characteristics of the latter as their specific meanings.

König falls into this fallacy when he tries to derive a reading method for architectural language from the theories of Charles Morris; and also Umberto Eco, although in a different way, when he writes that 'the architectural object denotes a form of habitation and characterises a global ideology of habitation'.[79] Already Eco's distinction between *primary functions* (simply denoted) and *secondary functions* (characterised and symbolic) compromises the immediate distinction between the meanings of architecture and its functions. But the fallacy remains, despite the fact that Eco has acutely contested Lévi-Strauss's need to refer every communicative act to the context of interpretative models similar to the codes of verbal language.

Faced with Michelangelo's design for the S. Lorenzo façade in Florence, based on the intersection of architectural structures and sculptural space, or the vestibule of the Laurentian Library, where the entire grammar of Classical orders is altered, while the walls delimiting an unreal space are articulated polyphonically, any architectural reading based simplicistically on functionalist parameters is put into crisis. The same can be said about the spatial metamorphoses of Palladio, of the Dientzenhofers, and even about the works of De Stijl and Le Corbusier.

The contents of architectural language *contain* meanings derived from disciplines outside architectural planning, but not exclusively from them. The ideology underlying architectural works is always, after all, a vision of the world that tends to pose as a construction of the human environment. Nor can one consider decisive the fact that, as ideology, architecture is bound to see the failure of its purposes. The Humanist dream fails when the high moral and rational function attributed to architecture as the first element of the secular 'city of man' is frustrated by political realism, by the Church of Rome, by the short-sightedness and hypocrisy of sixteenth-century neo-feudalism. And so the revolutionary dream of modern architecture has not been frustrated by the political involutions of the only great revolution of early 1900, but by the ambiguous relations, from the start, between architecture and revolution, between form and planning methods, between history and avant-gardes. In this sense architecture is always the *construction of a utopia*.

The value and the meanings of architecture go beyond what architecture manages to *realise* in society: Chartres Cathedral, the Pazzi Chapel, S. Ivo alla Sapienza, the *salines* of Chaux, the Villa Savoye and Chandigarh are evidence of ideas that have value as messages beyond their immediate effect on social behaviour and beyond their historical consequences. When Persico – in a climate not so very favourable to the 'construction' of rational facts – spoke of architecture as the 'substance of things hoped for', he stated a paradoxical but absolute truth. Architecture has, therefore, a high degree of ambiguity. It presents itself as a *usable object* and projects into the future utopian needs that are, logically, bound to be frustrated.

But this is the reality of architecture, and this is what justifies or explains the tension that, today in particular, dominates the debate on architectural culture. On the other hand, this possibility of inserting a fragment of utopia into reality is a privilege that architecture – compared to other systems of visual communication – often manages to use to the very end.

For this reason, in defining the substance of an architectural code, we go to the formula elaborated by Roman Ingarden and by Welleck and Warren for literature: code as system of systems.

Let us explain ourselves better. One can fix, for example, the values configurating the architecture of Humanism only by proceeding with two streams of research at the same time. On one side the study of the various socio-cultural structures that enter into the architectural languages: the symbolic systems, the problem of knowledge, social behaviour, the modifications of these questions by the architects' proposals, the laws of vision, the condition of technology and its intrinsic meanings, etc. On the other is the study of the inter-actions between the various systems: the study, in short, of the deformations undergone by every system of values in becoming part of an artistic code.

From the view-point of the history of technology one could say that Brunelleschi's constructive systems have not made a substantial contribution to the development of modern technology. But if one confronts this observation with the revaluation carried out by Brunelleschi within the symbolic and perceptive systems (these systems have their own independent histories and can undergo independent analyses), then the initial abstract information totally changes: it becomes concrete and, from its point of view, throws light on a system that, by giving it meaning, can even contradict the original statement.

If Brunelleschi's technique is introduced as an element of an architectural code, it will assume a quite different weight of meaning. In the concreteness of the S. Maria del Fiore dome the reference to history, the absoluteness of the formal relations, the representation value of space, the symbolism of the organism and the evidence of technology react among themselves to form a code of permament values that – apart from all the super-impositions that will modify it, compromise it, criticise it to an extreme of tension that reaches breaking point –

represents the basic structure of European Classicism in the fifteenth and sixteenth centuries.

We do not mean, with all this, to stress only the integration of technology with the functions and spatial construction of architecture, but to point out, also, how the specific architectural values spring from the complex stratification of architecture itself.

It is clear, though, that in the architectural work the various components can be arranged according to extremely variable hierarchies, assuming successively different roles.

In Borromini's S. Carlino one cannot clearly separate the typological structure from the symbolic, technological or geometrical structure, but in the Casa dei Filippini the functional system has primary values, while the symbolical and technological values are simply episodical. The relation between the various systems changes completely in contemporary architecture, where clearly the concept of 'code' can be applied almost exclusively to planning methods.

In other words, what is specific to architecture is the way of relating the various structures that converge in it. And this constitutes, not by chance, the problem of architectural theories, from Vitruvius's to the treatises of the nineteenth century.

By interpreting architecture in its complex structure and not in its mere visual appearance, we have the means of bringing back that very structure into unity and organicity. But in order to do this we will have to find out how to re-insert past utopias into present reality, how and within what limits we can recover the original historical meanings of architectures that have become part of modern urban and territorial structures and how the present myths will allow the decoding of myths, values and involutions of architectural phenomena in the course of history.

The reading of the work [Eco writes] is carried out . . . in a *perpetual oscillation,* so that from the work we move to the discovery of the original codes suggested by it, from here to an attempt at a faithful reading of the work, from this latter back again to our present codes and lexicons in order to try them out on the message; and from here we proceed to a continuous comparison and integration between the various reading keys, enjoying the work also for its ambiguity, that comes not only from the informative use of the signifiers in respect of the starting code, but also from the informative use of the signifiers as related to our end codes. And every interpretation of the work, by filling the empty and open form of the original message with new meanings . . . brings out new message-meanings that enrich our ideological systems by restructuring them, and disposing tomorrow's readers towards a new interpretative situation in respect of the work.[80]

We should make a few observations on this point. First of all we will have to distinguish between unintentional operations and those that correspond to precise critical choices.

In fact, once we have achieved the philological recovery of the specific message of the work, the comparison with the present codes is not so simple and immediate as Eco's words may lead us to suppose. Which code, in fact? We know too well that the entire cycle of modern art is split into a series of streams dialectically connected: and it is well known that this dialecticity of contemporary art does not allow a unitary definition, apart, of course, from superficial generalisations. Nor can one simply compare the codes of the past with the multiplications of codes typical of the present.

Even in the identification of the new global meanings of the present processes with the structure of the *media* through which the architectural message is organised, one has to distinguish carefully between the message and the conditions of its formation. These have, of course, their own independent meaning, but only as structures underlying particular configurations.

The comparison between the codes of the past and those of the present happens, therefore, in several ways:

A. As comparison between the general structures of the conception of space in history: in this sense 'perspective as symbolic form' can, as regards late Gothic and Classicism, be compared with contemporary codes that assume, in their turn symbolic form, the manifold, the fragment, the lexicons and the co-presence of opposites.

B. As comparison, carried out by the artist, between his own particular lexicon and the lesson derived from past works (a typical operation of architects like Kahn and Johnson).

C. As actualisation of history realised by the critic (and here we are within the more general chapter of *operative criticism* that we have already dealt with).

D. As an automatic and not always controllable deformation of every product of the past, carried out in the very act of perception and interpretation.

We face an obvious polarity: the need for a philological recovery of the past clashes with the filter of present interpretative parameters. But what is the precise use of philology to the history of architecture?

According to Wellek and Warren:

> The literary work of art is neither an empirical fact . . . nor is it an ideal changeless object such as a triangle. The work of art may become an object of experience; it is, we admit, accessible only through individual experience, but it is not identical with any experience.[81]

For Wellek and Warren there is, then, a structure of the work that remains identical to itself, but that, at the same time, is available to different readings in the course of history: it is 'historical' in the sense that the development of the various interpretations raised by the work can be described, re-assembled and used to start the new interpretations.

> Our consciousness of earlier concretisations (readings, criticisms, misinterpretations) will affect our own experience: earlier readings may educate us to a deeper understanding or may cause a violent reaction against the prevalent interpretation of the past. All this shows us the importance of the history of criticism . . . and leads to difficult questions about the nature and limits of individuality.[82]

This confirms what we have previously observed about the importance of the history of criticism in reading the history of architecture, but poses, at the same time, a further problem: the meaning of the historical cycles in respect of the single architectural project.

Having got rid of the childish concept of 'progress' in the field of historiographical interpretation, we have still to explain the reason for the incessant substitution of artistic languages in the course of history, and, in particular, the reason for the unprecedented rate of acceleration of substitution in the history of contemporary art.[83]

The artificial and conventional character of language cannot be explained without recourse to the study of the context in which language has a sense. But, at the same time, we know that it is language itself that transforms the context, that enriches it with new values, that subjects it to pitiless criticism, that pushes it towards limits beyond which there is only a radical revolution of the meanings and behaviours.[84]

To remain in the specific sector of architecture, perhaps the best evidence of this is to be found in the historical study of the so-called times of *crisis* or of linguistic decay. We know too well that, in historiographic interpretation, the concept of *crisis* is very much a concept of convenience without effective reality. The entire motion of history is the expression of a perpetual crisis. Those who employ this term a-critically do not interpret the reason of a historical moment, but rather express a personal adherence to a context of values of which they, somehow do not accept the evolution.

The problem of the passage from late-Gothic to Brunelleschian Humanism, for example, shows clearly that the ideal revolution of methods, of the conception of artistic production and of its social meaning, depended on the re-organisation and restructuring of linguistic material and methodological instruments that were already extensively present in the figurative tendencies of fourteenth-century Tuscany. The concept of perspective, the use of classicist elements, the co-ordination of spaces, the subordination of decoration to the laws of the architectural organism, the rigorous control of form through proportional canons, are not Brunelleschi's *inventions*. They are, rather, elements that had entered pre-existing codes, making them transient, compromising their structurality and giving them a problematic form.

In this sense Brunelleschi can be seen as the artist who, witnessing the apex of the crisis of the Gothic world, chose a few elements from that context: he restructured the organising laws that held them together so deeply and radically so that he came to the point of reaching a new system – revolutionary because charged with new meanings – that sprang from the new relations between its constituent signs.

The great linguistic systems in the history of architecture can, then, be defined as, somehow, unitary systems. It is sufficient, in fact, to measure their unitarity with the yardstick of a dynamic conception, keeping in mind what seems now taken for granted in semiological studies: that every artistic code can only be defined on the basis of the contributions that transgress, offend and marginally contest that very same code. The problem is, then, in the criteria to be used in order to distinguish among the linguistic unities in the history of architecture. In the example just stated it is obvious that we have a true linguistic revolution when the enrichment of a given code – particularly the Gothic – is carried so far as to cause a crisis in the dynamic system of the relations that, in spite of eversions and contestations from within, sees its universe of discourse as unitary. From this point of view the exasperated naturalism of *Manueline* style, the anti-structuralism of the German masters of the fourteenth and fifteenth centuries, the lack of realism of the English *Perpendicular*, are, of course, obvious eversions of the language defined between 1144 and 1230 (between S. Denis's apse and Chartres's choir), without, however, definitely compromising it. Their contestations can be read within the symbolic dimensions determined by the Gothic linguistic world. For the same reason, one should reject a classification that puts Classicism, Mannerism and Baroque on the same plane as antithetical and distinct movements. On the contrary, Mannerism, Baroque and Rococo are all moments of one great historical movement: Classicism.

Between Brunelleschi's revolution and Michelangelo's and Borromini's eversions there is the same distance that separates those who introduce a new universe of meanings that dominates for about four centuries – all the time getting richer, larger and self-contesting to the point of exasperation – from those who quarrel with it, rebel against it, even invent new thematics and new expressive structures (but without carrying out a new radical revolution).

One could say that, essentially, in the historical development we can distinguish between fundamental codes (corresponding to the great cycles defined by the systems of meaning and by the relationship of homogeneous production), derived codes (the categories that specify the evolution of the code in the course of time), and undercodes relating to particular and individual semantic areas. Of course the historical acknowledgment of these homogeneous areas is always limited. Every historical structure reveals the coherence of its own internal relations only within parameters defined by the critical choices of the historian.

The classification into periods becomes, then, the instrument for an 'intentioned' reading of history. And it is clear that the structural similarities on which the acknowledgment of a homogeneous cycle is based lead to hypothetical historiographical 'models'. These constitute, also, conscious constructions elaborated by the historian as abstractions to be used in the more objective instrumentation of his particular readings.

Already Riegl's and Panofsky's *Kunstwollen* seize on the common and underlying nuclei of subjective expression. We will never find, in history, a work completely Romanesque, Gothic, Classicist, 'modern' or 'open'.[85] Panofsky quite correctly insisted on the independence of the *Kunstwollen* from the conscious intentions and psychological attitudes of the authors. We can add that one can identify the nucleus common to the various works of the same expressive system only if the historian becomes a sort of cryptoanalyst, an investigator of the unconscious and subterranean relations linking the members of a linguistic community, even if on different sides of the barricade, and a discoverer of the invisible laws presiding over the formation of artistic language. Historical structures must, then be considered dynamic systems, to be studied through the abstractions that will bring to light the thick networks of hidden relations.

We think that by now it must be evident that what we call 'historical structures' or 'architectural codes' is something very near Weber's concept of 'ideal type'. For Max Weber[86] the 'ideal type' (*Idealtypus*),

> serves to orientate the judgment of attribution in the course of the research: it is not an 'hypothesis' but it shows the way to the elaboration of the hypothesis. It is not a representation of reality but it supplies representation with an univocal means of expression . . . it is realised through a unilateral emphasis of one or several points of view and through the connection of a quantity of diffused and discrete particular phenomena, existing in great or small measure, or even absent, corresponding to those unilaterally emphasised points of view, in a conceptual scheme in itself unitary. In its conceptual purity this scheme cannot be found empirically in reality; it is a utopia, and it is up to the historical research to find, in each case, the greater or lesser distance of that ideal scheme from reality. . . .[87]

The historical development corresponds, therefore, to a succession of revolutions and radical changes in the universes of meaning: the need for such revolutions is the specific meaning that has to be discovered by the historian. And this applies also to contemporary art and architecture that have institutionalised, within artistic production itself, the concept of revolution: the perpetual overturning of linguistic links and of the systems of meanings seems to be the ideal reference code for the 'Modern Movement'.

Within this framework semiological research is not at all anti-historicistic. It will be sufficient to set aside the artificial extremist positions by which structural research identifies itself, *ipso facto*, with a total determinism, to realise how much genuinely critical and demystifying weight is contained in the insistence on the problem of the relations between codes and contestations. We fully agree with Eco, in fact, when he states that semiology reveals pitilessly 'the false acts of freedom', the mitigated infractions of the codes and the too many cases in which, rather than freely using the language, we '*are spoken*' by the language itself.[88]

The probing into the structures of architectural codes, the specification of the limits within which one can speak of artistic revolution and of radical contestation, the careful and realistic weighing of the constructive value and the ideological implications of languages are, consequently, the legitimate and unsubstitutable tasks of semiological studies. An exact knowledge of the margins of freedom of every linguistic system brings the disguises of convenience, the play of the false advances and the emptiness behind irony and the joke crudely to light. All the mystifications, in short, relentlessly heaped on during the course of history each time the consciousness of the crisis is not followed by realistic and courageous analysis of its ultimate motives.

Now, as the present historical moment is characterised precisely by a similar game of hide and seek with reality in its totality, and as architecture reflects even too faithfully its aberrations and duplicity, we have the possibility of a more rigorous historical explanation of why such a complex discipline as semiology has met with so much favour in architectural culture. To justify this interest we could point out two distinct motives: opposed and complementary at the same time. On one side the need to settle the world of images surrounding the architect, and by which he is enormously pressurised, answers to the necessity of recovering a stable reference structure, a linguistic 'horizon' and some laws of behaviour, if not some stylistic choices. In this sense the identification of the precise relation linking language and ideology acquires the flavour of a return to the more authentic origins of the Modern Movement: this is the explanation of the many examples of primitivism or archaism in architects particularly aware of the theoretical problems of visual communications.

On the other side is the continuous temptation to exploit operatively, to translate into planning terms, and to arrange the results of semiological studies into formal systems. It may seem paradoxical, but this second tendency has a precise historical reason also. As for the problem of history, so for the problem of the meanings, the pragmatist tries to neutralise something confusedly felt dangerous. In effect the rigorous semiologic exploration of the structures supporting the current artistic praxis is in itself a danger for a good part of contemporary architecture. After we have identified the type of operation hidden behind architecture's attempt to absorb and neutralise the critical moment within planning, we shall not need many words to explain how semiological analysis could be threatening architecture as institution.

After all, what is comfortable in the present confused and contorted cultural situation is the possibility of continuous exchange between game and eversion, essential needs and fashionable phenomena, research and rhetorical toying with worn-out instruments, honest critical commitment and conscious scepticism *à la jongleur*. We were saying that this is a desperate but comfortable situation. And we begin to suspect that it is mainly comfortable, as the anxious search for a way out seems less and less dramatic. It is, in fact, easy to see that those who struggle so violently reject, after all, the only rational way able, at least, to state their problem:

the way to a deep penetration (and from the outside) of the structures of planning.

But instead of this penetration we see, on the contrary, an instrumentalisation of the disciplines derived from linguistics and semiology. *In other words, they are trying to translate into language the discourse on language.* As a result what should have been a demystifying weapon is being coaxed, flattered, seduced, made harmless and compromised by operations absolutely outside its competence. So we shall have to identify without equivocation the legitimate fields of architectural semiological research, firmly excluding any possibility of its immediate application to the discovery or justification of new figurative structures.

Boyd has tried to establish a chronology of the recent history of architecture, and has recognised some common features in many tendencies at their peak between about 1950 and 1962: the 'monolithic' and 'sculptural' emphasis of the forms, the polemic against the International Style, and the return to figurative symbolism.[89] He sees works by Stone, Yamasaki and Eero Saarinen as the main examples of what he calls the 'second phase' of the Modern Movement. A 'second phase', we note in passing, that the late Robin Boyd declared closed with the construction of that enormous 'mistaken symbol' – Saarinen's Air Terminal at Kennedy Airport.[90]

What is of most interest to us, though, is the fact that the Australian critic, together with many other English speaking critics and the very same architects taking part in the Counter-Revolution mentioned by Boyd, have insisted on using the expression 'significant form' to define the search for a new density of the architectural image. 'Significant form', 'imageability', 'figurability' are, in any case, terms that frequently recur in the writings of Saarinen, Stone, Rudolph, Yamasaki (and of some of their Italian followers), while the studies by Kepes and Lynch originate from the same confusedly expressed needs.

We know very well that the theory of art as *significant form* has been the ambiguous battle horse of, first, Clive Bell and, then (in an even more uncertain and ambiguous way, if that is possible), of Roger Fry, and that the neo-Symbolist theories of Susanne Langer and of a good number of the American scholars have in various ways stressed the 'significant' values of images.[91]

The misunderstanding – perfectly expressed by the results of those architectural researches – is in the attempt to establish an artistic language derived from research carried out in order to set up reading techniques.[92]

De Stijl managed to establish a language, on the extreme border line with criticism; by probing the compositive technique of a new code of visual communications: but it did not confuse planning methods with methods of reading planning. (For De Stijl, and for the Bauhaus, *Gestalt* psychology was nothing more than a working tool; in the same way that for Mondrian and Van Doesburg the Theosophical studies were nothing more than an ideal reference horizon.)

A more recent example of the misunderstanding is given by such a 'fashionable' architect as Robert Venturi in his *Complexity and Contradiction in Architecture*.[93] Venturi's exaltation of the category of *ambiguity* may, at first sight, seem stimulating. Only after realising that, in his historical analyses, tensions, contradictions and complexities become critical parameters *bons à tout faire*, able to explain Blenheim Palace and Fuga's double church at Calvi, and also work by Furness, Lutyens, Francesco di Giorgio, Sullivan and Alvar Aalto, one sees that the adoption of the concept of 'ambiguity' in the work of art, borrowed from the analytical texts of Empson and Eliot,[94] is aimed at justifying personal planning choices rather more equivocal than ambiguous.

Venturi does, of course, make many perceptive observations on the structures of complex architectural organisms, uncovering their less evident cultural matrixes. What we criticise is: on one side, the failed historicisation of architectural ambiguity, that becomes, therefore, an *a priori* category with only generic meanings; on the other, the conclusions of his research that, through historiographical flattening and confusion between analyses and planning methods, manages to justify personal figurative choices. (Apart, of course, from the great modesty of Venturi's designs and realisations.)

This said, we are unable to understand how such a serious and perceptive scholar as Vincent Scully could write, in his introduction to Venturi's book, that it has been, after Le Corbusier's *Vers une architecture*, the most notable cultural event in the architectural debate.[95] Venturi's book employs 'fashionable' analytical methods, turning them, without any mediation, into 'compositive' methods. In this way the values of *ambiguity* and of *contradiction* lose their historical consistency and are reproposed as 'principles' of a poetic. And it is difficult to understand how one could find, in this intellectual salvage operation, a new meaning in respect of Le Corbusier's 'five points', as Venturi himself shows that Le Corbusier's *purist* work is also dominated by multi-significance, by dualism and by complexity.

What, then, is the difference between Venturi's proposal and the poetics of many historical avant-gardes – most of all Paul Klee's – that recognised the introduction of the unconscious, of the irrational, of ambiguity and of the unsolved tension between opposite polarities, into the structures of artistic activity? Klee does not start from *a priori* categories (not even from historically defined categories) in order to identify the dimensions of his poetic. The high didactic content in *Theory of Form and Figuration* is in Klee's continuous comparison between subjective choices and formal processes in the reality of perception. For Klee, irony, complexity, and soundings on the verge of the rational are end results and not starting points.

So the theoretical clarification that today's linguistic and semiologic disciplines could introduce runs the risk of being instrumentalised and finalised according to mystifying theories. But, of course, the sin of immediate instrumentalisation of the analyses rules architectural culture. And with this we go back to a proposition repeated many times: the 'official' climate of architectural debate tends to absorb every external contribution, not in order to exercise self-criticism, but in order to neutralise criticism. In this way, the fidelity to the myths of the 'modern tradition' fully reveals its interested character.

The *use* we suggest for semiology and structural analyses should be to undertake a pitiless scrutiny of the meanings underlying apparently 'innocent' forms and choices; it should bring to light the system of conditioning accepted or unconsciously undergone by architect, critic and public, and should face the doer with his responsibilities. One could even accept a worn myth, or, in an extreme case, a mystification, provided one were fully aware of this acceptance, and willing to show it as such within the work one is shaping. (This has been, after all, Brecht's method.)

All this has a strong influence on stating the problem of objectivity in critical judgment. We will deal with this theme, to a greater extent, in the next chapter, but we must make immediately clear that, up to now, architectural criticism seems to have ignored Max Weber's equivocal lesson on the method of historiographical analysis and the problem of judgment values.

We offer . . . [Weber wrote in 1904] to those who act the possibility of measuring the unwanted consequences of their action, and to answer therefore the question: what is the 'cost' of realising the intended aim, in terms of the foreseeable losses of other values. As, in the majority of cases, every aim one is striving for either 'costs' or may cost something, the self-reflection of the men who act responsibly cannot avoid the mutual measure of the aim and the consequences of the action; one of

19.   Paul Klee, *Air-Tsu-dni*, 1917. ('Industria' written back-to-front)

the main functions of the technical criticism is, in fact, to make it possible. . . . The translation of that measuring into decision is not the responsibility of science but of the man who acts freely. . . . What we can do in helping him to decide is to offer the knowledge of the meaning of what is wanted.[96]

And with this, from a discourse on the instruments of historiography and criticism we return to the problem of the why of history and criticism: to the problem of their tasks. It is a problem that must be tackled by leaving the generalities used, necessarily in this chapter, in dealing with questions relating to the instrumentalisation of analytical methods, and immersing ourselves once more in the specific thematics of the architecture of the present historical moment, the starting point of our analyses.

Notes to chapter 5

[1] Cf. the introduction to the present book, particularly note 2. Cf. also: Antonino Pagliaro, *Nuovi Saggi di critica semantica*, Messina 1956; id., *La parola e l'immagine*, Naples 1957.

[2] E. Garroni, *La crisi semantica delle arti* op. cit., p. 154. Cf. L. Anceschi, *Progetto di una sistematica dell'arte* Mursia, Milan 1962, p. 162 ff.

[3] Cf. again E. Garroni, op. cit. p. 147 ff.

[4] Ibid. pp. 170–8.

[5] René Wellek and Austin Warren in *Theory of Literature*, Harcourt, Brace & World, New York 1963, have made some perceptive comments on the problem of the evaluation and implicit judgment in exegesis. Cf. also, on the same range of architectural problems: Renato De Fusco, *Architettura come mass medium. Note per una semiologia architettonica*, Dedalo libri, Bari 1967, pp. 123–47. Cf. also the results of the Prague and Bratislav Congress on 'Essenza funzioni e strumenti della critica d'arte' (participants: G. C. Argan, P. Bucarelli, J. P. Hodin, L. Novak, H. Read, M. Vaross), published in *Marcartrè* 1967, nos. 34–6, p. 8 ff.

[6] Cf. P. Collins, *Changing Ideals in Modern Architecture* op. cit.; id. 'The Interrelated Roles of History, Theory and Criticism in the Process of Architectural Design' in *The History, Theory*, etc. op. cit. pp. 1–10; id. 'Oecodemics' op. cit. On the relations between history of architecture and the possible tasks of a theory of architecture, see also the symposium on the theme: 'Architectural History and the Student Architect' (Participants: S. Moholy-Nagy, P. F. Anstis, W. L. Creese, L. K. Eaton, A. Jackson, S. Kostof, Fr. D. Nichols, E. F. Sekler, M. Whiffen) in *Journal of the Society of Architectural Historians* (U.S.) 1967, vol. XXVI, no. 3, p. 178 ff.

[7] Cf. Christian Norberg-Schulz, *Intentions in Architecture*, 1963, in which the author relates the crisis of modern architecture as a communication system to the lack of a solid *Theory of Planning*. In spite of the interest of many of his analyses, Norberg-Schulz's 'theories' are ambiguous in their aims: in part trying to define methods of historical research and in part methods of planning. Furthermore, Norberg-Schulz is a supporter of the division between history and architectural criticism (cf. op. cit. p. 290 ff.)

In Italy, Rossi's and Grassi's publications represent the newest methods of analysis applied to planning theory. But their distortion of the historical phenomena should always be considered instrumental: one should oppose the claimed objectivity of their readings, that translate into a new literary form some extremely subjective 'poetics'. (Cf. A. Rossi, *L'architettura della città* op. cit. and G. Grassi, *La costruzione logica dell'architettura* op. cit.) We just mention in passing, because their study goes beyond our terms of reference, the well known work by Alexander and Asimow, and also the anthology edited by Giuseppe Susani, *La metodologia della progettazione*, Marsilio, Padua 1967.

[8] This theme is central to V. Gregotti's *Il territorio dell'architettura* op. cit., and to Norberg-Schulz's *Intentions* (see preceding note).

[9] 'To the possible meaning of the idea of the logic structure of architecture on the

plane of individual ideation – on the plane, that is, of the image that the artist makes of it – is contraposed the logical principle of architecture, that is to say its substantial tautologicity. This, in my opinion, represents a positive direction: the aspiration to this logic form as an essential element of architecture constitutes a precise purpose, and a definite tendency; it represents, in fact, *the analytical quality of architecture taken as its aim.* Making this choice means giving a fundamental function to the didactic aspect of the theorical construction.' G. Grassi, op. cit. p. 108.

[10] Cf. Gennaro Sasso, *Passato e presente nella storia della filosofia*, Laterza, Bari 1967, chap. I; Edward H. Carr, *What is History?*, Macmillan, London 1961. No need to mention the well-known texts by Lévi-Strauss (however, the theme of history is dealt with in the introduction to the *Pensée sauvage*).

[11] Cf. E. Gombrich, *Art and Illusion* op. cit.; Gillo Dorfles, *Le oscillazioni del gusto*, Lerici, Milan 1958; *Il divenire della arti*, Einaudi, Turin 1967; *Simbolo, comunicazione, consumo*, ibid. 1962; *Nuovi riti, nuovi, miti*, ibid. 1965; Max Bense, *Aesthetica, IV*, Agis Verl., Baden Baden 1965; Abraham Moles, *Théorie de l'information et perception esthétique*, Paris 1958; R. De Fusco, *L'architettura come mass medium* op. cit.

[12] R. D Fusco, op. cit. p. 146.

[13] Cf. notes 38 and 85. 'The historicity of human actions [Argan wrote] appears today tormented by a crisis, of which the crisis of art constitutes only one aspect. The entire past appears like a period of which we have reached an end, like a "field" of which we have touched the boundaries, a system whose functional possibilities have been exhausted: seeing the failure of the goal that the process seemed to be aiming at, we hear of the "checkmate" of the human enterprise. As if for a sort of defensive attitude one looks everywhere for non-historicistic structural schemes, almost to prove that history has not been and is not now the great structure of human activity and that, therefore, *lucus a non lucendo*, history can follow, by changing the historicistic pattern of its development. This would explain why the problem of the structures rises from the general crisis of the structures in every field of knowledge: not as the problem of the auxiliary insertion of structuralism into historicism, but as the problem of a historicistic structuralism or of a structuralistic historicism.' G. C. Argan, 'Strutturalismo e critica' debate organised by Cesare Segre, in *Catalogo generale 1958-65*, Il Saggiatore, Milan 1965, p. LXI. Cf. Argan's observations on the problems analysed in the first chapter of this book. Worthy of note are Argan's indications about the possible use of structuralism for re-defining the historical cycles in the field of history of art.

[14] Recently Bonelli has taken up again this theme in polemic with Bettini, Paci and Della Volpe, stating that 'the pictorial and architectural language, constituted of figurative elements, because of the fact that it "represents" only itself without the possibility of referring to other acts and facts, reveals itself unable to communicate and signify'. Cf. Renato Bonelli, 'Critica e linguaggio architettonico', in *Arte lombarda*, 1965, X (volume in honour of Giusta Nicco Fasola), pp. 291-3 (later in the volume in honour of G. Caronia-Roberti,

Palermo 1967). This article follows the essay by the same author: 'L'estetica moderna e la critica dell' architettura' in *Zodiac*, 1959, no. 4, p. 22 ff., in which Bonelli polemicised Sergio Bettini's article: 'Critica semantica e continuità storica dell'architettura europea' in *Zodiac 2*, 1958, p. 7 ff. Bettini answered Bonelli indirectly in the article: 'L'architettura di Carlo Scarpa', ibid. 1960, no. 6. Cf. also Bettini's 'Possibilità di un giudizio di valore sulle opere d'arte contemporanea' in *Arte e Cultura nella Civiltà Contemporanea*, Quaderni di San Giorgio, Sansoni, Florence 1966.

[15] Cf. A. Schmarsow, *Das Wesen der architektonischen Schöpfung*, Leipzig 1894; P. Frankl, *Das System der Kunstwissenschaft*, Brunn 1938; H. Sedlmayr, *Die Architektur Borrominis* op. cit., and *Kunst und Warheit*, Hamburg 1958. Cf. also, on these structuralistic anticipations: Ch. Norberg-Schulz, op. cit., p. 118 ff., Werner Hofman, debate on *Strutturalismo e critica*, in vol. cit., pp. xxxv–xxxix.

[16] S. Bettini, 'Introduzione' to: Alois Riegl, *Industria artistica tardoromana*, Sansoni, Florence 1953.

[17] Cf. S. Bettini op. cit., pp. xiii–xv.

[18] 'For us, as for Early Christianity [Bettini writes (op. cit., p. lx)] there is no longer room for an art of the third dimension, that is to say of space as depth: this was the space of nineteenth-century "nature" and human illusion. In the Christian basilica as in the present architecture there is, therefore, a "dissolution of the plastic space" ... The early Christian sets up a spatial image of his church and the beating of time adjusts to it: inside this image he feels himself sheltered and safe. ... Today this serenity, this metaphysical trust is gone. We have no longer fixed points and immovable structures to lean on.' In this essay, as in many others, Bettini appears the most direct heir of Wickhoff's and Riegl's methods, opening up his criticism to actuality and operativity.

[19] S. Bettini op. cit., p. xv.

[20] S. Bettini, *Critica semantica* op. cit.

[21] Ibid., p. 12.

[22] Ibid., p. 11.

[23] C. Brandi, *Le due vie* op. cit., pp. 35–6.

[24] Cf. Umberto Eco, *Appunti per una semiologia delle comunicazioni visive*, Bompiani, Milan 1967, p. 171 ff., and *La struttura assente*, Bompiani, Milan 1968.

[25] Francesco di Giorgio's drawings of the Oratorio della Santa Croce are in Turin's Codice Saluzziano 148, ff. 80 v. and f. 81. The Oratorio della Santa Croce was built by Pope Ilario (461–68 A.D.) and was demolished by Urban VIII in 1629. Cf. *I trattati di architettura, ingegneria e arte militare*, Francesco di Giorgio Martini, edited by Corrado Maltese, Il Polifilo, Milan 1967, pp. 281–2, plates 148–9. Giuliano da Sangallo's survey is in the Codice Barb. Lat. 4424, f. 30v and f. 31 and can be considered an almost faithful copy of the fifth-century organism. Cf. also the drawing by the Anonimo Palladiano (vol. XIII, pl. 3) at the RIBA, London, about which cf. G. G. Zorzi, *I disegni delle Antichità di Andrea Palladio*, Neri Pozza, Venice 1959, fig. 269. Peruzzi's drawing, with elements of both the Oratorio della Santa Croce, and the Aula della Piazza d'Oro di Villa Adriana, is in

the Gabinetto diss. e stampe at the Uffizi, Florence, no. 529 A.

[26] Peruzzi's drawing merges, as we have already mentioned, the model of the Oratorio with that of the Aula della Piazza d'Oro. The typological synthesis, tried by the Siena master in his studies, taken up and vulgarised by Serlio, represents a sounding of the material offered by Antiquity as a historicistic rather than erudite *exploit*.

[27] Cf. Ernst H. Gombrich, *Art and Illusion* op. cit. Gombrich, in defining the activity of artistic perception as meetings and clashes between a 'system of expectations' and the unrealised content of the work, leans on the studies by Kris, who has used, with unquestionable methodological coherence, psychoanalytic techniques in the study of artistic phenomena. 'For some time [Kris writes] we have realised that art is not achieved in a vacuum, that every artist relies on precedents and models and, like the scientist and the philosopher, is tied to a precise tradition and works within a clearly structured area of problems. The degree of mastership of this structure and, at least in certain periods, the freedom to modify these ties, are part, presumably, of the complex scale with which the problems are judged.' Ernst Kris, *Psychoanalytic Explorations in Art*, New York and London 1952, p. 21. Gombrich too has explored the possibility of an alliance between psychoanalysis and history of art. (Cf. E. Gombrich, *Psychoanalysis and the History of Art*). In spite of the limited field that Gombrich, quite rightly, sees as valid for such an alliance, it is of interest to note that some conclusions derived from psychoanalytic methods concide with those obtained by analysing the works by the methods of information theory. Cf. also Ch. Norberg-Schulz, op. cit., who uses the researches of Gestalt psychology, of Piaget, of Ehrenzweig and of Max Bense.

[28] C. Brandi *Struttura e architettura*, Einaudi, Turin 1967, p. 38.

[29] Ibid., p. 39.

[30] Cf. Serge Doubrovsky, *Pourquoi la nouvelle critique. Critique et Objectivité*, Mercure de France, Paris 1967. (*The new criticism in France*, Univers. of Chicago Press, Chicago & London, 1973.)

[31] S. Doubrovsky, op. cit., p. 99.

[32] Cf. AA.VV., 'La critica discorde' in: op. cit. 1965, no. 4. p. 20 ff. in which was tried the first assessment of the stream that Eco would call 'apocalyptic': those who oppose the modern world with its myths and its values (from Huizinga, therefore, to Ortega and Sedlmayr).

[33] S. Doubrovsky, op. cit., p. 106.

[34] Claude Lévi-Strauss, 'Strutturalismo e critica', answer to the discussion by Cesare Segre in: *Catalogo generale Il Saggiatore*, 1958–65 op. cit., p. li.

[35] Cl. Lévi-Strauss, op. cit., p. lii.

[36] Ibid., pp. lii–liii.

[37] Roland Barthes, 'L'activité structuraliste' in *Lettres Nouvelles*, 1936, and in: *Essais critiques*, Editions du Seuil, Paris 1963.

[38] We find a proposal of a diachronic and historicistic structuralism in Barthes's and Argan's answers to the discussion *Strutturalismo e critica* op. cit., and in Umberto Eco's *Appunti per una semiologia delle communicazioni visive* op. cit. Cf.

also, although fairly contrived, the contributions by P. Vilar, M. Charles Morazé and L. Goldmann in *Sens et usage du terme structure*, Mouton et co., The Hague 1962.

[39] Armanda Guiducci, *Dallo zdanovismo allo strutturalismo*, Feltrinelli, Milan 1967, pp. 353-4.

[40] Cf. in particular: Susanne K. Langer, *Feeling and Form. A Theory of Art*, Charles Scribner's Sons, New York 1953, and *Problems of Art*.

[41] H. Wölfflin, *Kunstgeschichtliche Grundbegriffe*, Munich 1915.

[42] C. Brandi, *Struttura e architettura* op. cit. p. 32.

[43] Erwin Panofsky, 'Das Problem des Stils in der Bildenden Kunst' in *Zeitschrift für Aesthetik und allgemeine Kunstwissenschaft*, X, 1915, p. 460 ff., and in: *La prospettiva come 'forma simbolica' e altri scritti*, Feltrinelli, Milan 1961.

[44] E. Panofsky, op. cit., p. 164.

[45] Ibid., p. 162.

[46] Ibid., p. 165.

[47] Ibid., p. 169.

[48] E. Panofsky, 'Ueber das Verhältnis der Kunstgeschichte zur Kunsttheorie' in: *Zeitschr. f. Aesth, u. all. Kunstwiss.*, XVIII, 1925, and in: *La prospettiva come 'forma simbolica'* op. cit., p. 179.

[49] Ibid., p. 188.

[50] Ibid., p. 189.

[51] Ibid., p. 206.

[52] Cf. A. Dorner, 'Die Erkenntnis des Kunstwollens durch die Kunstgeschichte', in *Zeitschr. f. Aesth. u. all. Kunstwiss.*, XVI, 1920, p. 216 ff. Panofsky's answer was published as an additional note to the article already quoted. Cf. also Aldo Masullo, 'Kunstwollen e intenzionalità in E. Panofsky', in op. cit., 1965, no. 3, p. 46 ff.

[53] E. Panofsky, op. cit., p. 208.

[54] On this theme cf. Panofsky, *Meaning in the visual Arts; Papers in and on Art History*, 1955; and *Studies in Iconology*, Oxford University Press 1939. Of interest are the results from the 'Inchiesta sul simbolo nella cultura italiana', edited by Rubina Giorgi, in *Marcatrè*, 1966, nos. 19-22, and 1967, nos. 30-3 (contributions by Maria Corti, Mario Costanzo, Emilio Garroni, Eugenio Battisti, Maurizio Calvesi, Diego Capitella, Antonella Guaraldi, Filiberto Menna and Manfredo Tafuri), underlining many of the limitations of the iconological fashion. Cf. also: Ezio Bonfanti, 'Iconologia e architettura' in *Lineastruttura*, 1967, nos. 1-2, pp. 12-17. Rudolf Arnheim, in *Art and Visual Perception. A Psychology of the Creative Eye*, University of California Press, Berkeley and Los Angeles 1954, tried to absorb the iconological themes within an analytical technique based on *Gestalt* psychology, with, in our opinion, not very happy, nor very successful results.

[55] E. Panofsky, *Die Perspektive als 'symbolische Form'*, *Vortrage 1924-1925*, B. G. Teubner, Leipzig-Berlin 1927.

[56] Ibid.

[57] Cf. Pierre Francastel, 'Espace génétique et espace plastique' in *Revue*

d'Esthétique, 1948, I, no. 4, p. 349 ff. Id., *Peinture et Société. Naissance et destruction d'un espace plastique*, Lyon 1950.

[58] Cf. E. Panofsky, *Gothic Architecture and Scholasticism*, Wimmer Lecture, 1948, The Archabbey Press, Latrobe (Penn.) 1956. On the same theme Panofsky's *Abbot Suger on the Abbey Church of Saint-Denis and Its Art Treasures*, Princeton 1946; and 'Postlogium Sugerianum' in *Art Bulletin*, XXIX, 1947. A criticism of *Gothic Architecture* is to be found in Paolo Marconi, 'Art Ogival' in *Marcatrè*, nos. 8–10.

[59] Cf. E. Panofsky, *Gothic Architecture* op. cit., introduction and paras. I–II.

[60] Ibid., pp. 1–2.

[61] Cf. Frederick Antal, *Florentine Painting and its Social Background*, Routledge & Kegan Paul, London 1947. C. Brandi criticised Antal in *Le due vie* op. cit., pp. 96–8. 'In the period between about 1130–40 and about 1270 [Panofsky writes (op. cit., p. 20)] we can observe . . . a connection between Gothic art and Scholasticism which is more concrete than a mere "parallelism" and yet more general than those individual (and very important) "influences" which are inevitably exerted on printers, sculptors or architects by erudite advisers. In contrast to a mere parallelism, the connection which I have in mind is a genuine cause-and-effect relation; but . . . this . . . relation comes about by diffusion rather than by direct impact. It comes about by the spreading of what may be called, for want of a better term, a mental habit – reducing this overworked cliché to its precise Scholastic sense as a "principle that regulates the act", *principium importans ordinem ad actum.*' The cause-and-effect relation, takes, therefore, for Panofsky, a very particular meaning that justifies our interpretation of his text.

[62] E. Panofsky, op. cit., p. 23.

[63] On these arguments considered from a more strictly philosophical point of view, cf. R. Assunto, *La critica d'arte nel pensiero medievale*, Il Saggiatore Milan 1961.

[64] E. Gombrich, 'Vom Wert der Kunstwissenschaft für die Symbolforschung' in *Wandlungen des Paradiesischen und Utopischen*, Berlin 1966.

[65] Cf. E. Gombrich, op. cit., p. 76 ff.

[66] Ibid., p. 79. Gombrich, in *Psychoanalysis and the History of Art*, quotes a very significant passage by Ernest Jones on the theory of Symbolism, where the double process of probing into a system of values and of the critical leap towards new values, typical – for Jones – of every human institution, is very clearly traced. '. . . on the one hand the extension or transference of interest and understanding from earlier, simpler and more primitive ideas, etc., to more difficult and complex ones, which in a certain sense are continuations of and symbolise the former; and on the other hand the constant unmasking of previous symbolisms, the recognition that these, though previously thought to be literally true, were really only aspects or representations of the truth, the only ones of which our minds were – for either effective or intellectual reasons – at the time capable.' Cf. Ernest Jones, *Papers on Psycho-Analysis*, London 1948, p. 87 ff.

[67] Cf. for iconological readings of the quoted works: Maurizio and Marcello Fagiolo Dell'Arco, *Bernini*, Bulzoni, Rome 1967; id., 'Villa Aldobrandina

Tuscolana', in *Quaderni dell'Ist. di Storia dell'Arch.* 1964, XI, nos. 62–4; Nino Carboneri, *Ascanio Vitozzi, un architetto fra Manierismo e Barocco*, Officina, Rome 1964; Eugenio Battisti, 'Retorica e Barocco' in *Rinascimento e Barocco*, Einaudi, Turin 1960.

[68] Cf. P. Portoghesi, *Borromini, analisi di un linguaggio* op. cit., cf., in contrast: Hans Ost, 'Borrominis römische Universitätskirche, S. Ivo alla Sapienza' in *Zeitschrift fur Kunstgeschichte* op. cit.

[69] Cf. E. Baldwin Smith, *Architectural Symbolism of Imperial Rome and the Middle Ages*, Princeton University Press, New Jersey 1956; R. De Fusco, *Architettura come mass-medium* op. cit. Also Wittkower's *Principi architettonici nell'età dell'Umanesimo* can be seen as a study that justly limits the use of iconological analysis techniques.

[70] A similar result came out of the discussion on the 'culture of the symbol in Italy', published in the prev. quoted numbers of *Marcatrè*, and summarised by R. Giorgi, ibid., nos 30–3. On the same theme see also Portoghesi's observations in *Borromini* op. cit., and, in particular, the criticism of Ost's iconological reading of St. Ivo. (Cf. note 68.)

[71] R. Barthes, *Critique et vérité* op. cit., p. 40.

[72] Cf. Peter Collins, 'The Interrelated Roles of History, Theory and Criticism in the Process of Architectural Design' in *The History, Theory,* etc. op. cit., p. 7; and id., *Changing Ideals* op. cit.

[73] Cf. Galvano Della Volpe, *Critica del gusto*, Feltrinelli, Milan 1960, 1964. (The brief passage on architecture, the most unsatisfactory of the entire volume, is in the second edition only.) On Della Volpe's aesthetics see: Rocco Musolino, *Marxismo ed estetica in Italia*, Editori Riuniti, Rome 1963, p. 49 ff. and A. Guiducci, op. cit., pp. 229–303.

[74] See the debate on the *Critica del gusto* at INARCH, Rome, published in *Marcatrè*, nos. 8–10.

[75] Umberto Eco, *Apocalittici e integrati*, Bompiani, Milan 1965, p. 100.

[76] Cf. U. Eco, *Appunti per una semiologia*, etc., op. cit.

[77] Cf. U. Eco, op. cit. But see now, Garroni's study in *Semiotica ed Estetica*, Laterza, Bari 1968.

[78] B. Zevi, 'Alla ricerca di un "codice" per l'architettura', in *L'Architettura cronache e storia*, XIII, 1967, no. 145. Id. 'Povertà della filologia e Verso una semiologia architettonica', in nos. 146 and 147 (1968) of the same magazine, in which Zevi carries on the discussion on Eco's *Appunti* and on *Il linguaggio moderno dell'architettura* op. cit.

[79] Cf. Giovanni Klaus König, *Analisi dell linguaggio architettonico*, Libreria editrice fiorentina, Florence 1964; and U. Eco, *Appunti per una semiologia* op. cit. In a recent essay, Morpurgo-Tagliabue has opposed the 'elementary functionalism' of the theories that see the meaning of architecture in the show of its functions. Cf. Guido Morpurgo-Tagliabue, 'L'arte è linguaggio?' in op. cit., 1968, no. 11, p. 5 ff. Cf. also: Emilio Garroni, *Progetto di semiotica*, Laterza, Rome-Bari 1973.

[80] U. Eco, *Appunti* op. cit., p. 88.

[81] R. Wellek and A. Warren, *Theory of Literature,* op. cit. p. 155.

[82] Ibid, p. 156.

[83] In *Art and Illusion,* Gombrich applies information theory to the history of the figurative arts, reaching results similar to Dorfles', who has justly distinguished between the *aesthetic* and *semantic* consumption of art. (One should, however, verify the functionality of this second expression, because the term 'semantic' has in itself the totality of the meanings of a work.) Cf. also Ch. Norberg-Schulz, op. cit.

[84] One should compare this proposition with some theories of form, such as those of Focillon, and with some formalist analyses such as those of Sklovskij.

[85] Cf. U. Eco, 'Modelli e strutture' in *Il Verri,* 1966, 20, p. 11 ff. In this essay Eco takes up again Hjelmslev's thesis of the hypothetical character of the structural description. (Cf. Louis Hjelmslev, *Essais Linguistiques,* Travaux du Cercle linguistique de Copenhague, vol. XII, Copenhagen 1959.) Eco seems to us very near to our hypotheses, when, in referring to the ideal discussion between Riegl and Panofsky, he recognises that 'a model is worked out in order to indicate a *form common to different phenomena.* The fact that we think of the open work as a model [he writes (op. cit. p. 19)] means that we thought it possible to identify a common operative tendency in the various ways of operation – a tendency to produce works with *structural similarities,* from the view-point of consumption. Just because this model is abstract, it can seem applicable to several works that, on other planes (on the level of ideology, of the material employed, of the artistic *genre* to be realised and of the kind of appeal to the consumer) are indeed very different.' This *antimetaphysical* interpretation of structuralism, completely shared by us, implies a close relation between the parameters chosen for the description and for the analysis, and the aims of the analysis itself. This implies, particularly in the definition of the historical cycles of architecture, the possibility of identifying various structural similarities according to the aims assumed by the historical analysis.

[86] Max Weber, *Gesammelte Aufsätze zur Wissenschaftslehre,* Mohr, Tübingen 1922, 1951.

[87] 'When properly used [Weber continues] this concept can be used for research and illustration', but on the other hand 'the fulfilment of a science always implies ... going beyond the ideal type, whether it is conceived as empirically valid or as a generic concept.' (Ibid.)

[88] 'If semiological research has a definite direction [Eco writes (*Appunti per una semiologia* op. cit., p. 8)] this consists in reducing every communication phenomenon to a dialectic between codes and messages.... The message with an aesthetic function is an example of *ambiguous* message, that puts in doubt the code, and, because of its context, creates such an unusual relation between the signs that our way of looking at the possibilities of the code will have to change. ... But every type of information has to rely on zones of redundancy. One can only transgress the code within certain limits, always retaining some degree of respect. Otherwise, instead of communication we would have noises. ... 'Eco, summing up the most rigorous results of the recent studies on artistic

communication, finds himself in total agreement with Gombrich, on one hand, and with some results of Norberg-Schulz on the other. Cf. E. Gombrich, *Art and Illusion* op. cit., p. 211 ff.; C. Norberg-Schulz, *Intentions in Architecture* op. cit., p. 212 ff.

[89] Cf. Robin Boyd, *The Puzzle of Architecture,* Melbourne University Press, London and New York 1965.

[90] Cf. R. Boyd op. cit. pp. 125–7.

[91] The above-mentioned work by Boyd gives the measure of the influence of Langer's theories on American architectural culture. Boyd recognises three phases in the Modern Movement: after the orthodox phase the Counter-revolution follows, dominated by the myth of significant form, of the monolithic, of the sculptural and of the symbolic, that finds expression in the monumental work by Stone, Johnson and Saarinen. The third phase (Kahn, Tange, Rudolph, etc.) is seen as a recovery of the original values of the Modern Movement, enriched by the positive contributions of the Counter-revolution. Though rather simplicistic, Boyd's historiographic view exemplifies very well the myths of English and American culture in relation to the objective crisis of modern architecture.

[92] But the phenomenon is not limited to America. The contradiction between the search for a disciplinary autonomy of architecture and the need to justify architecture through other disciplines is one of the common characteristics of the international architectural debate. In this sense speculations on language and on communication systems assume the evasive role that a few years ago was played by the *exploits* carried out rather amateurishly by architects in the field of sociology and economy.

[93] Cf. Robert Venturi, *Complexity and Contradiction in Architecture,* The Museum of Modern Art (Papers on Architecture, 1), Doubleday & Co., New York 1966.

[94] Empson's *Seven Types of Ambiguity* and Eliot's *Essays* are, of course, the bases on which Venturi founds his analogies between architectural and poetic language. In this way the concept of 'ambiguity' loses the functional character it had (particularly in Empson), and is used as a parameter for homogeneous expressive values. Cf. also: Alan Colquhoun, 'Robert Venturi' in *Architectural Design,* vol. XXXVII, 1967, no. 8, p. 362, and Rykwert's review of Venturi's book in *Domus* 1967.

[95] Cf. Vincent Scully, *Introduction* to Venturi's book op. cit., pp. 11–16.

[96] M. Weber, op. cit.

6

The Tasks of Criticism

In trying to clarify the function of some instruments of critical and historiographical analysis, we have intentionally avoided the problem of outlining a theory of architectural syntax and grammar. In defining the architectural codes as a bundle of relationships linking a complex series of 'systems', we were attempting to stress something that seems to us typical of architecture as compared with other means of visual communication: the fact, that is, that the typologies, the techniques, the production relations, the relations with nature and with the city, can in the architectural context, assume symbolic dimensions, charge themselves with meaning and force the limits within which every one of these components plays its own role in the historical context.

Clearly, then, architectural language is multi-significant: and not only as an analogy with painting, but in the specific sense. When El Lissitzky on the one hand and Van Doesburg on the other theorised the experimental function of the new linguistic systems within the field of art, and established the *constructive* use in industrial production as the specific task of visual art, they had very much in mind the close link between artistic communications, the new methods of production and the new systems of reception of the communications themselves.

The only way to describe the structures of architectural language seems to be through historical synthesis. All the naïve attempts to single out a component from the complex heap of architecture and elect it as a parameter of architectural language, are bound to fail before the impossibility of outlining a complete history of architecture in this way. Neither the functions nor the space of the tectonic elements can be at the base of a semiological analysis of planning. In the very moment in which we stress the term *project* in order to designate architecture, it becomes clear that, each time, we should evaluate which new materials have become part of the universe of discourse of architecture itself, what are the new relations between the traditional materials, and which of these materials has a prominent role.

One cannot evaluate Laon Cathedral, the Pazzi Chapel and Berlin's *Siemensstadt* within the same linguistic parameters: if one chose purely formal criteria, the symbolic dimension of the first two works would escape completely, while one would miss the intimate contradiction of the third; if one chose the traditional iconological method, one would have to remain mute before Berlin's *Siedlungen;* and if one were to trust the analysis of space, one would find no terms of comparison between the spatial narrative of the first, the anti-narrative rigour of the second and the leaving behind of the concept of 'space' itself on the part of the third.

The language of architecture is formed, defined and left behind in history, together with the very idea of architecture. In this sense the establishment of a 'general grammar' of architecture is a utopia. What one can do is recognise and describe syntaxes and 'codes' that are historically defined, useful as 'ideal types' in historiographical analysis. Already criticism can derive a few specific tasks from what we have just said. If, having been forced to admit that, in the course of history, it is the roles attributed to planning that change radically, one then, in order to simplify, wants to keep alive a unitary concept of architecture, this can only be defined empirically, being very careful not to take this convenient simplification as a 'category'. Strictly speaking, between a Roman Triumphal Arch and a project for urban renewal, the gap is so great as to make one doubt the functionality of a history that would embrace both in the same linear series of phenomena. Nor can one project onto the past the parameters and interpretative codes typical of the Modern Movement. One can always read the Domus Augustana as an element of landscape planning or the Via Sacra as a series of architectural *objets trouvés:* but then one has to keep in mind what makes these readings possible (that is, the lack of adequate architectural studies on Antiquity and the 'semi-natural' state proper to the ruin) and their limited functionality (didactic, operative, etc.).

Beyond all this, the task of history is the recovery, as far as possible, of the original functions and ideologies that, in the course of time, define and delimit the role and meaning of architecture. That this recovery is always subjective does not constitute a real problem. We have quoted on this point Weber's propositions on the problem of objectivity in historical evaluation, and, anyway, contemporary criticism has long since worked out parameters able to set up a productive dialectic between the work and its analyst. One could say, in fact, that the critic, in making historical the meaning of an architecture or a cycle of works, finds an operative field in the activity of composition, description, comparison, and recomposition of the 'materials' that make up architecture itself in a new order, in all the bundles of relationships that join it together. By showing the 'pieces' of that organic whole which is architecture, the historian can reveal the multiple meanings and contradictions hidden – by definition, we are tempted to say – behind the apparent organicity with which architecture presents itself.

Finding the source of the crisis of Humanist naturalism in, on the one hand, Brunelleschi's spatial tensions and, on the other, in the early Giuliano da Sangallo's orthodoxy; seeing in the misunderstanding of Classicism in the Middle-European countries a 'historical' revenge carried out by 'popular', empirical and 'anti-Roman' cultures; identifying in the manifold ways followed by the avant-gardes of our century the contradictions that today shake architectural culture in a macroscopic way and expose the origins of the shortcomings of modern urbanistics; these are all examples of how, by recovering philologically the events of the past, it is possible to propose new questions to the present. New questions, we repeat, not new solutions. History cannot offer solutions (or, if you prefer, *can no longer* offer solutions).

It is not from the historical context that the present tasks are born. (It is not up to the historian to take on the job of sanctifying the historical continuity of the discipline.) Rather the dissection carried out on the body of history must precisely 'place' the problems debated at present, recognise their ambiguity, values and mystifications, offer the architect an endless vista of new and unsolved problems, available for conscious choice and freed from the weight of myth. In other words the historian accentuates the contradictions of history and offers them crudely, in their reality, to those whose responsibility it is to create new formal worlds. But at the same time history and criticism set a limit to ambiguity in architecture. By leading the works back into more general contexts, and in the very moment that it hypothesises an historical role for them, criticism delimits a field of values within which it is possible to attribute unequivocal meanings to architecture. In this way architecture's availability to a completely 'open' reading and use is reduced, restricted, circumscribed within the limits of recognisable meanings.

But in this activity criticism must be aware of the artificiality of its own operations: it must be prepared to reveal the instrumentality of its own attributions of meaning.

From this point of view the 'truth' of criticism is in its functionality. One can accept or reject a certain chain of historical facts only after having put the questions: what does it tell us about the hidden reasons determining architectural choices, and what present contradiction does it bring to light? Does that historiographic hypothesis manage to pose new *positive doubts* or is it not rather superfluous, consolatory or taken for granted? And in its probing into the structures of the phenomena does it take into account from the beginning the subjective deformations of the critic? Identifying criticism with history means, in fact, accepting the continuous co-presence of the unsolved problems of history.

The question marks left pending by the *late Antique* architectural experimentalism, the paradoxical fragmentation of structural organicity by paleo-Christian architectural experiences, the dilution of Gothic Rationalism into an unreal *assemblage* of 'things', the failure of Classicism, the crisis of Illuminist ideologies, the ambiguous relation between art and revolution set by twentieth-century avant-gardes are not themes exhausted and resolved in their historical developments: they are, on the contrary, problems still open, urgently in need of a solution, that have to be considered by those who operate in the present as perennially open 'questions'.

It may seem paradoxical to ask an architect to consider at one time, in his planning, Brunelleschi's utopianism and Gaudí's ambiguity. But the paradox presented today by history is just such a request, for an all-embracing attitude as the only guarantee of relative validity.

It is of little importance that the architects of the seventies are far more willing to snobbishly 'partialise' the sphere of their historical interests immediately frozen within the narrow rails of a perspective that claims to be 'critical', but is, in fact, only mystifying.

It is the historian that must kill the 'instrumentality' of history. The independence of the 'values' from any institutionalised historicism that was discovered by the historical avant-gardes, still applies today. Today, too, we are obliged to see history not as a great tank of codified values, but as an enormous collection of utopias, failures and betrayals. Today, too, hope for a new world rests on faith in violent fractures, the jump into the dark, the adventure accepted without reserves: if this were not the case we should resign ourselves to seeing our capacity for action and understanding slumber in the evasive celebration of the past.

But, and this is more important and serious, today we are also compelled to feel 'betrayed' by history. The 'betrayal' today is felt as a consequence of contradictions within the very tradition with which we cannot help but identify. The success of all the poetics of *ambiguity,* in architecture as well as in urban design, is due, in fact, to the following reason: those who propose ambiguity, complexity and contradiction as communicative and formative materials of architectural and urban experience, know they are employing real conditions, know that they are making explicit something felt, more or less confusedly, by everyone. In a certain sense, history has a tendency to become ambiguous. Offering no certainties, history seems to offer itself as a mere collection of facts and things that wait to be given a meaning, in their turn, by each successive planning choice. It is not history, any more, that offers the architect a horizon of stability and values. It is, rather, architecture that, in its making, in its changing, in its attempt to recreate from nothing its own purpose and values, gives a constant metamorphosis of meanings to history.

The somewhat hidden and perhaps not completely conscious objective of Kahn, Rudolph and, even, the later work of Wright, was to establish, through planning, the values of the past: to weed out from the shapeless heap of pure 'signs' still called 'history' everything that is not, somehow, related to the *hic et nunc* of every single work, and to include in it, as values, those other 'signs' that can, somehow, justify its existence.

In this way to the relative *availability* of architecture one adds the absolute availability of history. Provided that, in the very moment in which the more divided architects decide to find some terms of super-historical relationship with the past, as a compensation for the fall of their ideal tensions, the to and fro play between the ambiguity of history and the ambiguity of architecture closes itself in a circle with rather fragile boundaries. The relationship turns into baby-talk, mysterious silences, a whirl of banalities *à la Ionesco,* into winks meant to be light-hearted but revealing tragedy in all their haunting emptiness. Given this situation, let us try to re-state our initial proposition: criticism sets limitations to the ambiguity of architecture.

This means that the historian has to oppose the 'camouflaged anti-historicism' of present architecture. By writing past events into a field of meanings, the historian gives sense to the ambiguity of history: from abstract and completely available the ambiguity is rendered concrete and instrumentalisable. He will refuse to read in late-Antique architecture the premises of Kahn or Wright, in Mannerism those of Expressionism or of the present moment, in the pre-historical remains the premises of organicism and of some abstract experiences. And this refusal is a precise contestation of the mythologies of the pseudo-avant-gardes.

There is in fact only one way of uncovering the ideologies of renunciation hidden behind the rejection of history, the exaltation of the pure event and the illusory objective of the permanent revolution of language. Rejecting history means, today, giving oneself up to the most vulgar and, at the same time, the most subtle mystifications. It is myth that takes the place of history. One has to choose between being aware of one's actions and capitulating before heterodirected stimuli.

Equally, to think of being able to act solely on the plane of language, with the illusion of continuing, in this way, along the way opened by the historical avant-gardes, conceals new mythologies. The very character of complex structure that, we have seen, is typical of architecture, prevents a radical renewal derived from acting on only one of its component systems. The reality of production and technology in which we find ourselves has not left behind the great problems relating to the 'technical reproducibility' of the work of art, to the crisis of the object and to the 'fall of the aura'. What is new is the awareness of the links between instruments of communication and collective behaviours, that has come into being with the sophistication, rapid renewal and extension of the mass-media.

The way, for architecture, is not then the retreat into the silent night of pure form, relating only to itself, nor that of charging itself with allusive representations and showing with guilty blindness an utter alienation mistaken for independence. Reference to the specificity of the basic problems of architectural discipline will be useful only if it is then able to invest the global nature of the planning process, precisely identifying the margins of meaning of the discourse on language.

At this point a history able to unearth the intrinsic possibilities of the instruments employed by the architect becomes indispensable. Much more so if we realise that, after the 'great crisis' of the thirties all the 'projected hopes' of the avant-gardes reveal only their ineffectuality. To ignore either the limitations of the possibilities of communication or the new horizons opened by the means available to architecture leads to a clearly evasive attitude. Walter Benjamin's analyses of the semantic, operative, mental and behaviourist consequences of modern technology remain an isolated case in the history of contemporary criticism (and we suspect that it is not by chance). The misunderstandings that have dominated architectural culture from 1945 onwards derive in great part from the interruption of Benjamin's analyses: analyses, we must stress, authentically *structural,* beyond any evasive or fashionable meaning of the term or of the concept.

The historicisation of structuralism has, therefore, the following meaning for us: the exact and objective identification of the mechanism, the communicative potential, the mystifications and values of the context in which the act of planning is placed.

This implies giving up the attempt to work out new *solutions* beforehand, in history and criticism. As instrument of planning history is sterile, it can only offer solutions and indications already taken for granted. A new solution implies, on the other hand, a jump, a radical re-shuffle of the data of the problem, a risky adventure.

History can only prepare the bases for this adventure and explain why it is not feasible today. By rigorously identifying the structures of the real conditions along the entire range of their problematic, it can throw light on the terms of the contradictions in which daily behaviour is entangled. We need, then, to give up simplifying history, and to accept its internal contradictions and its plurality, stressing its dialectical sides, and exalting it for what it really is.

What is certain is that a history of this kind would reject any type of instrumentalisation. Not because the instrumentalisation of history is *wrong*, but because our goals are different, they aim at another type of 'productivity', they want to enter the architectural operation in a mediated and indirect way, suggesting a multiplication of the problems rather than solutions to the existing ones.

One could object that to try to act indirectly on such a wobbly and complex cultural world as the architectural world implies a desperate enterprise, whose productivity and incidence, furthermore, elude concrete examination. Of course the historian following this path will have to face the danger of the isolation of the praxis, but he will be comforted by many signs, first of all by the renewed interest of the younger generations for a historiographical method that is intimately dialectic and, at the same time, analytical.

Rather than turning to the past as a sort of fertile ground, rich in abandoned mines to be successively rediscovered finding in them anticipations of modern problems, or as a slightly hermetic maze good for amusing trips leading to a more or less miraculous *catch*, we must get used to seeing history as a continuous *contestation of the present*, even as a threat, if you like, to the tranquillising myths wherein the anxieties and doubts of modern architects find peace. A *contestation of the present:* but also a contestation of the values accrued by the '*tradition of the new*'.

In fact it is no longer possible to make history by posing as the Vestal of the Modern Movement. Those who, realising the waste of the values accumulated by the heroes of our century's artistic revolution root themselves in neo-Constructivist, neo-De Stijl, neo-organic and neo-avant-gardist positions, have all our admiration for the generosity and courage they have shown by disdainfully withdrawing from the chaos of frustrated intentions and false prophecies crowding the present landscape, but must also agree – as bravely – to take on, their choice whole-heartedly. This is no longer the choice of the revolutionary, but that of the conservative even if it is a conservative who wishes to recreate the ethical and subversive *élan* of the heroic age of the Modern Movement.

As the main dangers are scepticism, lack of confidence, tiredness, evasion into passive or playful activity, we would always value the position of the Vestal more highly than that of the many mystifiers and smugglers of false innovations who daily exhibit a verbal libido that verges on the pathological. And it is for this very reason that, having discarded the way of uncontrolled prophecies and of end-in-itself coherence of the *conservatives* of the Modern Movement, our renewed appeal to history may, perhaps, help to reconnect the threads of such a discourse as the one on modern architecture, that is too complex to be artificially simplified.

In a certain sense this type of historiographical criticism is waiting to be contested and left behind by historical reality. Since it places present praxis before its objective responsibilities historical reality cannot help judging, after the systems of values have been identified, that the various contrasting tendencies refer to the concrete response of the adopted instruments to the intended goals. But it must also be ready to take as a real datum the contradiction of history and its sudden jumps towards the unforeseen.

To be as historians and critics against indicating, prophesying, forecasting these jumps towards the future, does not imply a disbelief in them. On the contrary, it is just because one has faith in the positiveness and possibility of revolutions, that one can and must prepare a solid platform for those who intend to oppose the stability of values. But the distinction between the activity of demystification and the activity of planning must be kept at all costs, even if the price may seem too heavy for those critics that persuade themselves they are able to plan with the pen rather than with the drawing board.

At the same time the de-mythisation carried out by criticism has two, complementary, effects: (a) by breaking the link between architectural language and the ideologies underlying it, it appeals to the responsibility of the planner, asking him to make conscious, analytical, and verifiable choices; taking him away, in fact, from the automatism into which the architect inevitably slides when he tries to shorten his approach to the form; (b) it stresses, exasperates, takes to an extreme, the consumption of the thematics, methods, and languages: and, as *consumption* as such is one of the emblems of contemporary art (nor does architecture seem to escape its laws), this exasperation introduced by criticism reveals, at the same time, both the transience and the tragic quality of the present condition. In other words, criticism, by pushing away the temptation to become an explanatory note, a literary translation, a disinterested analysis or the depositary of prophetic perspectives, takes on the role of litmus paper checking architecture's historical validity. Today, solely because of the objective absurdity of the architect's present condition this check may seem to imply a continuous and often cruel inquiry.

Bound to 'build' – because by definition the architect cannot just give voice to his protest, dissent or nausea – but with no trust in the structures that condition their planning, in the society that will use their architecture, in the independence of their specific instruments, those architects who are more aware find themselves in an ambiguous, contorted, almost ridiculous situation. If they try to follow their (rare) eversive impulses through to the end they are shocked at having to decree, as the only possibilities, either the death of architecture or refuge in utopia. If they take the road to self-critical experimentalism, they are bound, in the best of cases, to produce pathetic 'monuments', isolated and extraneous to the dynamic of urban reality. More often they accumulate blueprints and plastic models in their ineffectual studios. In this situation, criticism continually risks becoming an instrument of falsity, opium guiltily supplied, superfluous and ornamental rhetoric.

It would be useless and wrong to judge the uneasy contortions and sophisticated balancing tricks of present-day architecture as if we faced a 'normal' situation. It would be useless and even more wrong to take into consideration (and, moreover, in abstract and obscure language) the absurdities that appear in relentless succession on the pages of magazines and in the production of architectural 'academies', ignoring the tragic quality of this evidence of anxiety and unease. For since this anxiety and unease can only be partially justified through the specific analysis of architecture, and is linked to the embarrassment felt by the intellectual, impotent but conscious clown before the dynamic of capitalist development, criticism has a duty to increase the unease, to make precise and operative the 'dissent' of the architect, to exasperate his objective situation.

So by contesting present-day architecture, taking it back to an historicity that would increase rather than reduce the problematics, continually forcing into crisis the apparently advanced objectives on which research and debate seem about to die down, the critic must present – with a rigour made necessary by the historical events with which he is involved – the exact picture of an absurd but real situation, more and more stimulating conscious doubts, constructive dissent and general uneasiness.

If structural analysis can manage to carry out such a task, the demystification operated by criticism will have formidable theoretical and technical support. But if it were to resolve itself in an a-historical exercise, we could no longer go on speaking of 'criticism'.

Nor can one say that the aims outlined above reduce criticism to terrorist and nihilist activity. Sartre stated that the task of literature is to 'call to freedom by exhibiting one's own freedom'. If, today, architecture is not able to call anyone to freedom, if its own freedom is illusory, if all its petitions sink in a quagmire of 'images' at best amusing, there is no reason why one should not take up a position of determined contestation towards architecture itself, as well as towards the general context that conditions its existence.

In that case historical activity, totally indifferent to *positive action*, becomes 'criticism of architectural ideologies' and, as such, 'political' activity – even if indirectly political. It must then be recognised, by those that intend to force the institutional role given to intellectuals from Illuminism onwards, that to find out what architecture is, *as a discipline historically conditioned and institutionally functional to, first, the 'progress' of the pre-capitalist bourgeoisie and, later, to the new perspectives of capitalist 'Zivilisation'*, is the only purpose with any historical sense.

It is not at all certain that, by placing historical demythisation in opposition to the myth of anti-history, criticism can solve this fundamental aporia of our century: on the contrary, it can be demonstrated that an abstract historicisation of planning leads directly to sudden stops and contradictions that are, to say the least, dispersive. Once again we must be able to accept reality and debate in dialectical terms. On the other hand, it is really illusory and completely unjustifiable to pretend somehow to 'dominate' such a transient and fragmented cultural situation as the present one. Just as contradictions now have their own autonomous reality, criticism must be able to recognise its particular and limited (but indispensable) role within their context.

In this sense we can borrow the statement that Weiss puts in the mouth of the 'divine marquis' at the end of *Marat-Sade:*

in these dialogues we had the intention
to put a few antitheses in question
and make them clash
so that
the doubts might clear;

nor does it matter that the critic must then – like Weiss's Sade – declare that in the present situation he is obliged to 'despair of finding the solution'.

Solutions are not to be found in history. But one can always diagnose that the only possible way is the exasperation of the antitheses, the frontal clash of the positions, and the accentuation of contradictions. And this not for a particular form of sado-masochism, but in the hypothesis of a radical change that will leave behind both the anguished present situation and the temporary tasks we have tried to make clear to ourselves in this volume.

Illustrations

Chapter 1: Modern Architecture and the Eclipse of History

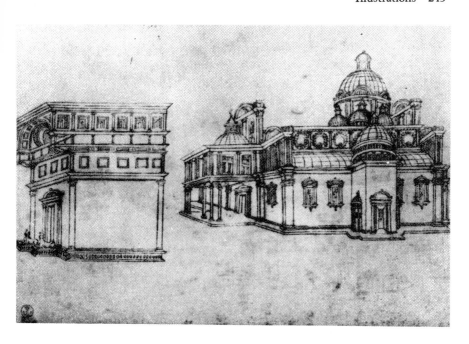

I   Simone del Pollaiolo, known as Il Cronaca (?), Fantastic project for a religious
organism and ideal reconstruction of Roman buildings (circular temple and baths).
Gabinetto diss. e stampe, Uffizi, Florence

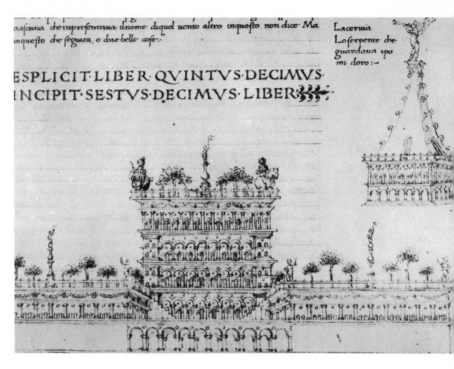

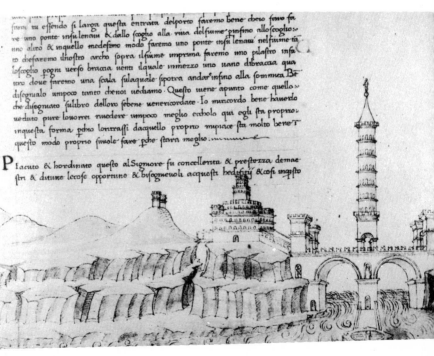

IV   Giulio Romano, Detail of the connection between the central nave, the cupola
and the circular choir of S. Benedetto in Polirone. The Gothic pre-existences and the
Mannerist restructuration 'speak' to each other in a restless play of transparencies

II & III (Opposite)   Antonio Averlino (Il Filarete), from the *Trattato di Architettura*
(1461–4), book XIV, fig. 109 e, and book XV, fig. 122 r

V   Andrea Palladio, Existing and ideal reconstruction of the Romulus temple.
R.I.B.A., London

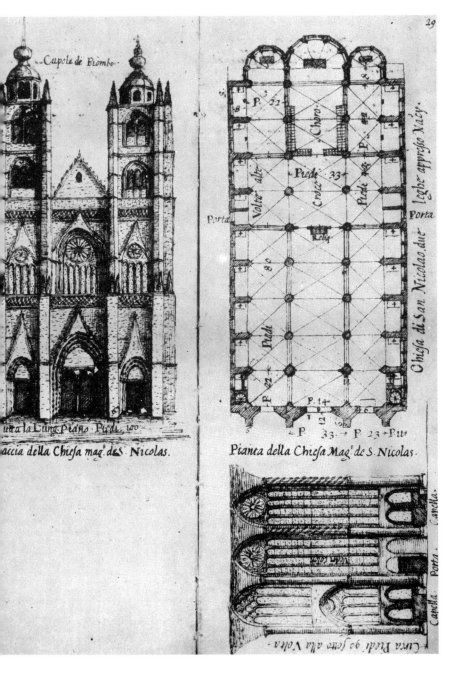

VI   Vincenzo Scamozzi, Measured drawing of St Nicolas cathedral near Nancy.
(From the *Taccuino di viaggio di V. S.*) The interest in the Gothic is filtered through a
classicist reading and a perspective of both the organism and the details

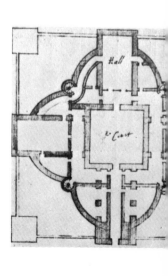

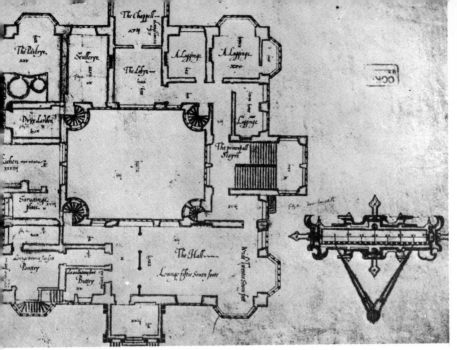

IX   Robert Smythson, Study for a country house (unidentified). R.I.B.A., London

X   Francesco Borromini, S. Ivo alla Sapienza. Kunstgewerbe Museum, Berlin

VII (Opposite above)   Worksop Manor (completed in 1586), engraving by Richard Hall in *Nottinghamshire* by Thoroton (1677)

VIII (Opposite below)   John Thorpe, Drawing for a house, based on the combination of geometric themes of Y, the circle, the hexagon and the triangle (*left*); house plan in the *Smythson Collection*. R.I.B.A., London (*right*)

XI (Opposite)
Francesco Borromini,
Cardinal Giussano's
tomb in S. Giovanni in
Laterano: the Gothic
mullioned windows, the
paleo-Christian elements
and the '*cosmateschi*'
mosaics, inserted in the
unreal space of
Borromini's 'perspective
theatre', assume the
value of ready-made
objects, joined in a
caustic *bricolage*

XII   Christopher Wren,
Tom Tower, Oxford

XIII   Christopher Wren, Project for the restoration of Westminster Abbey North transept. (On the right the present transept, on the left Wren's project)

XIV   J. B. Fischer von Erlach, Ideal reconstruction of the Phidian statue of Jupiter, from Pausania's description. From *Entwurff einer historischen Architektur*, Vienna 1721, Plate V

XV   J. B. Fischer von Erlach, Ideal reconstruction of Ptolemy's Light-house in Alexandria. From *Entwurff*, etc. op. cit. Plate IX

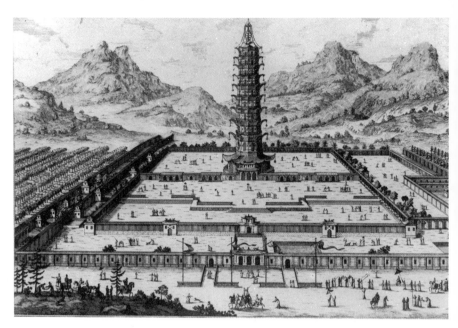

XVI   E. Fischer von Erlach, Nanking Pagoda. From *Entwurff*, etc. op. cit. Plate XII
XVII   E. Fischer von Erlach, Project for a fortified country house. From *Entwurff*,
etc. op. cit. Plate XX

XVIII   Nicholas Hawksmoor, Three projects for All Souls College. In these projects
we can read an empirical and 'sceptical' attitude towards historical tradition:
Classicism and Gothic are considered wholly available languages

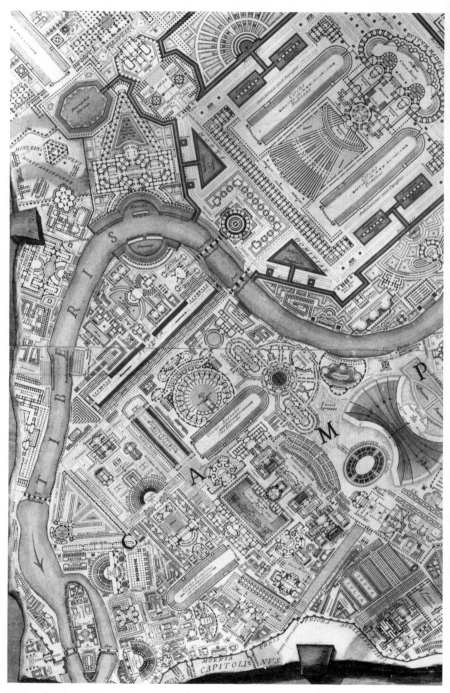

XIX   Giovan Battista Piranesi, Particular of the *Campo Marzio* (1761–2)

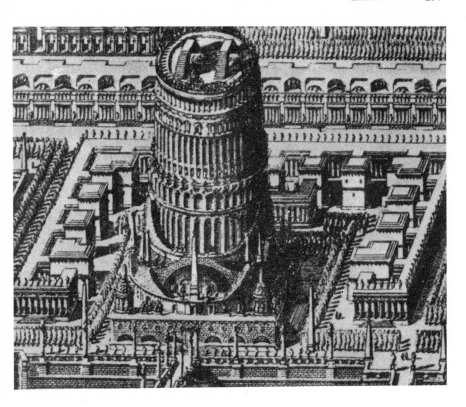

XX & XXI   Giovan Battista Piranesi, Hadrian's Mausoleum and the multi-apsed rotunda near Marcello's theatre. From *Campo Marzio*, op. cit

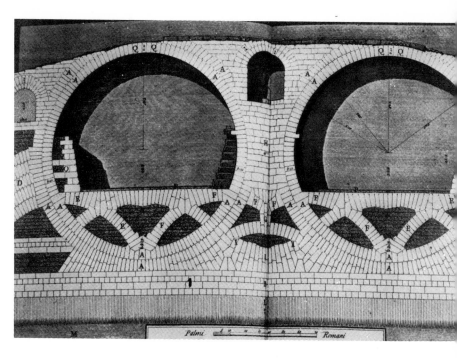

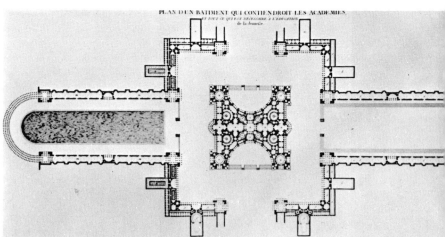

XXIII   Joseph Marie Peyre, Project for an Academy. From: Peyre, *Oeuvres d'Architecture*, Paris 1765

XXIV (Opposite)   Karl Ludwig Engel, Project for the University of Helsinki: ground plan and upper floors. Helsinki Archive

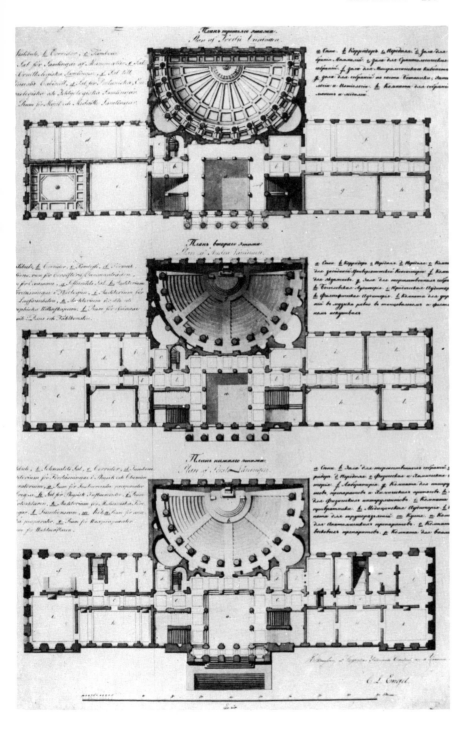

XXV   Karl Ludwig Engel, Project for the Imperial Senate of the Grand Duchy of Finland in Helsinki. Helsinki Archive

XXVI   Ch. Nicholas Ledoux, Project for Industrial Building in the Royal Salt-works at Chaux

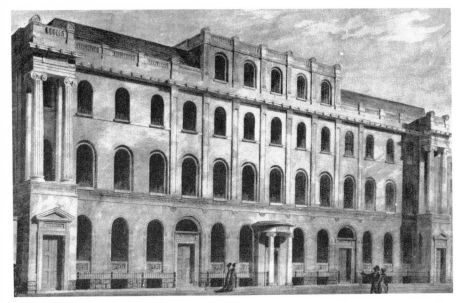

XXVII   John Soane, Project for the New Bank of England, London

XXVIII   John Soane, Port Eliot, Cornwall. In Soane's pre-Romantic eclecticism the 'sceptical' tradition of English architecture merges with a compositive rigorism derived from Illuminism

XXX   Emile Hoppe, Architectural study (1902). Historicism, Monumentalism and pre-Futurist motives all merge in the drawings of the *Wagnerschule*

XXIX (Opposite)   Staircase of Old Louisiana State Capitol (William A. Freret, 1880–2, in the existing building by James H. Dakin, 1847–9)

XXXI   Antonio Sant'Elia and Italo Paternostro, Competition entry for Monza cemetery, 1912

XXXIII Frank Lloyd Wright, G. Moore House, Oak Park, 1895–1923. The client's request (in 1895) was for: 'a house in late-Gothic style'. In 1923 Wright rebuilt the upper storey, destroyed by fire

XXXIV (Opposite above) Frank Lloyd Wright, 'Tahoe' project for a barge for two, almost contemporary to the rebuilding of the Moore House

XXXV (Opposite below) Frank Lloyd Wright, Studies for tall office buildings

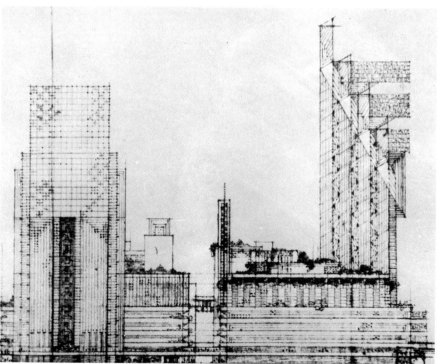

XXXVII   A. L. & V. Vesnin, Competition entry for the Central Telegraph Building (1925). From: *SA*, 1926, no. 2

XXVI (Opposite)   Ernst and Günther Paulus, *Kreuzkirche* at Wilmersdorf, Berlin, 1928–30

XXXVIII (Opposite)
Le Corbusier, Detail of
Chandigarh Capitol
showing The Legislative
Assembly Building; in
the foreground is the
ramp of the Secretariat

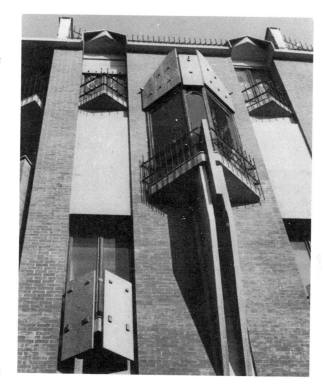

XXXIX   Roberto
Gabetti and Aimaro
d'Isola, The 'Bottega di
Erasmo', Turin (1955–6)

XL   Roberto Gabetti and Aimaro d'Isola, Casa Pero at Pino Torinese (1966–7)

XLI (Above) Philip Johnson, Project for a Museum in Washington, 1960

XLII (Left) Louis Kahn, Studies for S. Cecilia at Albi

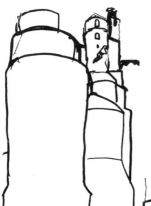

XLIII & XLIV (Opposite) Louis Kahn, Vaulted substructure to the Assembly Building at Dacca

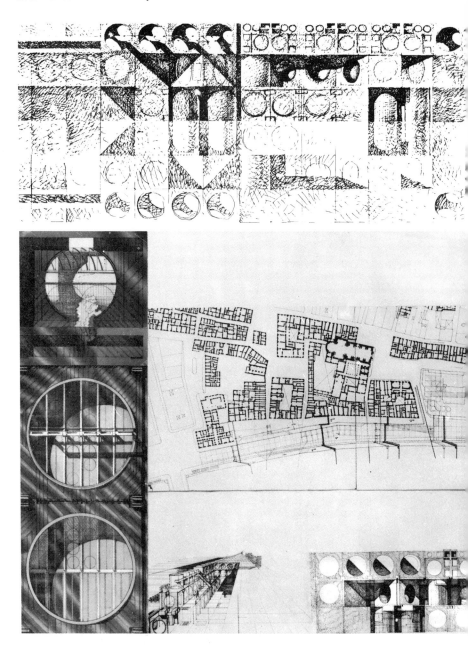

XLV   Franco Purini and Laura Thermes, Project for the reconstruction of the Tiber river-side in Rome (1966–7)

Chapter 2: Architecture as 'Indifferent Object' and the Crisis of Critical Attention

XLVI   William Chambers, View of the Alhambra, the Pagoda and the Mosque in Kew Gardens. From: W. Chambers, *Gardens and Buildings at Kew*, London 1763

XLVII   William Chambers, View of the Lake and the Island, with the Orangery, the Temple of Aeolus and Bellona and the 'House of Confucius' at Kew Gardens op. cit.

XLVIII   William Kent, Section of 'Merlin's Cave' in The Royal Gardens of Richmond. From: J. Vardy, *Some Designs of Inigo Jones and William Kent*, 1744, Plate 32

Chapter 3: Architecture as Metalanguage: the Critical Value of the Image

XLIX   'Critical' model by the students of the Istituto Universitario di Architettura di Venezia, relating to the Sforza Chapel by Michelangelo in S. Maria Maggiore in Rome

L   'Critical' model relating to the Medici Chapel in S. Lorenzo, Florence, at the 1964
Michelangelo Exhibition in Rome

LI   Hughues Libergier, Façade of the Cathedral of St Nicaise at Rheims (c. 1230–63), no longer extant, engraved by N. de Son in 1625

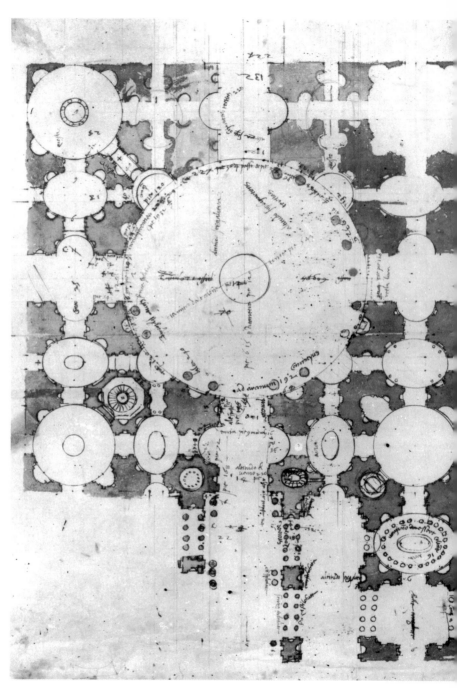

LII   Baldassarre Peruzzi, Study for a polycentric organism. Gabinetto diss. e stampe, Uffizi, Florence

LIII   Giovanni
Battista Montano,
Original drawing for
the *tempietti*
engraved by Soria.
Milan, Raccolta
Bertarelli, Collez.
Martinelli

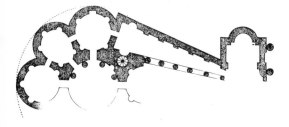

LIV   Giovanni Battista
Montano, Antique Temple in
the Roman countryside,
engraved by Soria

LV   Andrea Moroni & Andrea da Valle, Interior of the church of S. Giustina in Padua. (*Photo: E. Monti*)

LVI   Giorgio Spavento, Interior of S. Salvador in Venice, completed by T.
Lombardo & J. Sansovino. (*Photo: E. Monti*)

LVII   Gaelazzo Alessi, Study for the façade of Palazzo Marino in Milan. Raccolta Bianconi, Tomo I, p. 24 (A 4041), Milan

LVIII   Andrea Palladio, View of the choir of S. Giorgio Maggiore in Venice. (*Photo: E. Monti*)

LIX   Pietro da Cortona (?), Architectural study. Raccolta Bertarelli, Collez. Martinelli, Milan

LX   Christopher Wren, 'The Warrant design' for the North Front of St Paul's, London

LXI   Christopher Wren, Interior of St Stephen's, Walbrook, eighteenth-century engraving

LXII (Opposite)   Domenico Martinelli, Plan for a church in Poland. Raccolta Bertarelli, Collez. Martinelli, Milan

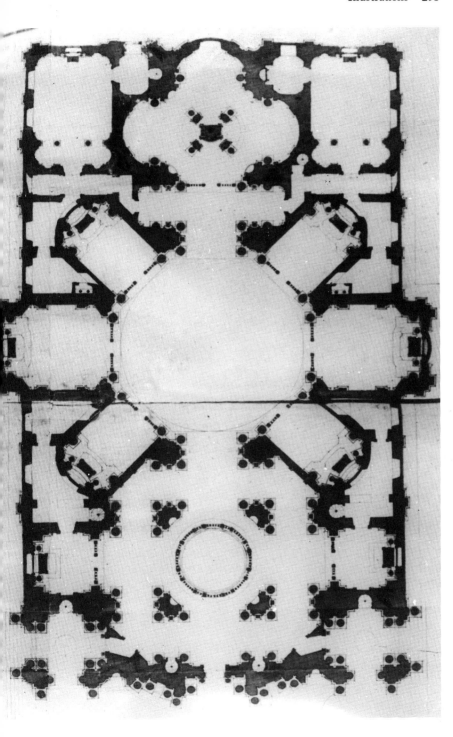

LXIII   Giuseppe Jappelli, Project for the new prison in Padua, on a panopticon system (1824). Main façade, sectional elevation and longitudinal section

LXIV   Viollet-le-Duc, Project for a covered market. From *Entretiens sur
l'architecture*

LXV & LXVI   Peter Behrens, Apartment block in the Bolivarallee in Berlin, 1930

LXVII   Paul Rudolph, Project for the Boston Government Service Centre, 1964

LXVIII   Paul Rudolph, Project for a house

LXIX   James Stirling, Engineering Laboratories, Leicester University

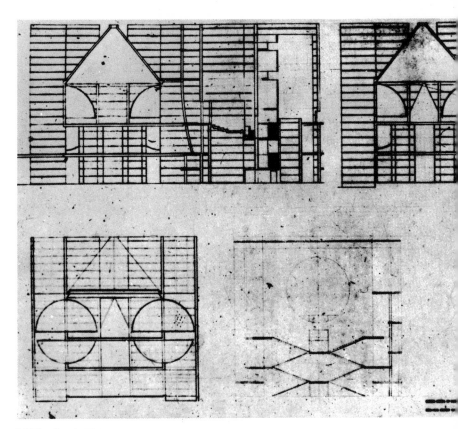

LXX   Louis Kahn, Project for Dacca's Capitol

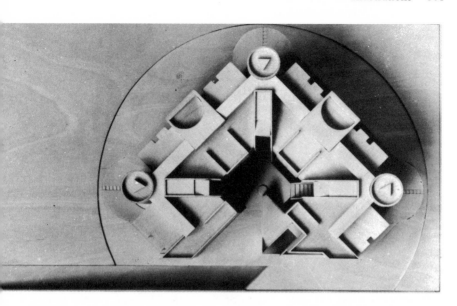

LXXI & LXXII   'STASS' Group, Project for residential unit near Rome

LXXIII   Kallmann, Knowles and McKinnell, Boston City Hall Project

LXXIV (Opposite)   Aldo Rossi, Research into form: 'the triangle in architecture'.
Top left: study for the portico from the project for the Piazza del Teatro Paganini in
Parma (1965–7); *Right and bottom:* plans and elevations of the monumental fountain in
the Piazza del Municipio at Segrate

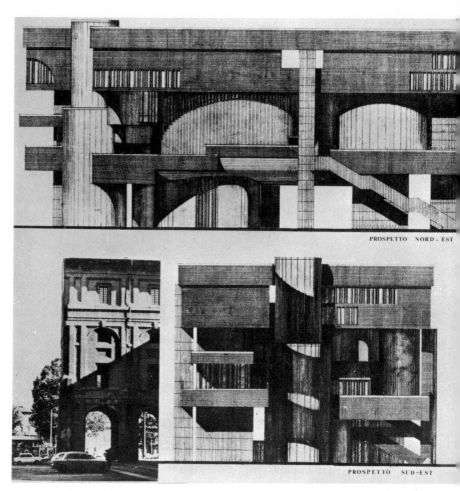

LXXV   Carlo Aymonino, Competition entry for the reconstruction of the Teatro Paganini in Parma

LXXVI   A 'critical' photograph that shows the complex dialogue between Michelangelo, Maderno and Bernini in the basilica and the 'porticato' of St Peter's. (*Photo: Lenci*)

Chapter 4: Operative Criticism ('Town design' and urban typology)

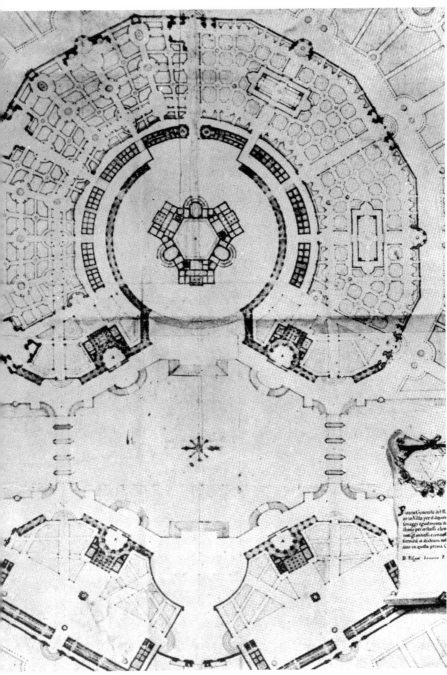

LXXVII   Filippo Juvarra, 'Regio palazzo in villa per tre personaggi'. General plan of
the palace and the park: project presented to the 1705 Clementine Competition.
Archivio dell'Accademia di San Luca, Rome

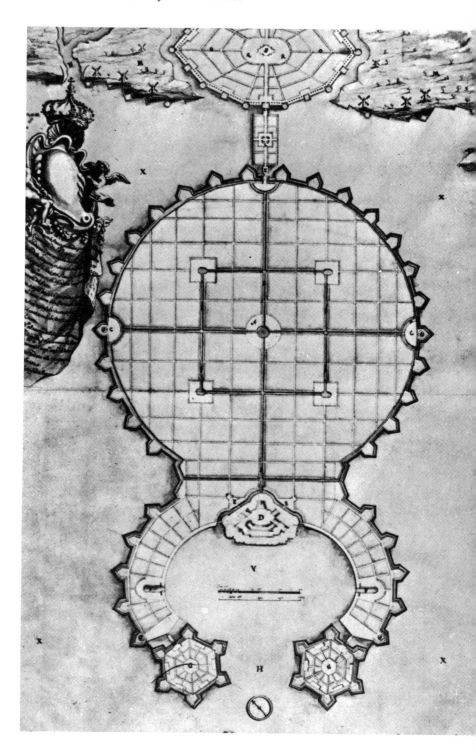

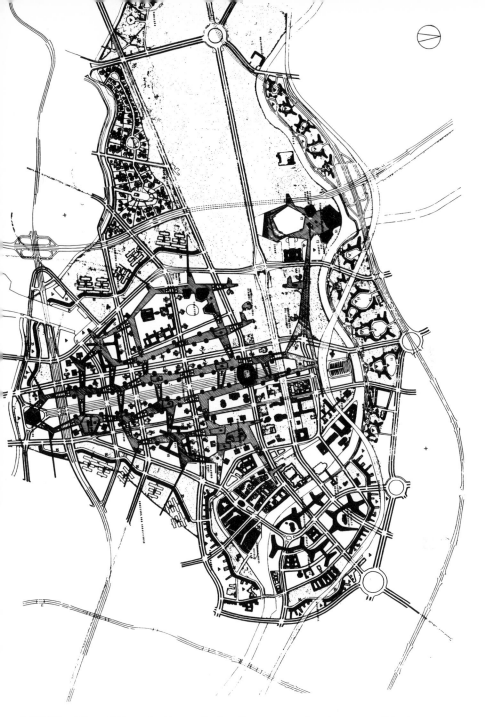

LXXIX   Alison & Peter Smithson, Project for restructuring the centre of Berlin

LXXVIII (Opposite)   Bernardo Antonio Vittone, Project for a 'town in the middle of
the sea'; 1732 Clementine Competition, Archivio dell'Accademia di San Luca, Rome

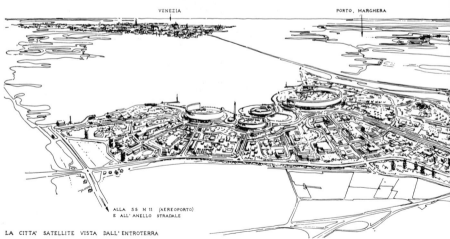

LXXX & LXXXI   Ludovico Quaroni and colleagues, Project for the CEP of S. Giuliano at Mestre, lay-out plan and birds-eye view

LXXXII Paul Rudolph, Project for the urban development of Stafford Harbor in Virginia

LXXXIII Kenzo Tange, Detail of the first project for the rebuilding of Skopje

Index of Names

Index of Names